BORN OF WATER AND SPIRIT

RICHARD C. TRAYLOR

BORN OF
WATER
& SPIRIT

The Baptist Impulse
in Kentucky, 1776–1860

The University of Tennessee Press / Knoxville

Library of Congress Cataloging-in-Publication Data

Traylor, Richard C. (Richard Claude), 1969-
Born of water and spirit : the Baptist impulse in Kentucky, 1776-1860 / Richard C. Traylor.
—First edition.
  pages cm
Originally presented as author's thesis (Ph. D.)—University of Missouri-Columbia, 2003.
Includes bibliographical references and index.
ISBN-13 978-1-62190-095-5
1. Baptists—Kentucky—History—18th century.
2. Baptists—Kentucky—History—19th century.
3. Kentucky—Church history.
I. Title.
BX6248.K4T73 2015
286.09769'09034—dc23
                2014028634

Contents

Acknowledgments

Historically, and taken as a group, the people called Baptists seem ever ready to amaze and confuse, inspire and frustrate. Likewise, the task of analyzing the Baptists in Kentucky from their roots to the brink of the American Civil War has been, at various times, amazing and inspiring as well as confusing and frustrating. Similar words might also describe the long and winding journey of understanding, writing, and then publishing their story. Along the way, I have incurred many debts that this mere mention can only begin to repay.

Many of the professors among the history faculty at the University of Missouri–Columbia assisted me intellectually as I created the first version of this work as a dissertation in 2003. First and foremost among these was my advisor John H. Wigger. Sincerely, no one could ask for a better advisor, and it was my deep honor to be his first graduating doctoral advisee. He showed great patience as I tried to come to grips with early American religion and the Baptist place in that story. His confidence in my ability to convey this story invigorated me when my own enthusiasm waned. His thoughtful and kind criticisms kept my thought processes clear and my writing in line. I appreciate his willingness to re-read chapters and offer his insights as I prepared for publication.

Of the other professors I owe for their guidance and assistance, Steven Watts stands out. As a student in his classes and as his teaching assistant, I reaped an intellectual harvest and learned from a master of the craft. To see him at work is to witness a wizard at play and it was my honor to briefly serve as this sorcerer's apprentice. From him I gleaned the greater cultural import of American

religion, and I will always remember the kind words from this prolific and brilliant historian after he read the first version of this work. Robert M. Collins influenced the work indirectly when he introduced me to Ellis W. Hawley's *The New Deal and the Problem of Monopoly*. Hawley's study of Roosevelt's New Deal policies fundamentally deals with the difficult task of harmonizing the seemingly irreconcilable ideological values of liberty and order, individualism and organization, democracy and security. Hawley notes how the values were ever present in American history and how the natural conflict between them has colored most of Western civilization. Though certainly the issue is not original to Hawley, my encounter with his clear presentation of the problem influenced the way I approach the study of history, affected the tenor of this work, and continues to influence my teaching. Among the religious groups of the early American republic, as the experiences of those within this work reveal, the Baptists came closest to reconciling these values, and their success and tribulations have derived from their vacillating ability to maintain the balance.

Production of this work at its early stages would have been more difficult had it not been for the financial support offered by the Department of History, University of Missouri–Columbia, including research grants that subsidized trips to Tennessee and Kentucky. The Southern Baptist Historical Library and Archives in Nashville, Tennessee, provided a Lynn E. May, Jr., Study Grant to fund a very productive week of research at their repository. I appreciate the help and attention of Bill Sumners, the archive director. Also, thanks go to the staff at the Margaret I. King Library, University of Kentucky, for going beyond the call of duty to help a wandering scholar. The staff in Special Collections at the Boyce Centennial Library, Southern Baptist Theological Seminary, also maximized my limited research time there. The affable staff in the interlibrary loan departments at Ellis Library, University of Missouri, and the Richardson Library, Hardin-Simmons University, eased my research burden considerably. Bill Taylor, director of the Serials Department, Roberts Library, Southwestern Baptist Theological Seminary, helped me locate just the right documents just when I needed them.

My colleagues in the Department of History, Hardin-Simmons University in Abilene, Texas, have provided the encouragement needed to produce this work while focusing on teaching. Many thanks go to Scot Danforth of the University of Tennessee Press for his editorial assistance, but more for his patience, understanding, and his belief in this work. The excellent guidance of

the readers he selected helped me find the strengths of the story and cull out some of the weaknesses. I also appreciate Jay Norrell for the work he did as copyeditor to improve the clarity of expression. Portions of chapter five previously appeared as "Sallie Rochester Ford: Fiction, Faith, and Femininity," in *Baptist History & Heritage* 40 (Summer–Fall 2005), pages 91–99. I am grateful to Bruce Gourley, Executive Director of the Baptist History and Heritage Society, for permission to use this material.

Finally, this work would never have begun without the unfailing love and support of my wife, Ruth. Her typing efforts on the first draft, taken from hand-written copy, helped immensely and, I am sure, damaged her eyesight permanently. Her patience, encouragement, dedication, and compassion are measureless. The hours she spent caring for our children, Mallory, Madison, and Grayson so that I could be about this project are countless. She is the epitome of a virtuous woman and I am blessed exceedingly beyond reason to call her my wife. I dedicate this work to her.

Introduction:
The Baptist Impulse and Kentucky

"**T**he success of our denomination is an illustrious example of the triumph of truth over error." So began a letter sent by the members of the Baptist Association in 1850 to the members of all the churches that affiliated with the association in central Kentucky. Their boastful tone reveals the clear sense of pride that these Baptists took in their role as propagators of the Baptist brand of "truth" in the pluralistic religious environment that characterized post-Revolutionary America. This group's boasts, however, were as loud as their particular contributions were small. Just ten years before, in 1840, the association had been struggling for its survival amidst doctrinal disputes, and had reached a low point of only five churches totaling 251 members. By 1850, though, they had rebounded to three times that number. The struggles and successes that they experienced in their short history had occurred in different ways and at different times in the dozens of other associations in their state, and in the hundreds from Maine to Mississippi. Thus, when these Kentuckians wrote of triumph, they viewed it locally, nationally, and even globally. With this in mind, their letter continued, "Without any settled organization by which the whole body could be wielded for the accomplishment of given results, and held together by no bonds but those of affection, we have come up through afflictions, and now exert an influence that will tell upon the destinies of the religious world."[1] This small band of believers could not have imagined how right they were.

Between 1776 and the mid-1800s, the number of Baptists in America grew at a staggering rate, rising from fifty thousand at the outbreak of revolution to over one million as the nation fractured into civil war. To some degree, this

success was foreshadowed in the American colonial experience. Before the revivals of the 1730s and 1740s labeled the First Great Awakening, the Baptists were a marginal religious group. Their separatist sentiments flew in the face of the established religion. The revival movement that affected the established order offered a new and radical message of experiential religion, wherein God's grace shines into one's sinful soul and gives new life. This "new birth" or "new light" message invigorated the religious landscape from Massachusetts to the Carolinas, accentuating the relationship between God and the individual. With the new worldview, New Light converts, many of whom had been christened as children in their Congregational churches, desired to affirm their new birth through re-baptism. Finding their churches theologically lacking and politically attached to the state, numbers of converts found welcome haven in the Baptist churches. Thus, the Baptist movement in America became the primary beneficiary of an Awakening not of their creation. Their expansion into and subsequent success in the South began a new phase of Baptist persecution based upon their continued challenges to the establishmentarian Anglican social and political order.[2]

Though the Baptist's dissident ethic appealed to a scattered and growing faction of colonists in pre-revolutionary America, the period between 1776 and 1860 marked the movement's coming of age as the old, colonial patterns of deference and privilege faded after the revolution. Unbound by British regulation, citizens of the nation moved west in great masses and explored opportunities for profit and social mobility. Old-guard political patrons lost ground to a new and increasingly populist political class that garnered the support of an ever-widening voting base. Such rapid and turbulent change brought with it a host of anxieties. The early republic's fluorescence deferred the true flowering of independence for all its inhabitants, since the democratizing trend largely excluded women and African Americans.[3] Innovations in transportation and technology paralleled increasingly obvious class stratification. Reform movements organized voluntaristic American men and women to combat the social evils that had cast dark shadows over the anxious early republic. While more and more Americans joined the westward quest for land, riches, and opportunity, the rift between the North and South dilated with mounting social, political, economic, and cultural disjunctures.[4]

In the late eighteenth and early nineteenth centuries, the westward immigrants from the seaboard states brought their faiths with them, and among these Baptists were the largest religious group. From Virginia and the Carolinas,

Baptists traversed the Cumberland Gap; from the mid-Atlantic states, Baptists floated down the Ohio River. As they met in the central, Bluegrass region, Kentucky acted as filter through which the migrants brought their customs and traditions. The Baptists brought their factions of Regular and Separate to Kentucky, where they blended, creating a synthesis that would characterize the vibrant Baptist movement in the nineteenth-century South.[5]

Among these westward migrants were Baptist preachers like Thomas Tinsley and William Hickman. Kentucky's Baptists mark Tinsley and Hickman's 1776 preaching at the first permanent white settlement (Harrodsburg) as the first Baptist preaching in the region. At the end of the year, Virginia's House of Burgesses designated these western land claims Kentucky County. As settlers moved in, three Baptist churches were established in 1781: the first two being the Severn's Valley Church in Elizabethtown and the Cedar Creek Church twenty miles east in Bardstown. The third church planted in Kentucky had actually formed in Virginia years before and was transplanted by the membership in Kentucky under the leadership of their pastor, Lewis Craig. Making a journey of over six hundred miles, the "Travelling Church" settled near and named themselves after Gilbert's Creek, some twenty miles southeast of Harrodsburg. Less than a year later, Craig and most of the congregation moved thirty miles north, near Lexington, and established themselves as the South Elkhorn Baptist Church. By 1785, eighteen churches had formed in Kentucky County, and six of these bonded together as the Elkhorn Association, the first such association west of the Alleghany Mountains.[6]

In 1790, with Kentucky on the cusp of statehood, one in every twenty-three of its residents were Baptists, a relatively high concentration on par with other states like Virginia (1:33), Rhode Island (1:20), and Georgia (1:25). Early growth in Kentucky's Baptist numbers came not from other traveling churches or immigration from Virginia. Indeed, over the next ten years, the Baptist population failed to double. Between 1800 and 1803, however, the number of Baptist church members tripled, largely due to the Great Revival. The Methodist population in Kentucky tripled as well in these years of revival. Numerical growth for the Baptists continued apace, doubling in the next decade and reaching over 45,000 by 1829.[7] The advent of preacher Alexander Campbell, discussed with greater detail in a later chapter, nearly devastated western Baptist churches in the 1830s. Campbell's "Reformation" provides a striking example of how the movement's democratic values could strain Baptist identity, particularly during periods of intense theological crisis. In the next few years, numerous

churches would divide over Campbell's ideas, and some ten thousand of Kentucky's Baptists would join his movement.[8] Despite such internal crises, Kentucky was the state in the South and West where Baptists most outpaced their rivals. By 1840, the Baptists had regained and surpassed their previous numerical strength. The number of Baptists grew dramatically, from 49,308 in 1840 to 74,965 in 1850, then to 94,759 in 1860. As Mark Noll has observed about Methodist and Baptist competition, contentions "existed wherever these two aggressive forms of populist Christianity overlapped." Nationally, Methodists outpaced Baptists in the early nineteenth century. In 1850 there were three Methodists for every two Baptists in the United States. The same year in Kentucky, though, there were five Baptists for every 3.3 Methodists. By 1860, one in every twelve Kentuckians was a member of a Baptist church and the adherence rate was likely much larger.[9]

The success of Baptists in Kentucky, in many ways, reflects their success in America in the early national period. Indeed, the Baptists constituted one of the major forces of the Second Great Awakening. With important exceptions, American historians in the early to mid-twentieth century tended to ignore the religious vibrancy of the Second Great Awakening, and much more the Baptist presence. Narratives on American religion tended to highlight, and perhaps exaggerated, the early influence of the seventeenth-century New England Puritans and the revivalism of the eighteenth and nineteenth centuries. Such studies tended to emphasize the intellectualism of the New England religious elites or the emotionalism of the mainstream evangelicals elsewhere.[10] In a kind of backlash, the "new social historians" sought to recover the voices of marginalized groups, such as the Mormons, Shakers, Catholics, and a host of minor prophets who led colorful—but ultimately doomed—movements.[11] While these studies promoted an appropriate sensitivity to the "variegated patterns of the American religious kaleidoscope," they also overcompensated for the consensus historians' failings and too often characterized more traditional religious groups as boring or bourgeois or both. Further, these studies sometimes presented such fringe groups as oppressed victims of the market economy or as indicative of Christianity's tendency toward social control.[12]

The recovery of a middle ground occurred in the 1990s in the wake of highly influential studies, including those of Nathan O. Hatch and Jon Butler. Hatch writes that democratization is thematically "central to understanding the development of American Christianity, and that the years of the early republic are the most crucial in revealing that process." Painting with broad strokes

and relying on fragmentary evidence, Hatch left it to future scholars to unpack the strengths and weaknesses of his thesis. Butler, in contrast, agreed that Christianity in the early republic had contributed to "a developing American democracy," but only as it "rested as fully on its pursuit of coercive authority and power as on its concern for individualism or its elusive antiauthoritarian rhetoric." In both of these major works, the Baptists appear as a significant movement with which historians must reckon. Both works also subtly note how the Baptists fail to fit with the other movements. Hatch, for instance, analyzes Methodists, Mormons, the Christian Connection, Baptists, and black religion and acknowledges that "it is easy to miss the democratic character" of the first three, whose ecclesiastical structures "turned out to be less democratic than . . . the New England Standing Order." Regarding leadership, Butler included Presbyterians, Congregationalists, and Methodists among the groups wherein "authority continued to flow down from the top" in the post-colonial period, while Baptists and Quakers "continued to hold complex notions of the ministerial role."[13] Thus, for both Hatch and Butler, the Baptists represented a major religious group difficult to categorize with the others.

Other influential works which contributed to the late twentieth-century renaissance of appreciation of early American religion, such as Christine Heyrman's *Southern Cross,* have deemphasized the important differences between the early nineteenth-century evangelical groups. Scholarly studies attempting to recapture those differences seem to simplify matters in the opposite extreme.[14] Still other works challenged Hatch's broad analysis of democratic faith by reasserting the centrality of the Congregationalists to religion in the early republic. For Congregationalism to avoid being marginalized, these scholars had to replace popularity with political activism in discussing "successful" religious movements.[15]

While the study of Baptists remained comparatively dormant, Nathan Hatch's challenge to historians to unravel the "puzzle of American Methodism" generated numerous scholarly studies of the most successful religious movement in the Second Awakening. These works examined the Methodists from diverse angles, nationally and regionally.[16] The resultant shelf-full of books helped explain the reasons the Methodists grew from a minor upstart group during the Revolution to "the largest, most geographically diverse movement of middling and artisan men and women in the early republic," numbering over 1.5 million adherents by the Civil War.[17] While the studies of Methodism help expose the myth of a monolithic evangelicalism

in the early republic, they have also overwhelmed understandings of religious pluralism in the period. In other words, if the scholarly recipe for early American religion first included copious amounts of Puritanism, followed by heaping spoonfuls of revivalism, to which were added dashes of spicy fringe movements, then the gallons of Methodism drowned out most of the other flavors. As a consequence, the study of Baptist expansion, which nearly matched the Methodists' phenomenal growth, has been, in the words of Mark Noll, "scandalously neglected."[18]

Certain scholars have claimed that the nature of Baptists hinders the historical study of them. Nathan Hatch, for example, notes that Baptist centrifugalism gave "free reign to regional distinctives and take-charge entrepreneurs." Dissenters like William Miller in New York and J. R. Graves in Tennessee led factions within the larger movement, which, Hatch claims, created such a haze that historians have failed to pin the Baptists down. Paul K. Conkin likewise comments that the Baptist "lack of organization makes elusive their early history and has consistently won them less historical attention than their numbers justified."[19] That Baptists were divided amongst themselves over theology and style cannot be denied. After the eighteenth-century revivals, Baptists largely divided between those who supported the New Light and those who did not. So-called Regular Baptists opposed the revivals and valued an orderly and sober worship style. They found virtue in inter-congregational unity, tended to be better educated, and flourished in large towns and cities. Separate Baptists, on the other hand, took part in the Awakening and believed the Holy Spirit could inspire the individual conscience. Therefore, they relished congregational autonomy, engaged in raucous and enthusiastic worship, and demanded strict discipline among their membership. Their preachers were fiery exhorters rather than educated expositors. They denounced doctrinal statements, or "confessions of faith," as man-made additions to scripture and tended to flourish in small villages and rural areas. These divisions and others challenge those seeking a comprehensive interpretation of Baptists as a group.[20]

Despite the supposed hindrances, recent scholarship has sought to capture the important role Baptists have played in American religion and national development in the early republic. Several works emphasize prolific and influential preachers such as Isaac Backus, Francis Wayland, and Basil Manly.[21] The abundance of Baptist church meeting minutes, ripe for statistical analysis, have led scholars to emphasize Baptist discipline as part of the movement's culture. While these discipline studies have improved understandings of gender and

racial issues among Baptists, their tendency is to limit a more holistic view of the Baptists as a movement.[22] As this study will demonstrate, Baptist centrifugalism and factionalism need not hinder research or understanding of Baptists. Indeed, if anything, they constitute a key part of the resiliency of the Baptists and deserve analysis.

Toward achieving a holistic view of the Baptist movement, certain distinctive characteristics of Baptists provide the basis for analysis. Collectively, I have labeled these characteristics "the Baptist impulse." First, Baptists placed a high priority on the act of baptism, demanding their converts undergo the immersion ritual before entering into full membership in the church. More than a mere initiatory rite, the act confirmed publicly the convert's transformation from one existence to another. Baptism, in their theology, was an act undertaken by a believing individual; thus they refused infants, frowned upon children partaking in the ritual, and demanded a public confession of conversion. Second, Baptists elevated the status of the individual in their cosmology so that, regardless of race or gender, human beings had direct access to God without the arbitration of any church body or hierarchy. Salvation of the convert's soul came from God's directly bestowed grace and not through church membership or the sacramental privileges dispensed through the church. From this individualistic ethic flowed their emphasis on religious liberty and subsequent practical commitment to disestablishment of religion. Third, even as the Baptists elevated the individual, they also privileged the local church as the free and corporate manifestation of God's people. While converts had full reign to commune with the divine, part of their new existence entailed respecting the consensus of all other converts who, it was assumed, had also received guidance. Divine wisdom, in other words, was found in many mouths. Working from this commitment, Baptists held congregational autonomy high, as the only form of church government approved by God. Divine wisdom also came through the Bible. Thus, Baptists tried to establish their theology and practice on their understanding of that ancient source. Fourth, these priorities contributed to the understanding of ministers as those called by God and by his people. Baptist clergymen were first among equals and were accountable to both their God and their church.

In short, the core of the Baptist impulse—the movement's fluid structure and democratic spirit analyzed herein—have proven to be its greatest strength and the source of its most terrible struggles. It was crucial to the growth of the Baptists in Kentucky, a state that serves as a window into the elements of

Baptist life that transcended region. Kentucky offers an excellent, representative site for understanding who the colonial Baptists had been, who they were becoming in the early national era, and who they would be after the Civil War. In essence, this work is a regional study of the Baptist impulse, and of how the religious turbulence of the Second Great Awakening was actually worked out on the ground.

In this largely topically arranged study of the Baptist impulse, the first three chapters unfold the primary elements in the impulse and how they were embodied in the Kentucky experience. Chapter one explores the three primary rituals in the Baptist movement: experiencing conversion and relating the conversion narrative, undergoing public immersion baptism, and partaking in communion. Beyond their religious significance, the three are analyzed by how the movement used them to negotiate tensions between the individual and the community. Chapter two examines Baptist preachers, particularly focusing on how Baptists conceived of them as first among equals, how the preacher was both product and shaper of the movement's priorities, and how he personified the democratic Baptist ethic. Chapter three highlights the significance of the local church to the Baptist movement, a point difficult to overstate. Each individual church represented the body of Christ on Earth, which bestowed high honor and entailed heavy burdens and responsibilities. Kentucky Baptists prized their local democracies as more biblical and more American than any alternative. The use of "associations," or affiliations of churches in a region, also reveals how Baptists tentatively approached inter-church cooperation.

Beginning in the 1820s, various forces of change in Kentucky encouraged internal examination of the movement's faith and practice. Chapter four focuses on those forces of change which affected the movement between 1825 and 1845, including Alexander Campbell's Reformation and schism, Andrew Fuller's influential revision of Calvinism, the quest for institutional refinement, the resultant anti-institutional resistance movement, and the challenge of Methodist successes. As these challenges and changes intersected, the movement emerged from the period prepared for a new era of denominationalism with a more institutionalized version of the Baptist impulse. Chapters five and six focus on the roles that Baptist women and black Baptists played in shaping, articulating, and propagating the movement. The opportunities and challenges they faced reveal much about the nature of the impulse. The conclusion, chapter seven, captures how the continued quest for

refinement and a new view of the Baptist past reoriented the movement's priorities between 1840 and 1860. Success encouraged a boldness which skewed the Baptist impulse in Kentucky toward greater rigidity, denominational arrogance, greater institutionalization, and the belief that the American future was theirs for the taking.

1

From One World to Another: Conversion, Baptism, and Communion

Head hanging low, nineteen-year-old John Taylor walked westward to the lonesome mountain on the horizon, where he was sure that he would die. Perhaps he would perish by his own hand or meet his fate at the hands of another; either way the young man was confident that God was his ultimate executioner. As the setting sun cast shadows across his path and a chill wind pierced his soul, Taylor reflected on his last two years and upon the cosmic crimes that had earned him the decree of death.

Taylor had enjoyed his youth in Virginia on his father's farm along Happy Creek in the Shenandoah Valley. His parents, earnest Anglicans, provided John what education they could in the Great Valley, but the young man tended to fill his free hours with frolic. In the winter of 1770, the jovial boy sought his amusement at a religious gathering near his family's farm. The famous Baptist preacher William Marshall, known for thunder-gust preaching and drawing crowds of hundreds or thousands, had come preaching repentance down the Great Valley and gathered a crowd outside an old chapel. A vast concourse

of hearers stood in the snow, captivated by Marshall's powerful New Light preaching, but Taylor moved among the congregation quietly, amusing himself at their foolish weeping and shouting. As he neared the stump from which Marshall proclaimed the awful destiny of the unrepentant, Taylor spied his fourteen-year-old friend Thomas Buck. Tears streamed down young Buck's face as he listened to the preacher. Marshall starkly depicted the final throne of judgment whereupon God would administer justice on the souls of the wicked. Seeing his grim future afresh, Buck cried out loudly for mercy. Taylor himself stood agape, struck dumb, staring at his friend in wonder. When his senses returned, Taylor began to hear Marshall's proclamation in a new light. As the blistering exposition of impending doom sunk in, Taylor's scoffing proclivity subsided. While listening intently to Marshall's warnings, he felt as if struck by lightning, and sensed that his "heart was touched with a dagger." In a moment, his frame of reference changed and he felt love for those he had mocked, especially for Marshall, the messenger of condemnation.[1]

For the next year, however, young Taylor lived despondently. He continued his folly and vice, but felt guilt rather than pleasure. As the year wore on, his grief overwhelmed him to the point where he felt like roaring aloud. He had to excuse himself repeatedly from his friends' company to bemoan his hopelessly sinful state. He took to reading the Bible, but could not muster the boldness to approach God in prayer, lest he offend an infinitely holy deity. Beginning in the summer of 1771, Taylor forsook his old folly-loving friends and endeavored to control his behavior. His initial success in this effort led him to believe that he would "get to Heaven as well as the noisy Baptists."[2]

With his self-proclaimed holiness, Taylor felt no need to attend any worship meetings until October 1771, when his newly converted boyhood friends Joseph and Isaac Redding began preaching in their Happy Creek neighborhood. The perspicuous proclamations of these two Baptist brothers encouraged Taylor to keener consideration of his plight. He discovered that while he may have corrected his external vices, inwardly he remained "a perfect blank of darkness, from which dreadful darkness all manner of evil was constantly flowing." His perceived new light had "blown out as with a puff" and he felt every possible effort to correct himself to be futile, as his corruption multiplied itself beyond mastery. Throughout the winter, Taylor had no appetite and found his sleep fitful and restless. Perhaps, he thought, he had missed his chance for salvation and reconciliation with God. Then in February 1772, while chopping firewood in a deep snow, a more troubling

possibility occurred to him. Perhaps God hated him and had condemned him for eternity. With this thought, Taylor dropped his axe, convulsed in a tremor, and fell to his knees, not praying for mercy but believing in the justice of his eternal sentence. For the next month, young Taylor agonized over his plight, ruing the day he had been born. He felt that he "had better be in Hell than alive here." At last, Taylor concluded that "destruction was at the very door." In great anxiety, he resolved to meet his fate alone and he began his death march to the lonesome mountain.[3]

As night descended, Taylor passed under a high, overhanging rock at the foot of a mountain where he believed God would execute his sentence. As he had done countless times before, Taylor sank to his knees and felt again that his punishment was just, praying that God's righteousness would remain unimpeachable by this demonstration of wrath. But in that moment, while speaking, Taylor sensed a new release, "a sweet calm and peace of mind" that he had never known before. He felt a new possibility of salvation that altered his "resolution as to dying in the mountain." He repented at the Hanging Rock and "began to cry again for mercy" rather than justice. Energized with hope, Taylor returned from his spiritual precipice to his Anglican family and friends. But they received him coldly. His friends rejected his new found faith. His parents grieved over their son's "late, great delusion."[4]

In May 1772, Taylor attended a Baptist church meeting for the first time. The log meeting house stood on a bluff overlooking the flowing waters of the South Fork of the Shenandoah. Worshipers filled the meeting house and many more stood outside. Taylor listened through the open logs of the house. Eight people stood before the pastor and congregation, relating their conversion experiences so that they might be baptized and welcomed into the church. Hearing their professions, Taylor doubted that most of them had been truly converted and even wondered at the pastor for allowing these "poor, deluded souls to join the church." His friend Isaac Redding, who was inside the house, whispered out through the logs for John to come in and relate his experience, but Taylor doubted that he had been converted and felt the pastor was "sending people enough to Hell already." The next day, a Sunday, Taylor witnessed the eight converts baptized into church membership, surely sealing "their own damnation at the Lord's table."[5]

That night and the following day, Taylor pondered restlessly what he had seen and heard, comparing it with his own experience underneath the Hanging Rock. He resolved to take a hymn book, find a secret place, and pray

for answers. A familiar hymn verse occurred to him and he repeated it as he walked:

> *Jesus, my God, I know His name.*
> *His name is all my trust.*
> *Nor will He put my soul to shame*
> *Or let my hope be lost.*

As he wrestled with his thoughts and retraced his own spiritual journey, he finally embraced the genuineness of his experience at the rock and his salvation as complete and secure. So too were those people saved whom he had seen immersed in the South Fork of the Shenandoah. Two weeks later, at his next opportunity, Taylor himself entered the baptismal waters and became a member of the Lower South River Baptist Church in northern Virginia.[6]

Within a year of John Taylor's experience at the Hanging Rock and baptism, he became a preacher and a decade later moved to Kentucky. By the time of his death, sixty-three years after walking away from the Hanging Rock, he had become one of the most famous and influential Baptist preachers in the state of Kentucky. In 1812, Taylor returned to the neighborhood of his youth and, in the company of his old friend Thomas Buck, visited the now-worn stump from which William Marshall had preached his message of repentance. They found the exact spot where Buck stood and wept at the preacher's convicting words. Taylor then returned alone to "a lonesome, hanging rock in a rugged mountain," where he had gained hope and relief from guilt forty years before. One last time, Taylor knelt underneath that rock "with thanksgiving to my God for past favors and [with] prayer to Him for preservation for days to come."[7]

Taylor's lengthy search for sure salvation brought him into contact with elements which would be key in early Kentucky Baptist life: preachers traveling from stump to stump proclaiming messages from the Bible, crowds of hearers intermixed with mockers, an underlying Calvinistic worldview, the undulating passions of conversion, meeting houses overflowing with congregants, and the powerful meaning conveyed through hymn texts. Taylor's tale also portrays the church evaluating the supplicant's religious experiences, crowds witnessing a nearby stream become sacred baptismal waters, the sense of security and belonging that accompanied conversion and church membership, and the blurring of sacred and profane whereby stumps, fields, rocks, and streams are endowed with spiritual significance. Likewise, in these elements, the Baptists,

by the construction and revision of their distinct identity, delicately negotiated and often blurred the border between private and public, individual and community.

The rites of conversion, baptism, and communion are crucial to understanding who Baptists were and how they perceived themselves. The Baptists allowed only "regenerated," or converted, individuals into the church community. Each local church governed itself autonomously and thus held the power to examine each candidate's conversion account and decide whether the conversion was legitimate. The often lengthy conversion experience took the individual to intensely isolated depths both emotionally and physically. In relating their experiences to the church members, the individual's private and personal pilgrimage became the subject of public evaluation: an evaluation that determined if the individual could take part in a community kept pure by guaranteeing that all its members had each experienced similar spiritual journeys.

The validation of a person's conversion qualified him to be baptized into that church community. Of all elements of Baptist life, the rite of baptism was the most central to the movement's culture. Beyond the fact that the rite gave the movement its name, baptism served as the true entry into local church membership. It was also the most public and well-known of the Baptist practices, the first of the two "ordinances," or commanded rites of Christ—the other was communion—in which the movement engaged, and the most stridently defended Baptist doctrine. The act of baptism straddled the line between the individual and the community. For Baptists, the rite symbolized the death, burial, and resurrection of Jesus. Culturally, it also symbolized the crossing over from the dry wilderness to Canaan, the promised land of milk and honey.[8] The candidate entered the baptismal waters alone. On the banks of the stream or river stood three groups of people: the church members already baptized, those who were part of the congregation but had not yet joined the church officially, and often a number of curious onlookers unconnected with the church. The "administrator" of the baptism, usually the pastor of the local church, called the candidate out into the water, placed his hands on the candidate, and then momentarily immersed her below the rolling waters. The minister raised up the candidate to a new life as a church member, and she took her place on the bank with the clustered people of God.

A third element of Baptist life, along with the relation of the conversion experience and baptism, which visibly brought together the individual and the community, was the "Lord's Supper," or communion. While Baptists only

experienced conversion and baptism once in their lives, the ordinance of communion, as a recurrent event, symbolized their continual remembrance of Jesus's sacrificial death. Each church set its own schedule for taking communion, though typically it was practiced at regular intervals during the year. The communion ritual placed a heavy burden upon the individual. According to the Baptist interpretation of Paul's teachings, only the regenerate could partake at the Lord's table, and only those who examined themselves and were worthy to commune. At the same time, while the ritual seemed focused on the individual's relationship with God, the supper served as a unifying event for the regenerate church members to build a sense of community. Only those who had been converted, examined by the church, and baptized had opportunity to sit at the exclusive table.

Each of these three elements—conversion, baptism, and communion—reinforced the importance of the individual in the cosmos and the bond of communal identity. On the early Kentucky frontier these communal reference points served a critical function for socialization, but also for simple protection and psychological wellbeing. But even as the state developed and the frontier moved farther westward, these three important elements remained central to Baptist life. However, the meaning attached to each one evolved in a unique way to contribute to the movement's development.

In the early nineteenth century, for example, the Baptist conversion narrative was a familiar tale, easy to evaluate when related to the church. Indeed, the narrative at times seemed markedly formulaic. Converts related harrowing stories of their progress from unregenerate to regenerated, and their narratives typically followed a seven-step framework. In the first step, they gained knowledge of their sinful state and were made aware of their need for some kind of redemption. Second, they sought to reform themselves by doing good works. When this hoped-for reformation failed to occur, their spirits sank into the third stage, characterized by a forlorn sadness made more burdensome by an overwhelming sense of guilt. Fourth, to assuage their guilt and to find some kind of answers to their difficulty, the pilgrim turned to the Bible, other religiously oriented texts, or sources of religious knowledge. Whether they read or listened to others, they searched for redress and hope in the midst of their own hopelessness. But what they found in the Bible only confirmed the surety of their condemnation. Thus the fifth and worst state consisted of hopeless wandering and a growing awareness that all hope was eternally lost. In the pit of despair, the wanderers threw themselves on the mercy of God and sought, in

the sixth stage, pardon not only for vice but for their depraved nature as well. Finally, having arrived at their weakest, saddest, and most dependent condition, in the seventh stage, pilgrims were converted and experienced a radiant lightness of being, in stark contrast to the weight of sin that had bedeviled them for so long.[9]

Though most of the early Kentucky Baptist conversion narratives followed a pattern, each had its own peculiarities. James Pendleton, for example, in his period of self-reformation, considered himself so independent that he cursed God and said that he would have been "glad to annihilate Him." Reuben Ross, married and in his twenties when he was converted in 1802, had always perceived religion as solemn and gloomy and, even after his wife's conversion, looked at it with aversion. However, he became more interested in his own salvation after the death of one of his close friends who he believed had never been converted. In another instance, John Taylor's teenage sister Jane became convicted in the mid-1780s after she made fun of one of her brother's church members. Though the member was a devout man, he tended to belabor his preachers with endless questions. One Saturday evening, he called on Taylor to extinguish his doubts about his own salvation. During his extended lamentations to his preacher, Jane, "ready to burst with laughter at . . . this foolish man's talk, left the house to vent her levity to her satisfaction." On Sunday, she saw the man and it "occurred to her that he was the most holy-looking man she ever saw"—if this holy man doubted his security, then what fate was in store for her? Within a month, she was among the first baptized in a local revival.[10]

Another variance in the conversion experience was the incident that prompted or motivated the struggle. For many, hearing a preacher hold forth on the impending judgment of those caught unaware in the last days naturally compelled fear and trembling conducive to a conversion experience. However, seventeen-year-old Jeremiah Vardeman, though converted during a religious revival in 1792, denied that the revival preachers had anything to do with his awakening. Instead he attributed it to the teachings of his parents and his own Bible reading. For others, like Thomas Smith, Jr., being present at a baptism could lead to contemplation of one's spiritual destiny. William Vaughan's conversion in 1810 began when he witnessed the dying suspirations of a man he considered wicked and profane. Samuel Greathouse began pondering his own fate when, during a house-raising, a falling log killed two nearby men instantly. Sometimes the most trivial event could goad a person toward contemplation. Collin Hodge, on his way to a western Kentucky horse race, chanced

upon a group of people returning from a revival meeting. As he passed the group on the road, the well-read Hodge ruminated upon the thought that as he and the revivalists traveled in opposite directions now, so they might also at their deaths. The next day, Hodge joined a Methodist church; but within a year he had left that movement to join the Baptists. Other converts had more unworldly awakenings. In 1809, Samuel Vancleave, a fun-loving man of means in his forties, was building his brick home with the help of some workmen. While discussing the celebration he intended to host upon the work's completion, Vancleave danced a jig back and forth across the scaffolding. Suddenly, he claimed, he heard a voice clearly repeating in his ear, "Thou fool! This night shall thy soul be required of thee!" The formerly gregarious Vancleave immediately took to his bed expecting to die soon. For several days after, he remained alive, though he ate little. Within a short time, he converted and joined a nearby Baptist church in northern Kentucky.[11]

Dreams could also play a role in conversion. Wilson Thompson claimed to have suffered terrible nightmares of judgment from which he would awake "trembling with alarm and terror" during his conversion experience. Two weeks into deist William Vaughan's conversion distress, he had "a remarkable dream." In the dream, he said, "I was on the farm my father died on. I had a vision of hell. I saw the smoke of the torment of the damned ascending up out of the open crater of a mound. Then I seemed to be at a place in the woods where there was a collection of people, and several ministers preaching." A week later, Vaughan followed a small company of people going to a Baptist church meeting three miles away. When he arrived, he saw a preacher he had never encountered before, but whom he recognized from his dream, "Even to the minutia of his dress." Within six weeks, Vaughan was baptized into a local Baptist church.[12] Dreams suffused the religious experiences of early Baptists and other religious groups. In addition to the role they played in conversion, they foreshadowed revival and were taken to be a means of divine communication. However, as biblicists, Baptists tended to view their dreams skeptically. They did not prioritize their dreams and visions over the Bible. Thus, they did not see dreams as revelations that would add substantially to the revelation in the Bible, in the manner of Joseph Smith and William Miller. In contrast, historians of early Methodism reveal how dreams served as one of the most subjective and purely democratic influences in that movement. While not theoretically elevating their dreams to the level of scriptural revelation, Methodists in practice gave dreams substantial credence in decision-making.[13]

Wilson Thompson's written account of his earlier conversion included contemporary Baptist beliefs on juvenile conversion. He began his struggle in 1799, shortly before the "Great Revival" spread across central Kentucky. Thompson grew up in a Baptist family and his father was a respected leader in their local church. So frequently did traveling preachers lodge in the Thompson home in northern Kentucky, neighbors labeled it the "Baptist Tavern." With religious conversations in abundance, young Wilson grew particularly interested in "the awful realities of a future state, the miseries of the wicked, and kindred subjects." Fearing an eternity in hell, eleven-year-old Wilson "resolved to do good, get religion, and thus get clear of future miseries, and at last reach a happy heaven." Having passed through the expected first and second stages, Thompson began to experience the third; as he grew tired of doing good and dreaded the prospect of spending "a whole long life in this irksome way, and never see any pleasure in youth or manhood."[14]

As Wilson Thompson wrestled with his tiresome future, he overheard his mother and aunt discussing the recent death of his young cousin. The crux of their conversation was whether the girl had passed the "line of accountability." As the women explained it, the line represented that point in a young person's life when he lost the innocence of his infancy and became accountable to God for his sinful nature. Upon discovering this novel idea, Thompson immediately felt "a very deep interest in the doctrine" and set out on "a close search for this line." He wished to consult the Bible, but his marginal literacy hindered this kind of search. So any time he heard the Bible read, he listened intently to hear evidence of the "line." Shortly thereafter, he heard a reading from the book of Luke in which a twelve-year-old Jesus tells his parents that he must be about his Father's business, leading Thompson to conclude that the "line" must be at twelve years of age. Thus pre-teen Thompson determined "at once to drop all my religion, and spend that year in taking my fill of sin, while yet an infant and in a safe condition . . . not accountable for anything that I might do while on the infant side of that line."[15]

During Thompson's year full of unrecorded sins, a religious revival occurred in northern Kentucky and he witnessed many of his pre-teen friends affected by the "powerful work of grace." Wilson's heart grew troubled since he had continued his indulgence in sin into his thirteenth year. The revival renewed Wilson's awareness of his sin-sick soul. Over the next few months, he sought answers in overheard conversations, sermons preached, hymn texts sung, or remembered excerpts of poetry instead of his own reading of the Bible. Like

John Taylor, Thompson found peace only when he embraced his dependence on God's grace rather than pursuing perfection on his own.[16]

Despite the variances, however, early Kentucky Baptist conversion narratives generally revealed a bias toward Calvinistic theology. John Calvin, a sixteenth-century reformer, emphasized the sovereignty of God in the process of salvation. His thoughts particularly informed the beliefs of the British Particular Baptists. These believed that God had predestined, before the creation of the universe, who would be included among the "elect," or the regenerate. The actual agent of this election was the death of Jesus, who made possible the "atonement," or reconciliation of sinful man to a holy God. If Jesus died for the elect and the elect had been chosen before time, there was nothing that anyone could do to pursue salvation; they either were elect or they were not. This Calvinistic understanding of the atonement dramatically affected Baptist development in Britain and America. If a Baptist preacher took this doctrine seriously, it abrogated his responsibility to preach sermons that would convict his hearers of sin, since the job of conviction rested solely in the hands of God, acting through the Holy Spirit. Preachers need not invite or exhort their hearers to accept salvation since whether those hearers would or would not accept God's irresistible grace depended upon a predetermined decision by God.[17] Preachers might instill knowledge—that is, they might encourage the first stage and inform the fourth stage of the conversion process—but the narratives clearly reveal the private nature of the experience, as the sinners wrestled with justice, grace, and mercy before finally arriving at the seventh and last stage.

William Conrad expressed just such Calvinistic influence. Conrad related in his conversion narrative how he gazed up at the sky and proclaimed his "soul was given the knowledge that on account of what Jesus had done, God would remain just and save a poor sinner" such as he. Likewise, fourteen-year-old Hannah Graves seemed almost unaware of her conversion when it occurred in the mid-1780s. She and her best friend Polly Woolfolk, during a revival at the Clear Creek church, would sit up late at night together worried to weeping over the state of their souls. Each took turns rousing the other from sleep with earnest inquiries such as, "How can you sleep when every drawing breath may terminate in eternal destruction?" As John Taylor recalled it, days later at a meeting Polly noticed something out of the ordinary in Hannah's expression and asked her, "'What ails you?' Receiving no answer she then replied, 'Hannah, you are converted! O Hannah, you are converted!' Joyful Hannah,

after a little, replied [that] something had taken place she could not well account for. But hoped it might be that great blessing."[18]

When converts related their harrowing tales of conviction to the church in a public profession, the church members listened for Calvinistic clues in the tale. In addition to a Calvinist pattern, hearers also expected a level of confidence in the telling. If the narration left out those important details, they might question the supplicant for clarification. Colonial Anglican missionary Charles Woodmason mocked such interrogation ceremonies. He called it a "farce" to see the church members sitting there "with fix'd Countenances and grave looks, hearing all this Nonsense for Hours together, and making particular Enquiries, When, How, Where, in what Manner, these Miraculous Events happen'd." What Woodmason betrays in his lampoonery is the seriousness and attentiveness of the Baptists as they heard the alleged converts' stories. Jane Taylor related her deliverance so clearly and confidently that no one asked her any questions. During a revival in 1822, Martha "Patsy" Scearce delivered an account of her conversion with such evidence and confidence that she proved a tough act to follow. Several of her young peers planning to relate their own experience after her grew discouraged and less persuaded by the evidence they themselves had mustered. College student Thomas Smith, Jr. had a more difficult time relating his experience at the church in Georgetown. Though he had training in public speaking, he said that in giving his experience, "The man disappears and the weeping and stammering babe takes his place. . . . He forgets all he ever learned about oratory, gesture, emphasis. The soul speaks in her own simple and unadorned language, despising the rules of rhetoric and the graces of delivery." When church members needed clarification or wanted to probe the candidate, they were all free to ask questions such as, "Have you now become good, or are you the same great sinners still? Have you had no temptations, evil thoughts, or rambling of mind in the worship of God since the time of your conversion? On whom do you depend for salvation?"[19]

Church members also had liberty to refuse membership if the conversion narrative failed to persuade. Since reception of a member typically required a unanimous vote, one objector could derail an application. Contention over a candidate's reception among the church could prolong the ceremony. The Boone's Creek Church experienced such an episode in the midst of a 1787 revival. At a Saturday church meeting in the woods, an Irishman named Watson related his experience, answered the typical questions, and seemed poised for acceptance when the pastor, John Tanner, stood and expressed his doubts about

Mr. Watson's faith. Tanner opposed the revival, fearing that it was the work of the devil. After the pastor gave his opinion, another man stood and said he wished to interrogate Watson on the subject of God's "eternal decrees"—that is, subjects related to predestination. The moderator, William Hickman, Sr., denied the request, claiming that such topics were too deep for new converts. Rather than refuse Watson, the church set his case aside and then received seven or eight others for membership before sunset. The meeting recessed for refreshment and then reconvened at a nearby cabin. During the recess, Tanner and Watson conversed until Tanner became satisfied with the veracity of the candidate's testimony. Only then was the church able to receive Watson into fellowship.[20]

Of course, the possibility always existed that those relating their conversion had learned the right words to say, but had not truly experienced that of which they spoke. Typically, church members looked for the familiar pattern and earnestness in the telling, but even then they could be fooled. In January 1823, fifteen African Americans sought admission to the Clear Creek Church and all were received. But the next day some members alleged that two of them, children roughly eight to ten years old, had simply "picked up what they stated to the church." Such concerns carried a great deal of weight—threatening impurity in the church—and the church agreed to postpone the children's baptism until these two could be reexamined at their home.[21]

The dramatic struggle of the conversion experience instilled in the Kentucky Baptist converts the desire to pursue personal piety, not because their salvation depended on it, but in thanks for the tranquility gained by unmerited favor. With the sacred charge to pursue holiness, the slightest slip could compel the greatest guilt. Young student Thomas Smith, Jr., illustrated this compulsion for righteousness the day after he had experienced his own redemption. Although he had attended church meetings for much of his life as part of a Baptist congregation, he had neglected to see Sunday as somehow special. But after his conversion he noted, "For the first time in my life I felt determined to keep the Sabbath day holy as far as possible." Yet, within a week of his regeneration, he found himself chatting with a schoolmate and thoughtlessly uttered a profanity. He immediately wondered, "What will he think of me, who have just taken up my cross? . . . Is it an evidence of my not having felt the change from darkness to light? Or is it rather an instance of the force, yea, the eternal tyranny of habit? This should teach me to exercise double diligence."[22]

Even years after conversion, the pursuit of holiness marked the Baptist quest to maintain the devotion produced by the first relief. For many Baptists, and especially for ministers, this kind of drive encouraged them to promulgate their faith and convince others of the commitment God expected of them. Even after an extensive preaching tour of the Missouri territory and serving as pastor of many growing churches, influential Kentucky minister William Warder condemned his own failings in this area. "I grieve and am ashamed," he recorded in his diary, "when I look back and see the great lack of fervent piety and zeal, which marks the most of my life. Indeed, when recollection causes the whole scene to pass before me, I find much to lament, and little to rejoice in." Rather than reveling in the many successes of his life, Warder's un-ending pursuit of holiness forced him to admit that "were it left to my choice to recall it . . . there would be no hesitating in letting it pass."[23]

The demand for practical piety after conversion affected Baptists not just individually, but also on a corporate level. In a pluralistic religious environ-ment, Kentucky Baptists were consistently reminded that their behavior as converts reflected upon the soundness of the movement itself. Neglecting the rigor and striving of the pious would mean certain defamation, not only of themselves, but of their church as a whole. Thus, in times of religious de-clension or dormancy, Baptist leaders urged their parishioners toward intense self-examination and a rekindling of righteousness. During one period of ap-parent stasis, one group of Baptists in central Kentucky asked themselves, "Have we not become so much conformed to the world, and indulged so much in pursuit of the things of this world, that we have lost (in a great degree) [Christ's] image?" They wondered, "Where is that Christian love and affec-tion?" They concluded the lack of love, "Together with that daily declension in practical godliness that is almost universally seen among us, calls aloud for serious examination and actual reformation." The same year, in the south-ern part of the state, other Baptists decried similarly languid conditions and argued for "the importance of growth in grace, because without it, we have no evidence of our being in a state of favor with God." They then encouraged increased piety and self-examination as "one of the means to be employed in promoting growth in grace," since such "a scrutinizing investigation of our hearts and characters will enable us to discover our deficiencies."[24]

The importance of individual conversion, the Calvinistic undertones in their narratives, the valuing of personal piety, and the role of the church in evaluating conversion experiences all remained western Baptist mainstays

throughout the early nineteenth century. During the 1830s, however, new understandings of Calvinism would encourage an appreciation of innovation in church practices and an ambiguous revision of the place of the individual in Baptist life. Both of these changes would in the end help the movement remain competitive in an increasingly pluralistic setting. Likewise, the rite of baptism would also move from a cherished part of Baptist life to an ordinance to be vigorously asserted and defended.

The practice of baptism historically had been a key source of pride for the movement and had made the early Baptists a controversial sect. By denying the validity of infant baptism (or pedobaptism) and by asserting that the true administration was by total immersion, the Baptists diverged from long-time Catholic and Anglican practices, making themselves targets of transatlantic persecution and ridicule for nearly two hundred years. Opponents in seventeenth-century England spread scandalous stories of Baptists immersing women naked or in see-through garments. They told terrifying tales of the victims of Baptists who were immersed in rivers only to sicken and die soon after. In the Carolina hinterland, Anglican Charles Woodmason found Baptist immersion practices offensive and uncivilized. He opined in his journal that "it would not be less offensive to Modesty for them to strip wholly into Buff at once, than to be dipp'd with those very thin Linen Drawers." In debates, opponents accused Baptists of child abuse by refusing infants the manifold benefits of christening. Some Baptists faced imprisonment for asserting their religious views. Baptists in Boston during the mid-seventeenth century faced harassment, exile, and imprisonment from the established church authorities. Even as late as the 1770s, Baptist dissenters endured religious oppression in Virginia.[25]

As religious liberty became more accepted in the United States after the American Revolution, the practice of baptism became less controversial and remained a very public Baptist distinction. Every member of the Baptist movement entered into the fellowship through this public ritual. They did not believe that the ritual had a regenerative purpose. The waters did not "cleanse" the sinner's soul from his or her depravity. Indeed, Baptists expected nothing supernatural to occur whatsoever.[26] That such an apparently vacuous exercise should be held by the Baptists in such high regard, as a significant part of both their lives and their movement's identity, reveals both the power of symbol in Kentucky Baptist faith expressions and their understandings of the biblical mandate for immersion baptism.

Baptists, who considered the Bible their authoritative guidebook both for faith and practice, attempted to follow the examples they saw in the New Testament for their practice of baptism. The first baptisms recorded in the New Testament are performed by John the Baptist before the beginning of Jesus's ministry. Jesus's own baptism at the hand of John is recorded in three of the gospels as the inaugural event of Jesus's ministry. Jesus himself never performed baptism, leaving that to his disciples, and the gospel writers record few of his teachings on the subject. His few references to baptism consist of metaphors. For instance, when two of his followers ask for seats of authority in the Messiah's kingdom, Jesus asks them if they are willing to "be baptized with the baptism that I am baptized with?" They reply that they are, and he assures them that they will surely experience that "baptism," suggesting that his followers not pursue greatness, but humility, service, and sacrifice. Again in the gospel of Luke, Jesus repeats that he has "a baptism to be baptized with, and how distressed I am till it is accomplished," referring to his own suffering and death.[27] Finally, the author of Acts records the resurrected Jesus telling his followers to expect another baptism, not like John's water baptism, but a baptism of the Holy Spirit, which is to occur after Jesus's ascension.

For Baptists in Kentucky, the actions of the New Testament Christians revealed the importance of baptism to building the Christian church. The fuller theological and practical meaning of the ordinance came from the writings of the apostle Paul.[28] As they read Paul's letters to the churches, Baptists saw baptism as an important symbol. In his letters to the Christian churches in Rome and Colosse, Paul elaborated upon the symbolism of baptism. To the Roman church, he asks, "Do you not know that as many of us as were baptized into Christ Jesus were baptized into his death? Therefore we are buried with him through baptism into death, that just as Christ was raised from the dead by the glory of the Father, even so we also should walk in newness of life." Paul repeats this theme to the Colossians, explaining that they have been buried with Jesus in baptism, and raised "with him through faith in the working of God, who raised him from the dead." In these letters, Paul not only explains the symbolism of baptism, but also notes the element of identification. Those who were baptized were "buried with" Jesus and were also "raised with" him. Paul extends this idea further in his letter to the church in Galatia by writing, "As many of you as were baptized into Christ have put on Christ."[29]

In the Baptist understanding, Paul's explication of baptism not only details its symbolic and relational aspects, but also the association between baptism

and unity. On this subject Paul writes, "By one Spirit we were all baptized into one body . . . and have all been made to drink into one Spirit." Elsewhere Paul repeats, "There is one body and one Spirit . . . one Lord, one faith, one baptism; one God and Father of all," emphasizing the level of unity expected of the church and the role that baptism plays that oneness.[30]

To some Baptists, being baptized was merely the final step in entering the "door into the church," the last of the initiatory rites. To others, though, it enhanced and completed the joy they had found in their conversion experience. In each case, early Kentucky Baptists viewed their baptism as the significantly public expression of their faith and the shift from one worldview to another. In 1845, when Thomas Smith, Jr. began his studies at Georgetown College, a Baptist school in northern Kentucky, he had not had a conversion experience. For the waggish Smith, Sunday church meetings were prime opportunities to meet young ladies. Heading to a church meeting at Great Crossing, Smith "found a large crowd assembled . . . all dressed in their Sunday and gayest attire." While the preacher delivered his sermon, Smith "caught the eye of many a shy damsel, as she looked slyly at the stranger." At the baptism of two of his college peers, Smith took in the mood of the moment. "The water's edge was crowded," he wrote, "with persons anxious to behold the ceremony. There is something in baptism calculated to allay the mirthful feelings of the mind and fill it with awe. It may be because it is the door of the church and a formal renunciation of all the pleasures of sinners." As he considered his newly converted friends, he continued, "We look upon our associate as he enters the water with the same feelings that would arise were he going to another country. We feel that we can no longer rank him among those ever ready to rush headlong into sin and we can but feel that our connection with him is in some measure dissolved."[31]

Smith himself may have been one of those feeling anxiety while he crowded the water's edge given that ten days later he himself began to feel the guilt pangs often associated with the conversion process. Seeking guidance, he attended a Baptist prayer meeting and asked for the prayers "of those who had given themselves to God." The next day, after relating his troubled mind to the pastor of the church of Georgetown and praying with him, Smith said, "When I arose from my knees I felt a sensation I never felt before; words could not describe my feelings." Within two weeks, Smith stepped over the water's edge and was baptized into the Georgetown church. Reflecting upon his immersion later that day, he wrote, "I felt that the line of separation between me and the

world was about to be drawn . . . that my back was turned upon the weak and beggarly elements of the world. . . . I arose from the water with a light heart and with a firmer resolution to live to the Lord."[32]

Forty years earlier, Wilson Thompson expressed a similar feeling about his own baptism, seeing it as a collision of worlds. "When I was raised from the water," he recalled, "the first thought that I recollect was, 'O! That sinners could but see and feel the bounties of a Savior's love!'" Like many newly baptized converts, Thompson seemed primed for preaching as he looked at those on the river's bank. "Such a weighty and painful sense of their blind and dead condition came over me," he wrote, "that I felt a strong desire to speak of the glorious plan of salvation. I remained silent in language but burst into a flood of tears, and came out of the water weeping like a child." One of the first persons he saw on the riverbank was his unconverted uncle, and Thompson's first impulse was to embrace him and "tell him of the fullness and worth of a precious Savior." But the emotional effect of the event prevented young Wilson from speaking, and he simply "gave vent to a flood of tears."[33]

Just as the conversion account helped mark this transition from one world to another, so too did baptism. In one's conversion, the place made sacred was private or secluded, as with John Taylor's Hanging Rock or Wilson Thompson's wooded grove. In baptism, however, the fusing of sacred and secular was public, and often the place was shared with all other members of the church community. Often Baptists built their church meeting houses purposefully near creeks, streams, or rivers not simply to have a source of drinking water, but with the baptismal rite in mind. Baptisms typically occurred on Sundays after a preaching service at the meeting house. When water flowed near the meeting house, members simply "repaired to the water." In some cases where water of sufficient depth could not be readily found, as was the case in Mayslick, Kentucky, in the early 1800s, Baptists in "long horseback processions were often seen traversing the woods along a narrow road to Lee's Creek or Johnson's Fork." During periods of revival, when many converts would appeal for baptism and many more sought to witness the spectacle, the processions could be enormous, gathering numbers as they traveled. After a lengthy 1837 revival at Crab Orchard in central Kentucky along the Logan Trace, two thousand people gathered to witness Moses Foley baptize forty-six converts in the Dix River, about one mile from the town. Just a few weeks later, three thousand onlookers crowded the same banks to see forty-nine baptized. When church members and onlookers met in some sequestered spot along the bank, a preacher would

deliver a brief sermon, sometimes on the topic of baptism itself. Then the pastor of the church would enter the water and call the candidates toward him or line them up in the water.[34]

The amount of time actually spent in baptizing the converted varied depending on the situation and the style of the administrator. John Taylor, looking back on several years of his ministry, doubted that he had spent more than ten minutes on baptism at any one time, even when there were multiple candidates. Other pastors seemed amazed and inspired by the speed of some baptisms. John S. Higgins, who witnessed Moses Foley baptize his forty-six converts at the Dix River, timed him at twenty-two minutes. Later, Higgins and his associate Burdette Kemper together immersed forty-nine converts in seven minutes and wondered how long it took Jesus's twelve disciples to baptize their first three thousand converts on the day of Pentecost, as recorded in the book of Acts. Some pastors took time to speak some words over those being immersed. Typically, they repeated Jesus's command in Matthew 28:19 to baptize "in the name of the Father, and of the Son, and of the Holy Ghost." James Lee, who baptized Wilson Thompson, seemed to offer a prophecy before immersing the teen, when he remarked, "I am now about to baptize one who will stand in my place when my head lies beneath the clods of the valley."[35]

The importance of baptism to the movement also compelled ministers to administer the ceremony despite inclement weather or the health of the converts. Baptism, until the mid- to late nineteenth century, took place outdoors in natural bodies of water, which had long been a source of controversy for Baptist critics. Even as the Baptist movement began in seventeenth-century England, critics decried the unhealthful effects of entering polluted or icy rivers for baptism. As one scholar of English Baptist history notes, the Baptists defended their practice and "countered with at least as many stories of people who, though immersed in rivers where the ice had to be broken, yet suffered no ill effects." Two hundred years later, John Taylor continued the debate with early Kentucky's most famous Presbyterian, David Rice. In 1789, the pioneer Presbyterian preacher published a tract defending infant baptism in which he also argued that immersing a victim of consumption would be fatal. Being familiar with Rice's arguments and without evidence to the contrary, Taylor confronted a dilemma when he was invited to baptize a few recent converts, one of whom was an elderly man named Wilson. The old man evidently suffered from the last stages of consumption and could barely speak above a whisper. Taylor described old Wilson's baptism as "a great trial to my faith." As he took

the candidate into the water, the experienced preacher trembled with fear, hoping his duty would not be the man's demise. Wilson alleviated Taylor's fears when he arose from the water and, with a fairly strong voice, cried, "Glory to God! Glory to God!" and continued in fine health for several more years.[36]

Kentucky Baptists expressed little concern about unclean water when they baptized, but icy water presented both a challenge and an opportunity to advertise the depth of commitment of the movement's adherents, among both clergy and laity. Preacher Alfred Taylor, after immersing converts in the winter of 1837–1838, expressed his devotion to the practice. "I have had the pleasure of baptizing three hundred and six converts since Christmas," he wrote, "and although the ice has sometimes been removed out of the way, I have found my Master's commandments not grievous, but joyous; and although I am both small and weakly . . . I have yet the first time to feel like shrinking from the task." On the contrary, Taylor stated, "The enjoyment to me was as much as it would have been to any of my pedobaptist brethren in sprinkling them." That same winter, W. C. Buck baptized twenty-six converts in the Ohio River near Louisville in twelve-degree weather with five to six thousand people watching from the bank. One Baptist witness of the event remarked on the frigid conditions, claiming, "No one was ever injured in the path of duty."[37]

Baptists succeeded so well in advertising faith and devotion through baptism that some converts placed a primacy on immersion over all else. Lewis Arnold had spent his adult life purging himself of the vestiges of his parents' religious influence, perfecting his reason, and studying physics and philosophy. In 1827, after his own private soul-searching and conversion experience at the age of fifty, Arnold resolved that he had to be baptized and set out in the dead of winter to find a minister who would baptize him. His friends in the town of Versailles, Kentucky, marveled at the folly of this reasonable man, who had ridden twenty miles through the numbing weather. They told him that the closest minister's house was still too far, that the minister was likely not at home, and even if he were, that the waters were frozen. Immersion was reasonably out of the question. Arnold relented, and shortly after, his aged mother convinced him to join the church she attended. When he eventually joined the church on a Saturday, he still could not wait until the regular Sunday baptismal service, instead demanding to be baptized that very afternoon.[38]

The Baptist doctrine and practice of immersion was not a difficult concept to understand, but if potential adherents failed to grasp what the Baptists advertised, difficulties could ensue. Elizabeth Ramey's experience at the turn

of the nineteenth century illustrates how powerful perceptions about baptism could affect the movement's prospective adherents. As the revival fervor of the late eighteenth and early nineteenth century moved across northern Kentucky, Ramey progressed through the stages of the conversion experience and became mentally lodged between the sixth and seventh phases of penitence and final relief. Her trouble surfaced when she made a hasty vow to God. She promised God that she would "believe and be baptized," thinking that baptism had a role in one's conversion. Soon after her vow, she became convinced that she had made two grievous errors: first, she realized that baptism was separate from conversion, and second, that she had not been really converted yet; and still she vowed that she would be baptized. With her superficial understanding of Baptist theology and with a Calvinist sensibility, she felt forever trapped in metaphysical limbo. To carry out her vow, she thought, she must join the church, and to do that while unconverted was a sin. Ramey grieved intensely for two weeks. She ate very little and neglected the domestic duties about which she had been so industrious before. Hearing of this mourner's condition, the influential and peripatetic Baptist preacher John Taylor visited the Ramey home. The minister advised Ramey to "comply with her vow to God . . . get baptized . . . go to spinning . . . clean your house and cook food for your husband and little children." In July 1800, Ramey attended the Baptist church meeting of Bullittsburg, hoping that the church would hear her story, reject her experience, and absolve her of the hasty vow. In the end, when the relation of her experience met the expectations of a conversion narrative, the church received her. Still, she remained afflicted with guilt and suffered tremors until she was baptized the next day.[39]

Despite the occasional quandaries which arose as Baptists publicized their faith through believer's baptism, more often the public performance of immersion served to stimulate the movement's growth. Thomas Smith, Jr.'s conversion process began after he witnessed a baptismal service. Elizabeth Ramey's husband, William, followed her in baptism seven months after she resolved her vow. Experienced pastor John Taylor felt that baptizing generally functioned as "the greatest medium of awakening sinners." He further believed that the act itself dramatically portrayed the essence of the nineteenth-century evangelical message and proved the veracity of the movement's anti-pedobaptist stand. He wrote:

The best proof that can be given on gospel baptism is to see a man rise up and hear him declare his faith in Christ, and [at] that moment for a proper administrator to lead him into water of a proper depth, and lean him back to figurate a burial, and in the name of the triune God solemnly [to] immerse his whole body under water. This reduces the doctrine of baptism to practice before his eyes. In this the Baptists have the advantage of all the sectaries in the world in the article of gospel baptism. And to this is much owing their success in the world.[40]

The Baptist practice of immersion clearly transcended a mere initiatory rite. It compelled an outward and public acknowledgment and expression of what had been a very personal and private change of condition. At the same time, it provided yet another bond to hold the church members together. In these ways, baptism, along with the conversion experience, represented an overt statement of communal belonging in a society growing increasingly fragmented socially, economically, and politically.

Whereas baptism served as the Baptist's most public ceremony and the conversion relation joined a private experience to a public examination, the Baptist practice of communion, or the "Lord's Supper," revealed the more private side of the movement. Most churches chose to close the meeting house doors to all who might threaten the purity of the church. The communion ordinance, as the only widespread Baptist ordinance that was repeatedly observed in a Baptist's lifetime, offered a symbolic reminder of both the individual's communion with God and the bond of belonging shared with fellow believers. Given the weight and meaning of the rite, non-church members were not allowed to participate in the communion rituals of most early Kentucky Baptist churches.

As with baptism, the Baptists adopted the practice of the supper from their understanding of certain New Testament passages. While all four of the gospel writers record an account of Jesus's last supper with his twelve disciples before he is arrested and crucified, the synoptic writers (Matthew, Mark, and Luke) reveal the details of Jesus's admonition concerning the cup and the bread. In each of these accounts, Jesus says that the cup from which they drink holds his blood and that the bread they share is his body. Only

Luke's description suggests that Jesus intends the taking of bread and wine to be a commemorative act. Baptists generally relied on Luke's account and especially the apostle Paul's writings for their practice of communion. Paul's first letter to the church at Corinth contains two references to the rite, which seem to emphasize its inherent unity and the importance of celebrating it purely. After commanding the Corinthians to "flee from idolatry," Paul writes, "For we, though many, are one bread and one body; for we all partake of that one bread . . . . You cannot partake of the Lord's table and of the table of demons." Later Paul encourages mutual submission in the church and avoidance of contention, noting that the Corinthians practice the supper shamefully and selfishly. Paul warns them, "Whoever eats this bread or drinks this cup of the Lord in an unworthy manner will be guilty of the body and blood of the Lord. But let a man examine himself, and so let him eat of the bread and drink of the cup."[41]

With little other mention of communion in scripture, early Baptists extrapolated the specifics of their practice from other principles and from social circumstances. The debate over communion in seventeenth-century England between William Kiffin and John Bunyan articulated the issues that would trouble Baptists well into the nineteenth century, even into the American frontier. Bunyan argued that since baptism was not necessary for conversion, then "any true Christian must be welcome at the Lord's table." Kiffin countered that such an allowance would water down the purity of the church. If a pedobaptist communed with an anti-pedobaptist and the two were in unity, what would it say about the veracity of either's conversion? Kiffin also alluded to the biblical order of the two ordinances, asserting that baptism always precedes communion. In the end, the question revolved around the proprietary nature of communion. Did it belong to the individual, as Bunyan averred, or to the church, as maintained by Kiffin?[42]

Early Kentucky Baptists, having so recently existed as a persecuted sect in many colonies, generally advocated closed or "close" communion restricted to those who had been immersed as adult believers. This more exclusive practice worked to maintain the purity of the sect and to manifest the bond of community. However, the alternative view, akin to Bunyan's, of "open" communion had its few adherents as well. David Kelley, for example, converted in 1812 and joined the Mount Pleasant Baptist Church in western Ohio County. A few years after joining, he began to have trouble with the practice of close communion. When he voiced these concerns to his church, the members voted to

exclude him from the church until he changed his mind, which he did after some time. The membership clearly held no grudge against Kelley, since they called him as their pastor in 1825.[43]

Most Baptist churches established their commitment to a restricted communion early on. The Baptist church at Beaver Creek in eastern Kentucky, organized in 1798, constituted themselves upon several doctrines, including their belief that baptism and the Lord's Supper were ordinances of Jesus Christ, and that only true believers were "the fit subjects of these ordinances." They specified further "that the true mode of baptism is by immersion." The church at Sardis, founded thirty years later, made the belief more explicit, stating, "None but those who with the heart believe unto righteousness and with the mouth make confession unto salvation are fit subjects for baptism . . . . And such alone should be admitted to the communion table." More pointedly, one group of Baptists south of Lexington agreed that baptism was the preparatory rite before one could take communion, arguing, "When this order is inverted, the beauty of the church is marred."[44] In the early nineteenth century, when Baptists alone practiced believer's baptism by immersion only, communion remained a relatively uncontroversial issue; but in the late 1820s, as the views of Alexander Campbell became more popular among Baptists, the leaders of the Baptist movement were forced to defend their restrictive understanding of communion, a defense that would only grow more strident as the century progressed.

Thus, in the theologically pacific first quarter of the nineteenth century, Baptists focused more on the pragmatic elements of communion. Since each church governed itself and drew upon the experience of its initial membership for its heritage, the first several years of the church's existence included a working-out of various issues, such as the proper procedures and times for communion. In 1801, when 100 congregants left the church of South Elkhorn to form the Mount Pleasant Church in Jessamine County, they determined to hold communion semiannually, at the beginning of summer and again at the end. They continued under this plan forty years before adding another observance in January. Bethel Baptist Church also agreed to a semi-annual communion schedule in 1811, and did away with the formal plan in 1823, agreeing that the church would "appoint the day of communion when they think most proper"; but they returned to the old schedule in 1824. The members of the church at Mayslick, meanwhile, voted to observe their communion season every other month. Even after agreeing on the timing of communion, some

churches wrestled with other pragmatic concerns. Members of Providence Baptist Church discussed early on if it was in order "for all the members present to take their seats at the time of communion." They agreed that such an expectation was in order, but that members were under "no compulsion to partake." A year later, the same church, after a discussion, agreed that it was not "becoming in a church after the communion to take the remainder of the bread and wine and eat and drink it before the congregation," that is before all the Baptist adherents who were not official church members.[45]

Generally, Baptist church members met privately on two occasions, each designed to promote solidarity and synergism. The first and more frequent was their monthly business meetings, in which they managed the church's practical affairs and exercised discipline over wayward parishioners. The second was the communion service. But these meetings, though both were private, contrasted sharply in tone. Whereas the debate of the business meeting could produce contention and distance members from one another, the communion service brought them together. In 1823, seventy-one year old John Taylor observed the rite of communion with more than three hundred members of the church at Clear Creek in central Kentucky, recording, "More communicants surrounded the Lord's table this day than I had ever seen at one time." He continued, "To see that number of people, after solemnly sitting and communing with their dying Lord, and many from floods of tears, rise to their feet as one man with sonorous melody (and many of them with all the warmth of young converts) sing the closing hymn was pleasant indeed." The special communion seasons in which Baptists "surrounded the Lord's table" rivaled in effect the prominent Methodist Love Feast which also employed an exclusivism that, as one historian has noted, "helped create for those present the sense of security and confidence necessary to develop strong group cohesiveness."[46]

In a very real sense, that conclusion could apply not only to the communion service, but to the conversion relation exercise and the baptismal service. Throughout the late eighteenth and early nineteenth centuries, in the midst of dramatic institutional growth, these most widely practiced of Baptist ceremonies reveal neither a celebration of the individual nor a constriction of conscience to the needs of the community. Instead, each ceremony was a melding of individual and community. In an emerging national culture, itself wrestling with the disorientation of rights and responsibilities, revision of social hierarchies, new opportunities and boundaries, and negotiation between republicanism and liberalism, the Baptist movement offered a religious worldview

with complementary values, one which balanced and fulfilled the needs of individual and community.[47] What resulted in part from these Baptist rituals were communities and associations bonded in a kind of fellowship that surpassed that of craft guilds and early labor leagues.[48] Their community predated and transcended in mission the early nineteenth-century reform movements, which also provided a high degree of comradery.[49] The Baptist movement could uniquely recognize the significance of the individual in several respects: in its early emphasis on Calvinistic determinism, wherein the creator of the universe condescended to touch the souls of individual people; in its recognition of particular variations of conversion narrative and the inherent solitude of the experience; in the symbolic watery burial and resurrection of the convert in a stream; and in the personal communion "with the dying Lord." Yet in each of these, Kentucky Baptists also upheld communal authority. Though conversion narratives might vary, each was to signal a salvation experience acceptable to all the members of the church community. Baptism might separate out the individual convert into the water, but served as the door into a community of like individuals. And while the individual communed with Jesus at the Lord's table, he did so only with the whole church and only under the guidance of a minister. If, as Thomas Smith, Jr. suggested, the rituals signaled the transition from one world to another just as if one were "going to another country," they also exhibited a fusion of values that were themselves being sorted out in the tumult of the early national period. Through their rituals, each central to the movement's culture, the Baptists advertised themselves as a distinct group in an increasingly pluralistic religious environment, but also as a movement playing in tune with the tones of America. And with this ability to publicize themselves through ritual, they attracted adherents eager for an environment which seemed to resolve the inherent tensions not only in a developing western society, but also in an American cultural transition.

2

First among Equals:
The Baptist Preacher

Rising to the podium, Basil Manly, Jr. looked out over a crowd full of Baptist preachers and laymen who had gathered in 1876 to celebrate the hundredth anniversary of the Baptist presence in Kentucky. Those in the audience had reason to celebrate, since Baptists could by then claim one in every nine Kentuckians as their own. Nationwide, Baptists represented only one in every twenty-four Americans. The substance of Manly's address dealt with explanations for the movement's significant progress and increase in the state. In his analysis, he admitted that migration to the state had helped the movement, but not much. Denominational writings such as tracts or books had been a positive consequence of growth, but not the cause. Manly himself served as president of the state's Baptist college at the time, but he denied that "learned men" had reason to claim credit for the movement's growth. Instead, he claimed that the key to Baptist increase must "be discovered in the silent, unperceived, and unrecorded actions of the thousands of unimportant individuals; in the sacrifices and zeal of the large number of comparatively unknown

ministers and private members." Speaking more plainly, Manly continued to credit "the old field, back-woods, country preachers," who he said had "done more to advance the cause of truth . . . than numbers of men of more shining qualities and sustained by the most generous expenditures." In concluding his appraisal of early Baptist preachers, Manly obliquely cited the stiff competition early Baptists had encountered from Catholics, Presbyterians, and especially Methodists, when he asserted, "By such means has grown to its present size and importance a body of churches . . . without bishops to plan its campaigns . . . without an organized conference of itinerant clergy to concentrate its powers, and bring into harmony of thought and effort its various parts, without . . . a general assembly which should bring its scattered members into . . . systematic cooperation."[1] What Manly observed was the clear irony that though the Baptists were a comparatively disorganized religious group with a largely uneducated, uncultured, and unsalaried clergy, the same band of preachers had effected and maintained the movement's dominance in Kentucky, keeping it competitive throughout the nation during the nineteenth century.

Baptist preachers in the early republic actually constituted a diverse group in economic terms and in educational background. For this reason the preachers were able to relate to their hearers, fashion common-sense messages in their preaching, and advance the movement among a populace primed by revolutionary rhetoric to accept a populist style of preaching from speakers of their own background. Baptist preachers tended to come from the same social backgrounds as their audiences. In the early westward migration of the 1770s and 1780s, Baptists and their preachers sometimes moved together. At times, whole churches moved west with their preachers leading the way. The most well-known example of this phenomenon was Pastor Lewis Craig's Travelling Church which moved from Virginia and settled at Gilbert's Creek in northern Kentucky in 1781. But few Baptists came to Kentucky in similar circumstances and the migration of whole churches does not explain the movement's growth after the flow of westward migration subsided. At the heart of the movement's expansion was the Baptist preacher's ministry and his ability to relate to his hearers. The most impactful catalyst for the early Baptist preacher's relational ministry was the bi-vocational nature of his work. By "relational ministry," I mean a minister's work that is based on and dependent on his ability to empathize socially with those to whom he ministers. It also involved his ability to build potentially long-term relationships with his congregation. In contrast, the peripatetic work of Methodist circuit-riding preachers demanded they

sacrifice these type of social relationships for the cause of spreading the gospel. As a consequence, their closest relationships were with other itinerants who trained them and with whom they maintained correspondence. Since most preachers received no salary for their religious work—indeed, many refused pay—they had to "keep their day jobs" and minister in the evenings and on Saturdays and Sundays.[2]

The "farmer-preacher" image of the frontier Baptist preacher, such as that remembered by Basil Manly, Jr. in his commemorative 1876 speech, has driven popular perception of the early movement. Nostalgic depictions in the late nineteenth century tended to overemphasize the importance of the farmer-preacher. During the Gilded Age, a time of social and cultural transition, evangelicals read an idealized "old-time religion" into history. Part of this construction was the farmer-preacher as symbol of agrarian purity. Nevertheless, many of the early preachers did indeed till the soil to support themselves and their family, as did a great number of Americans in the nineteenth century. The vast majority of the farmer-preachers managed small to medium-sized farms, considered themselves preachers first, and toiled in both professions year-round. As James Pendleton recalled, the early farmer-preacher would sometimes be seen "in Winter, having cut down a tree, sitting on its stump to rest, and while resting reading the word of truth with a view to the next Sunday's sermon; and, in Summer, after following the plow until his horse needed rest, stopping to open the blessed book of the Lord."[3]

However, the popular image of the farmer-preacher tends to obscure the Baptist preachers who worked in other trades between 1780 and 1840, helping the movement appeal not only to agriculturalists, but to tradesmen and artisans as well. The Baptist movement's prosperity and the preacher's relational ministry were reflected in the wide range of professions from which the Baptists filled their pulpits. Further, one of the keys to the ministerial success of the artisan- and tradesmen-preachers lay in the fact that while they pursued their consecrated vocations like the farmer-preachers, they maintained relationships with the business world. Many preachers taught common schools to support themselves, including William Downs, Walter Warder, Spencer Clack, Samuel Trott, James Nall, and Hiram Curry. Some of these teacher-preachers gained distinction among their peers in their promotion of education like, Gray B. Dunn, who established the first grade school in his region north of Russellville in western Kentucky, and Robert T. Anderson also of Russellville, whose school included instruction for the deaf.[4] Among

other bi-vocational preachers, William Vaughan, Alan McGuire, and Thomas Jefferson Fisher were tailors; Samuel Carpenter and Silas Mercer Noel were lawyers, as was Porter Clay, brother of Henry Clay; Joel Hulsey, David Hardisty, and Richard W. Nixon engaged in mercantile enterprises; William White Penny, Peter Bainbridge, James Fishback, and Farmer Rees all practiced medicine; and Orson H. Morrow and David Mansfield were surveyors. William Keller and his apprentice Benjamin Allen both ministered in Baptist churches while they practiced carpentry and cabinet making. Throughout Kentucky, the variety of trades in which preachers engaged matched the myriad pursuits of the population as a whole, including preachers such as Zacheus Carpenter, a house-joiner; Robert Stockton, a hatter; William Lowe, a wheelwright; Thomas Parker Dudley, a banker; John W. Young, a blacksmith; Robert W. Ricketts, a gunsmith; and William Conrad, a tanner.[5]

Baptist preachers in the early nineteenth century came from a variety of backgrounds and occupations and continued to work in those positions while preaching to their congregations. Because of this, they were able to draw upon their experiences for their sermons and exhortations. In an agrarian culture, the farmer-preachers and even the artisans and tradesmen were familiar with the natural rhythms of seasonal labor in a way that enriched their understanding of the agrarian metaphors in the Bible. Thus, even though they might have little formal education, the early Baptist preacher could not only grasp biblical ideas, but could transmit them clearly to hearers who were similarly attuned. Isaac Malin, one of the first Baptist preachers in north-central Kentucky, gained a reputation for his use of relatable illustrations in his preaching to explain biblical principles. In one of Malin's sermons he reportedly propounded that, "Christians are like fat-gourds. If there is any fat in the gourd, it is certain to show on the outside. And, so, if there is any grace in a man's heart, it will be seen in his works." Malin's congregation would have understood the allusion to the large gourds in which they stored their lard in the absence of more refined crockery unavailable in the most western settlements.[6]

A sense of egalitarianism pervaded the relational ministries of the early Baptist preachers. Their conversion narratives did not single them out as any more holy than others, nor were their conversions any easier to endure. Their baptisms had been the same as anyone else's since no one was baptized into the ministry. In fact, the only clerical mark of a Baptist preacher was the recognition he received from his congregation as minister. Such recognition did not elevate the preacher to a higher social status, as had been the case in the

colonial established churches, but it did promote him to a leadership position in the flock: a position of authority clearly rooted in and sanctioned by the consent of the individuals in his church. Though the Baptists used many of the old Puritan Congregationalist practices, in their philosophy of ministry they differed significantly. As Harry S. Stout has explained, in New England the "status of the clergy depended on the monopoly of speech they enjoyed; that more than anything else counterbalanced the lay majority's claim to power."[7] For the Baptist preacher, the authority to preach came from God, but it was the lay majority who best understood and had to affirm this call. Both initially and continuously, clerical power and status was derived from below. In contrast, the root of authority for Methodist preachers was more complicated. Candidates for local ministry in that tradition underwent examination by a committee composed of their peers and select church officials, such as circuit riders and presiding elders. These examinations took place at quarterly conference meetings superintended by the church hierarchy. Beyond this, each year the conference leadership oversaw the renewal of licenses for local preaching. Any preacher who sought to join the circuit riding elite faced years of official supervision before receiving a circuit. Though there are similarities between the early careers of Methodist and Baptist preachers, once in full-time ministry, Methodist ministers were more centrally controlled.[8] In the absence of overarching denominational oversight, the ties between Baptist ministers and those to whom they preached remained relational.

Even though the authority to preach often came from the minister's peers, the transition from congregant to clergyman could be turbulent. This extensive transition process, as much as anything else, both blurred and clarified the line between laity and clergy and culled the truly dedicated adherents out of the flock for positions of servant-like leadership. Baptists, in choosing a minister, typically looked for evidence of a calling from God to the ministry. That call could come to the unsuspecting future preacher in a variety of ways. Many times, members of a church diagnosed the call for a member, even for recent converts. Less than two months after Thomas Smith, Jr.'s conversion, he was shocked to discover that members of his parent's church saw the call in him. In his exclamatory diary entry, he confided, "The people in Henry [County] predict that I will be a preacher!!!!!! They know as much about my future occupation as I do myself." Smith doubted their collective wisdom, seeing himself as more comic than cleric. "I find that I am too much disposed to ridicule and mimicry," wrote Smith. Nonetheless, within five years, he was

among the most influential preachers in Louisville. In a different case, William Conrad's call seemed to develop from a personal crisis. In 1821, after four years of conflict in the Baptist church at Dryridge between two factions—the "Old School" Predestinarians and the "New School" Free-Will Baptists—young Conrad took it upon himself to find a new preacher who would either unite the church or lead off the Predestinarians like himself to form a new church. While Conrad found several men who he thought would serve his purpose, as he later wrote, "My mind would speak over and over: 'You will never make a preacher . . . you will never do for a preacher . . . you cannot talk plain . . . you stutter . . . you will never make a preacher.' This I cheerfully and heartily admitted, for I was only looking for a man who would make a good preacher." Sometime later he realized that he "had been made willing to preach," emphasizing his own Calvinist passivity in receiving a calling.[9]

In some cases, the ministers' experience of being called could be as unsettling as their conversion experience. Just as conversion represented a transition from one "world" to another, in many respects the transition from hearer to preacher instilled a profound sense of responsibility as the farmer or tradesmen also took on the mantle of spiritual leader. For those men deficient in literacy or whose communicative talents were never developed, a calling to preach could both tantalize and terrify. Wilson Thompson's tumultuous calling experience illustrates the way preachers responded ambivalently to the "impression" to preach. Thompson's impressions began shortly after his baptism in 1802 and for several years were something of an obsession for him. "Sometimes my mind would become so engrossed at the meetings and especially at prayer meetings, that I could scarcely refrain from expressing my feelings to the church," Thompson recalled. At each meeting, he felt compelled to preach forth "the fullness of Christ . . . and grace in the plan of salvation," but his own hesitance and fear of failure prevented him. He would then resolve to try again at the next meeting. His burden of guilt from this cycle of failure oppressed him to the point of sleeplessness and loss of appetite. A sudden and intense illness, possibly brought on by his own depression, gave him further pause, and he resolved to attempt "to preach Christ and Him crucified." But again, even as he recovered from his sickness, he resisted once more. "[I] was slow in speech," Thompson recalled, "and could not communicate to others the few thoughts I might have; I was a poor, backwoods, ignorant boy, knew nothing of books, and but little of the world. Indeed, I possessed no qualifications at all that are essential to a minister."[10]

In the months following his recovery, Thompson was asked to close two meetings with a brief exhortation. Like Methodists, Baptists differentiated between preaching and exhortation, though the content of the two was often indistinct. Being allowed to exhort on these occasions cleared Thompson's conscience, but shortly afterward he became plagued with doubts concerning the validity of his salvation. Such a state of doubt confused the continuing impressions he felt to preach even more, but still, he said, "The awful responsibilities of the station deterred me; my ignorance and imperfections forbade me; and my liabilities to err and perhaps to preach some false doctrine . . . were so important a matter that I trembled at the idea with dismay." To negotiate his predicament, Thompson began to exhort at the end of the day in the school where he taught. So moving were his emotional exhortations that people from around the region would gather at the school just to hear Thompson's powerful words. But still his frustration remained, compounding his depression. Thompson's parents, unbeknownst to him, knew of their son's exercised mind and feared he was tempted to suicide, so they contrived for him to sleep in their room. Soon after, however, Thompson's ordeal took a stranger turn.[11]

Tormented with insomnia, Thompson tossed and turned on the pallet his parents had laid for him. One night, well past the midnight hour, in the dim light of the fire's glowing embers, Thompson had a vision of a "shadowy form" which approached him, bent over, and said, "I know your trouble, and your great desire to know what you should do; and I have come to tell you." The dark figure instructed the young man to read the sixth and tenth chapters of the book of Matthew. He was told to say "I am the man" after he read each sentence. Only then, he was promised, would he come to know his duty. Thompson claimed the vision did not startle him, but rather had a calming influence. The figure appeared to him twice more before dawn, repeating the instructions verbatim each time. The next day, Thompson tore off to a secret place to read the two chapters as instructed. But reading them and responding "I am the man" after each sentence made no sense to him, and he could not discern the lesson the figure of the vision intended for him. He reread the chapters several times to no avail. Not wishing his parents to know of his exercises, but in want of advice, he told his aunt of his experience and read her the chapters. Before he could finish, she began weeping and to his surprise said, "You should not expect anything to be plainer. . . . You need not think you can conceal your impressions; they are already known to the church. I have known them for a long time, and your father and mother are much troubled on your account. . . .

You will have to preach the gospel. God has called you to that work. . . . You are injuring your own health, troubling your parents, and fighting against God." In spite of her consolation, Thompson was now vexed with the knowledge that others knew of his problem, and still he was burdened by his sense of responsibility. Sequestering himself once more, he sought a final word of direction by taking his Bible and praying, "O Lord, let the first words that my eyes shall rest upon, when this book opens, show me my duty and make it plain." He opened his Bible as randomly as he could and read a verse from the book of Isaiah. But thinking again, the young Thompson saw that Isaiah was in the middle of his Bible—the most likely place to open the book—and the verse was the first in a chapter, beginning with a large capital letter that would naturally attract the eye. Worst of all, he thought, "You have made the Bible your fortune teller, and all this may be wrong, perhaps even sinful."[12]

Wilson Thompson's struggles over his calling to the ministry were ended by the man he feared most: his pastor, John Beal. Thompson concluded that his own duty included sharing his burden with Beal, but as he wrote later, "When I saw him, my heart failed me. He was a very stern man, and I shuddered at the thought of introducing my subject to him." Beal had only been pastor of the church for a few years, and it is possible that young Wilson had never spoken with the preacher alone; but in the end Thompson was surprised at the kindness, tenderness, and respect Beal showed him when he divulged his secret. The preacher heard the young man's tale in confidence, and with permission, he would share Thompson's impressions with the church members, who already had an interest in the young man's calling. Thompson agreed, and in 1810, a full nine years after he had first felt the impressions to preach, his church ushered him into the ministry. The members afforded him the liberty, he recalled, "to speak, preach, or exhort, or exercise my gifts in any way or at any time or place" in their extended neighborhood in northern Kentucky.[13] Though perhaps extreme, Thompson's experience reveals the manifold concerns young Baptist men had once they "felt their call."

Regardless of where the call came from, whether a collective decision or a subjective impression, once a church saw one of their own as fit for ministry, they took up the matter in the church business meeting to determine if they should "license" him to preach. Licensure granted the preacher a degree of credibility, so that others in the surrounding community would accept his preaching based upon the church's own reputation. Since the public image of the licensing church hung in the balance, the licensing process could be brief or lengthy depending

on how well the church knew the prospective preacher or how quickly the licentiate took to the craft of preaching. Elsey Hickerson, for instance, had long-standing bonds with the church members who licensed him in 1842. His parents had affiliated with the church on Hardins Creek in Washington Country as early as 1808. Hickerson grew up in the church and succeeded his father as its clerk. When Hickerson turned thirty-five years old, the church honored him with another leadership role as a deacon. When he became licensed ten years later, his experience in the church helped him, and he became a fully ordained minister after just eight months. Likewise, William W. Ford, a deacon and the son of a deacon served only a four-month licensing period in 1824 before being ordained by the Fox Run Baptist Church.[14]

The typical licensing period lasted a year or two, but each autonomous church could evaluate their licentiates as they saw fit. The Mount Tabor Church chose to license Jacob Locke incrementally: first, in August 1800, they allowed him only to exhort, then in March 1801 added preaching to the offices he could exercise. Not only could churches place restrictions on the sort of preaching their licentiates delivered, they could restrict the location where the would-be preacher proclaimed his trial sermons. At times, churches even placed limits on the content of proclamations. Fortunate licentiates received few limitations. Brother Curry of Mayslick Baptist Church received positive feedback in 1793 from his fellow church members, who gave him "general license to preach the gospel wherever the Lord in his providence shall open a door." Others, less fortunate, received merely tepid approval. Daniel Lambert, for instance, could not have been completely affirmed in his gifts when his church limited his opportunities by telling him to "forbear traveling in strange parts except in company with older ministers." Further, he could not expound upon the scriptures as he desired, but instead was instructed to "be cautious of taking mysterious texts and attempt matter almost too great for our oldest preachers." Lest these instructions be unclear to Lambert, they clarified, "If you attempt to preach, . . . use the plain parts of the scriptures and avoid as much as possible those high words that will not mix well with our common language." In the end, Daniel Lambert's church sent him on his way with ambiguous encouragement. "We sincerely wish you to prosper in the Lord," they assured him, but continued, "Look entirely to him in confidence that you can prosper as a minister no other way, but always remember that every step you take in the ministry is not from any call from the church as we are not quite satisfied as to your call, [sic] therefore we are not willing to approve or disapprove until further evidence."[15]

If a church needed to hear the prospective licentiate preach to get an idea of his preparedness, the candidate preached a trial sermon. This proved to be a good test both of a candidate's gift for preaching and for his commitment to the arduous role of a Baptist minister. As a minister he would be at the front lines of the Baptist movement, and no half-hearted woolgatherer could be counted on to stay the course. Accounts of the anxiety suffered by candidates for licensing illustrate that even when the compulsion to preach motivated them greatly, the idea of preaching in front of their fellow church members, their friends and family, as well as older preachers they respected terrified them deeply. The ever-timid Wilson Thompson even saw the pulpit as "too sacred a place for me." The distress felt by William Conrad resembled Thompson's. One Sunday, Conrad mentioned to elder preacher William Glasscock some thoughts he had had during the older man's preaching. Unexpectedly, Glasscock smiled and told him that the young man would have an opportunity to preach the next week. "Oh, what a shock!" recalled Conrad. "Could I but have gotten back again those few words I had spoken in the presence of Elder Glasscock!" Conrad had an anxious week and when Sunday came, his dread overwhelmed him. He had hoped to avoid preaching in his home church somehow, but now the time was at hand. Despite his misgivings, he forged ahead even after Glasscock sat him down outside the meeting house before the service began and offered him a chance to back out. Later, after the meeting, Conrad remembered very little of what had happened in any part of the service, including his own sermon. But his compulsion to preach was satisfied, and he felt "a secret, inward quiet and consolation." Shortly thereafter, his church granted him a license to preach with no limitations.[16]

Such intense anxiety during a trial sermon could give the church reason to delay or dismiss a candidate. Baptists generally viewed a preacher's calling as being of divine origin, but since their authority went with the licentiate, they were sometimes slow or hesitant to vouch for this sense of calling. Nathaniel Hickson felt such a calling and petitioned his church for "privilege" to exercise his gift for them. At the next church meeting, Hickson "came forward and read a passage of Scripture, but being embarrassed in his mind was obliged to desist from speaking." The church members requested Hickson to wait outside the meeting house while they discussed his performance and his fate, but they could not agree. The members decided that they "could not at present determine whether he was called to the ministry." Still they encouraged him, saying he could "deliver a word of exhortation at anytime" and "give his views

of a passage of scripture." But he definitely was not to consider himself in "a state of probation for the ministry." If he was still desirous of preaching, he could resubmit his petition and submit to a "trial before the church." Hickson was determined and apparently improved himself enough to go to the church again seventeen months later, when they finally allowed him to preach "publically whenever he shall be inclined."[17]

After a licentiate had received permission from his church to preach, he was expected to strengthen his gifts. The probationary period between licensing and ordination gave the ministerial candidate an opportunity to practice the craft of preaching and public speaking. Still, despite these opportunities and helps, licentiates suffered numerous embarrassments and faced stern criticism from their audiences. Alfred Taylor's first attempt at preaching after receiving his license in 1831 seemed more likely to mortify the novice preacher than to develop his talents. Taylor, being the son of a pastor, might have been expected to take easily to pulpiteering, but that was not the case. In his very first sermon as a licentiate, Taylor stood at the pulpit and, according to custom, read the biblical text upon which he would preach. He looked at his audience, began to sound out a few hesitant words to begin his sermon, and then paused. An awkward silence filled the room as Taylor simply stood there in the stillness, which, according to witnesses, quickly turned painful. Taylor regained his composure and continued on for a few moments, then sputtered to a stop. Once again, in a dreadful silence, Taylor was overcome and sat down in weeping humiliation. Shortly after, an undeterred Taylor made another effort at preaching in western Kentucky. His second attempt began as poorly as his first, but instead of giving up, Taylor turned and preached to the wall rather than face the unrelenting gaze of his hearers. Despite this meager improvement, many who heard him expressed their sad opinion that young Taylor "had better quit." His high, whining tone of voice and poor delivery disappointed most who heard him, but he slowly developed as a preacher, was ordained three years later in 1834, and eventually became an influential figure among Kentucky Baptists in the mid-nineteenth century.[18]

Some licentiates became so discouraged during their probation that they almost hoped their churches would rescind their licenses. Even though they still desired to preach, their inability produced a dilemma. Their sense of calling compelled them to preach, but their own sense of unfitness appalled them. James Pendleton's first two sermons as a licentiate in 1831 went far better than Alfred Taylor's, but Pendleton realized thereafter that his two attempts "had

exhausted my scanty store of theology and [I] could think of no other subject on which I could say anything." Since he, like other licentiates, acted under his church's authority, and it was the church alone who could verify a call, Pendleton resolved the situation by telling himself, "I will try to preach, I will do the best I can, and when the brethren see that they have made a mistake, they will candidly tell me so, tell me that while they do not wish to hurt my feelings, they deem it their duty to say to me that I can never make a preacher." If the church did so, then he could clear his conscience and devote himself to his farm. Nonetheless, after three and a half years of ministerial probation, Pendleton was ordained.[19]

Still, the probationary period could provide licentiates opportunities for encouragement even though the men themselves might have been embarrassed by their first performances. R. T. Dillard had practiced law successfully for four years before he began to preach in 1824. Like many novice preachers, he saw his efforts as failures and might have given up, had not an older member of the congregation stood up at the end of his sermon and exclaimed, "I thank God that the good Lord has cheated the devil out of another lawyer." Such public affirmation offered support for licentiates wrestling with taking on a bi-vocational career and doubting their own worthiness. Walter Warder received valuable praise after he attended a large gathering of Baptists at the Elkhorn Association's annual meeting. Preaching to what may have been the largest congregation in his early career, Warder performed his task with much "fear and trembling." When the time came to dismiss the assembly, John Taylor, long a venerated presence in the state, stood and remarked that he and some of the older preachers, as well as many of the assembled brethren, "perceived the gift" that was in the twenty-seven year old Warder. Taylor compared the situation to the tenth chapter of Acts, when the disciples saw the gift in the preaching of Saul. Following Taylor's praise, the ministers gathered around Warder, welcomed him as a fellow minister though he was only a licentiate, and prayed a blessing upon him. Warder later recalled that this encouragement had been "one of the best occurrences" of his life, and that in his "desponding moments the recollection of that scene" gave him strength."[20]

In addition to the opportunities licentiates had to practice their preaching, either in itinerant appointments or appointments with a local church, they often paired up with older, more experienced preachers who apprenticed the novices in their new craft. This informal apprentice relationship not only allowed the licentiates to learn the skills of preaching, but also helped

the younger men feel a connection to the larger Baptist movement. The mentoring process also promoted a bonding of the Baptist clergymen one to another, contributing to a larger sense of belonging and pride in their craft. The mentoring preachers' influence could be seen in the pulpit when the mentor and apprentice preached together. Landon Robinson, licensed in 1820, lived in northern Kentucky and traveled widely in the exercise of his gifts. His mentor and traveling companion was Absalom Graves, a long-time minister and well-respected Baptist leader in the northern part of the state. To observers familiar with both men, the resemblance between the two preachers was uncanny, as Robinson took on the mannerisms and locution of Graves so that he "seemed a second edition of the same man." The two became closely related in the minds of their hearers and, coincidentally, would die within a few months of each other in 1826. In another case, John Henderson Spencer's attempt to duplicate his mentor, Mordecai Ham, did not have the same effect. When he tried to preach an interesting sermon previously delivered by Ham, he failed in many respects and claimed afterward to have been "cured of all my plagiaristic proclivities."[21]

Mentors could provide encouraging words when they were needed, or prodding ones if the licentiate seemed to be disengaging from his calling. When James Pendleton wished his church would rescind his license, one of his mentors goaded him, saying "You certainly could do better if you would try," and, "You are scarcely earning your salt." Still another experienced preacher pushed him to improve his style, remarking, "You say some pretty good things, but your preaching is neither adapted to comfort the saint nor alarm the sinner." In 1832, the twenty-year-old Pendleton spoke before some of the most well-known Baptist ministers in the state at a convention in New Castle. Afterward he was approached by Silas Mercer Noel, the moderator of the convention and a preacher among preachers in the early 1830s. Like Pendleton's mentors, Noel also spurred the young licentiate "to put more life" into his sermons. Pendleton recognized the truth in his elders' evaluations, but in the end, their observations only tended to depress him further. Nevertheless he sought to improve himself and his sermons.[22]

The licensing process had its advantage to the churches, the licentiates themselves, and the movement as a whole, but the probationary period had its frustrations beyond occasional discouraging words from mentors or hearers. One Baptist preacher in 1841 shared his frustrations in a letter to the popular Baptist newspaper the *Baptist Banner and Western Pioneer.* The writer

Eng.by Henry Taylor.N.Chicago

James M. Pendleton. Southern Baptist Historical Library and Archives, Nashville, Tennessee.

approved the system of licensing, but denounced the lengthy probation periods, which extended to "a year or two, or three." The author asserted that churches should be familiar enough with the potential of their "sons" to make a single year's probation sufficient. He decried the practice wherein a church would license one of its own and then fail to "assign him any labor in her own bounds, or request him at the time to perform stated service in her own body." Sometimes these licentiates were also deterred from preaching in other churches "for fear it may be said, 'O, he just wants us to call him to preach to us; his own church that ordained him won't have him.'" The result, according to the agitated writer, was harm to the church and the licentiate. The writer suggested that a church should act as "a kind and affectionate mother" to her licentiates: pointing out his foibles, correcting evil habits, restraining overenthusiasm, and rousing him from sluggishness. "In this way," he wrote, "she would prepare her son for usefulness in his own body and . . . wherever he might be." The editor of the newspaper, W. C. Buck, responded favorably to the letter, agreeing that the majority of churches were inattentive to "the due cultivation of the gifts conferred" on candidates for ministry. Buck asserted further that such neglect was "an evil too prevalent, especially in the West," and that those churches were "criminally negligent" of their responsibility to their licentiates. But Buck, who already sensed the direction Baptists were taking in the 1840s toward ministerial education, could not agree that churches should allow only one year for probationary preaching. "The truth is," Buck replied, "that the majority of our licentiates are unlettered young men, and it is impossible that their ministerial qualifications can be adequately developed, until they have sufficient time to improve their intellects." But intellect aside, Buck also agreed that churches needed time to evaluate the licentiates' "habits and general character." A lengthy probation period would reveal the level of sanctity licentiates had achieved, so that churches might be sure they would "give themselves wholly to the painful pleasure of preaching glad tidings to a lost world."[23]

When the licentiates had finally proven themselves and were called to pastor a church, they submitted to an ordination ceremony. This event marked the completion of their probation and, more importantly, the beginning of their life as a Baptist minister. When a church determined a licentiate was ready for ordination, it typically called for a committee of ordained ministers, who were often from nearby churches, to perform the ceremony. Generally churches held their ordination ceremonies on the same day as their monthly business

meeting. Each member of the church had a voice in the approval or rejection of the candidate, and the committee of visiting ministers could interrogate him and give their recommendation either for or against his ordination.[24]

Though each church had the liberty to conduct the ceremony on its own terms, ordination services generally contained similar elements. During James Pendleton's ordination service in 1833, likely typical of the solemn exercise, his "ordaining council" examined him on several topics. They asked about his "Christian experience," which probably included an account of his conversion. They also wanted to know about his "call to the ministry": why did he feel compelled to preach and what were the circumstances of his sense of calling? Finally, they interrogated him on his doctrinal views. Pendleton himself found the whole examination "far from being thorough," but the council seemed satisfied enough with his responses to favor his ordination. The inspection of a licentiate's doctrinal views could delve deeply into the more problematic issues of theology. Porter Clay's ordination ceremony in 1824 included questions on the doctrine of soteriology, specifically on the nature of the elect and whether they could fall away and lose their salvation. One member of Clay's council asked him, "Do you recollect, brother, that you ever knew a sheep turned into a goat or a goat into a sheep?" Clay pondered the question before responding, "I do not recollect that I ever knew such a circumstance." The question undoubtedly related to Jesus's designation of those who followed him as "sheep" and those who did not as "goats."[25] The likely intent of the question was to determine where Clay stood in regard to Calvinistic predestination. Clay's oblique response satisfied the questioner, but did not clarify his position.

Some licentiates sought to postpone their ordinations because of their own sense of inadequacy to the task. Lewis Deweese's church took up his ordination in November 1796, but during his interrogation, he made clear that he felt unready to take the next step in his career. In the end, his church agreed with him and put off his ordination. He finally submitted to ordination eleven months later. In September 1821, the Corn Creek church agreed that George Kendall had proven his gifts adequately. His strength in the pulpit, his ability to clearly explain passages of the Bible, and his zealous devotion to the Baptist movement convinced his church to ordain him. Kendall himself, though, lacked their confidence in his own talents and skills. He refused their ordination for almost two years.[26]

While the ordination examination could be unsettling, in a great many cases the composition of the examination committee more than likely put the

examinee at ease. In preparing for the ordination of a licentiate, a church invited ministers from the region, but given the close-knit nature of Baptist life, the odds were slim of facing a committee of unfamiliar faces. In fact, a good number of ordination candidates knew their committees well. When Theodrick Boulware came before the North Fork church for ordination in July 1812, he took questions from William Hickman, Sr., James Suggett, and John Ficklin. The connections between these men ran deep. Both Ficklin and Suggett had been ordained at North Fork, in 1807 and 1810 respectively. Hickman pastored North Fork's parent congregation, the Forks of Elkhorn church, and preached regularly at North Fork from its constitution during the revivals of 1800–1803 until his death in 1830. Boulware joined Forks of Elkhorn as a teenager while Hickman was pastor there. Shortly after Ficklin became pastor of North Fork, Boulware moved his membership to that church. Thus, between 1790 and his ordination in 1812, Boulware slowly built relationships with the men who would evaluate him for the ministry.[27]

The ordination of Robert Kirtley in August 1822 also bore the marks of a friendly rite of passage. Kirtley's family moved from Virginia in 1796 when he was ten and settled in Boone County within the northern bend of the Ohio River. His parents, former Episcopalians, joined the newly organized Baptist church at Bullittsburg, and his father Jeremiah soon took a leadership position in the church. When Robert converted in 1811, he joined the church of his youth and by 1817 had established himself as a leader at Bullittsburg, being chosen as one of the church's deacons. In the revival of religion that permeated the state between 1817 and 1820, Robert Kirtley revealed a keen interest in the salvation of others, and the church licensed him to preach in 1819. During these years, formative in Kirtley's ministerial development, the Bullittsburg church enjoyed preaching from two ministers, Absalom Graves, who had joined the church in 1797, and Chichester Matthews, one of the founding members of the church. In 1820, these two were joined by James Dicken. Thirty-five year old Dicken had experienced a life comparable to Kirtley's. He was born just a year earlier than Kirtley, had also married in his early twenties, converted in the same year, and then joined the same church. The Bullittsburg church members chose to license both Dicken and Kirtley on the same day in 1819. They might have shared their ordination together, but Kirtley declined his and only accepted it in 1822 at the urging of the church. Thus, when Kirtley finally accepted ordination in the church of his youth, the church of his parents, he faced examination from a three man committee: his two pastors, Graves and Matthews, who had known

him since his boyhood, and James Dicken, one of his closest friends. After his ordination, Kirtley joined in the ministerial labors at Bullittsburg. So close was the ministers' bond that when Graves and Dicken died within a few months of each other, it prompted aged preacher John Taylor to offer up a prayer for Kirtley, because "two-thirds of the world was swept from him at once."[28]

Though the connections between an ordination candidate and his committee were not always as close or distinct, the relationships tended to reveal not only the close community among the Baptists, but also the particular bonds formed among the preachers themselves as a guild of bi-vocational ministers. An example can be found in the 1860 ordination of Alfred C. Graves, Absalom Graves's great-grandson. Among the ministers on the young Graves's committee were Robert Kirtley and his son James A. Kirtley. In other instances, Zachariah Morris led Isaac Steele's committee in 1818 after both men had helped organize the Middle Fork church ten years before. Joseph Taylor headed his son Alfred's ordination committee in 1834. And J. H. Spencer's seven-member committee included at least one preacher whom Spencer had traveled with as a licentiate and several others whom he would have known from his preaching tours and the gatherings of Baptists who lived along the Kentucky-Tennessee border near the Barren River.[29]

The preaching tasks of the licentiate did not change substantially after ordination. One key difference, however, involved his new authority to administer the important ordinances of baptism and communion. Such new responsibilities could cause anxiety. Church members who attended a Saturday meeting of the Williamstown Church in April 1827 witnessed the ordination ceremony of William Conrad and Nelly O'Neal's account of her conversion experience. The following day it fell to Conrad to perform O'Neal's baptism in the nearby stream. Just as Conrad had felt incapable of preaching before he received his license, he felt an "unworthiness" and "poverty" in his ability to perform the public ritual correctly. Under the perceived pressure of the situation, the awkward and self-conscious Conrad took the new convert in hand and later noted that, "I baptized the sister so quickly, I felt that surely I had bruised her against the rocks in the bottom of the creek." That afternoon, those in attendance had to go to great lengths to assure the concerned minister that he had done it right. In a similar circumstance, James Pendleton illustrated that even after baptizing for a few years, he could still learn from those more skilled in the craft. In March 1840, with sixty new converts to baptize, Pendleton and visiting preacher John L. Burrows went down in the Big Barren River to perform the

ceremony. With so many to immerse, the preachers took turns. In the end, Pendleton thought to himself that Burrows "baptized more gracefully than I." Nevertheless, Pendleton does not record anyone ever criticizing his lack of gracefulness in administering the ordinance.[30]

Newly ordained ministers, licentiates, and experienced preachers did not always receive the approval of their congregations, as the populist spirit of the Baptists afforded congregants liberty to criticize their leaders—sometimes for the preacher's benefit, sometimes not. One of the cherished characteristics of the Baptist movement in early Kentucky was the status of the preacher as one of the people. As a matter of principle, Baptists honored the fact that ministers came from among them, were approved by them, and worked alongside them. Thus could one group of Baptists boast in 1820 that the difference between Baptist ministers and laity was "less than in almost any other denomination of Christians." This allowed parishioners a certain latitude with their ministers. In the months before James Pendleton's ordination, he heard about a layman's commentary on his performance in the pulpit. The parishioner criticized Pendleton's skills by wryly opining, "as God is omnipotent he of course can make a preacher of that young man." Pendleton winced at the suggestion that only the awesome power of a deity could improve his preaching skills. In a similar fashion, farmer-preacher Moses Pierson gained a reputation among his hearers in the early nineteenth century not for his eloquence, but for oddities in his word choice and tone. Pierson tended to overuse the word "peradventure" in his preaching, which might have been overlooked by his congregations had he not pronounced it as if it were spelled "paradventure." Among his facetious hearers, Pierson gained the nickname "Old Paradventure." Compounding Pierson's problem, though, was his painfully harsh voice, which reminded some of his congregants of a splinter's vibration on a fence rail during a stiff breeze. Thus, "Old Paradventure" also acquired the unflattering sobriquet "Old Splinter-on-the-Fence."[31]

Gender differences could also play a role in the pointed criticism of ministers. Hannah Graves, an influential member of the Clear Creek Church, immersed herself so well in Bible reading that she gained a reputation for knowing the book as well or better than her ministers. This knowledge emboldened her to deal bluntly with preachers and gave her criticisms a certain weight. When one of her church's preachers decided to leave the church during a time of trouble, she rebuked him. Using an analogy of Jesus in the book of John, she asked the minister if he was like a hireling who leaves his sheep when trouble comes, as opposed to the good shepherd who cares for his sheep.[32]

By the 1830s, biting criticisms had begun to wear away the communal nature of some churches and undermined the leadership of local pastors. As the movement began to mature in Kentucky, what once smacked of egalitarianism now seemed disrespectful. In 1837, the editor of Kentucky's Baptist newspaper rebuked those who promoted harsh opinions. Asserting that he blushed to record the fact, the editor condemned those Baptist church members who "too often go to meeting and bring nothing away but the faults of the sermon and of the preacher." Expanding the breadth of his indictment, he declared, "Some appear to esteem their orthodoxy only in proportion to the skill with which they can detect the faults and imperfections of their minister; and look upon piety as nothing more than the volubility with which a man recounts the errors in the last discourse to which he listened." What church members might have viewed as a right in an egalitarian sect now seemed to tear away at a more respectable institution.[33]

The issue of criticizing pastors and their abilities never disappeared in the early nineteenth century and compelled one group of Baptist churches in western Kentucky to address the issue publically. In 1840, the Baptists meeting with the Little River Association sent a letter to its constituents on the subject of the relationship between members and their pastors. The letter, most likely written by a pastor or group of pastors sensitive to the issue, encouraged church members to recall that their pastors were "men called and qualified of God for sacred services...men animated with a principle of love to Christ and the souls of men." Still, they were "but men, and men too of infirmities and imperfections." Proper conduct toward pastors, said the letter, was an "incumbent duty." Church members should never slander their pastors' character, lessen their reputations in the community, hinder their influence, and should avoid "making illiberal remarks upon their performances." The letter made clear that church members, as individuals before God, retained the right to decipher scriptural truth. Preachers had no monopoly on biblical truth. On the contrary, the letter encouraged Baptists to "compare the doctrines delivered by your minister with the sacred scriptures, and to judge for yourself respecting the truth of them." However, if they had any objections about the doctrines they heard or felt any disapprobation of their minister's performance, they should express their concerns delicately. The letter suggested, "Perhaps a free and affectionate conversation with them in private, about the unsatisfactory parts of their performances, would generally answer the best purpose."[34] Despite concerns over critical remarks, both the good-natured jibes and the

harsher criticisms expressed the nature of the preacher-hearer relationship in the Baptist movement. Baptists reveled in the thought that they had established the church of Christ as originally portrayed in the New Testament, in which each member of the church, even the pastor, presented himself equally before God.

Whereas an egalitarian sensibility generally characterized relationships between ministers and laity in a Baptist church, the administration of the ordinances was clearly a minister's prerogative. Based on their reading of the New Testament, most Kentucky Baptist churches only authorized ordained ministers to administer the ordinances of baptism and communion in the church. When unordained preachers tried to take on those duties, it led to difficulties. The Little Union Church, for instance, had to deal with this very issue in 1812. Their quandary apparently arose when a convert received immersion baptism by an unordained preacher, but their question focused on whether the convert needed to be rebaptized before reception to membership. Unable to resolve the question themselves, they sought the advice of other churches. Their association refused to answer the question of rebaptism, saying, "Each Church is the proper tribunal to determine the qualifications of the members she receives." But the association went beyond the question and reasserted the widely held belief that "baptism is not rightly administered by any person who is not regularly ordained as Minister of the Gospel."[35]

Other statements of Baptist theory by associated bodies of Kentucky Baptist churches made clear that while ordination gave the minister distinct rights, it also carried tremendous duties and responsibilities. One associational statement revealed the paternal character of the office of pastor by advising that ministers "exercise no authority [in the church] save the counsel of a tender father." Some Baptists in north-central Kentucky agreed in 1831 that the pastorate was a "high and holy calling." An earlier statement by the neighboring Long Run Association articulated this same idea and added their perspective on pastoral duties. These Baptists expected a higher degree of holiness and humility from the ministerial office. Their associational letter sent to the churches in the region declared, "As ministers are the most public, and ordinarily, the most influential characters in the Church, much depends on them." In their sermons and in their private conversation, the ministers' conduct should match the expectations of scripture. At the same time, the letter warned ministers directly not to "aspire to a state of superior and permanent dignity, as of higher office than their brethren" in the ministry, whose preaching gifts may not be

as developed or visible. Still another associated group of Baptists warned their ministers that "self-glory or self-interest should be forgotten." They claimed that no one minister had received a fullness of gifts, and each should engage in ministry only after "prayerful consultation with God and his own soul. . . . For there are no doubt many, whose usefulness is measurably destroyed by aspiring too high." These statements collectively reveal the Baptist ministry as an important calling with great expectations and one filled with dangerous temptations of pride and self-aggrandizement.[36]

One characteristic that distinguished Baptist clergy from laity was the frequency with which preachers put themselves at risk in the execution of their duties, particularly by traveling to appointments in dangerous outlying areas. The western frontier in the late eighteenth and early nineteenth centuries contained manifold hazards, including occasional Indian raids, bandits, wild animals, and the common dangers of long, solitary travel. One of the earliest Baptist preachers in Kentucky, William Hickman, Sr., encountered such dangers in the winter of 1788 and 1789 when he accepted a preaching appointment some twenty miles away at Owen's Fort in Jefferson County. Hickman and three companions set out in frigid conditions, making most of the journey after dark. Intermittent snowfall interrupted the little moonlight that shone on the travelers throughout the night. On horseback, they crossed Benson Creek nineteen times along their way. "At some fords," Hickman later recalled, "the ice would bear us over, at other fords some steps would bear us, the next step break in." The preacher and his coterie arrived at the fort after two o'clock in the morning. Hickman preached to several groups on Saturday and Sunday, and his hearers invited him to return in warmer weather. For his future visits, they arranged to send a guard with him to watch over the more perilous parts of his trip. When the warmer weather came, Hickman coordinated his preaching at several locations nearby the fort. Baptists traveled with the preacher as he rode from meeting to meeting, prompting Hickman to observe that the two or three dozen gathered "looked more like going to war than to meeting to worship God." Preachers like Hickman certainly did not enjoy the hardships they faced in pursuit of their calling. In fact, Hickman once had to be persuaded to venture into the frozen night. But such preachers took their ministerial duties seriously, believing that in their preaching they offered nothing less than eternal hope and joy.[37]

By the 1840s, two facts brought new anxiety to Kentucky Baptists and increased the burdens placed on ministers. First, Baptists began to elevate their

pastors to greater positions of honor and leadership. Second, though Baptists in Kentucky outnumbered other religious groups in the state, the Methodist juggernaut was quickly closing the gap. The notion of Kentucky as one of the last bastions of Baptist preeminence in the country heightened pressure to defend the state in the name of Jesus and democracy. A measure of success and their anxiety merged to promote an increasingly loud boasting. In 1841, for example, the editor of the Kentucky Baptist newspaper estimated that there were approximately 600 to 700 Baptist churches in the state. Based on that assessment, the editor claimed that "at least two-thirds of the entire population is decidedly favorable to and under Baptist influence." Indeed, there were about 700 Baptist churches in the state, but for the editor's estimate of adherence to be correct, there would need to have been ten adherents for every Baptist church member—an assumption too-optimistic by half. The burden and responsibility of defending what success there had been, however, largely fell to the Baptist minister. In such a competitive climate, it fell to the Baptist preachers to propel the movement and extend Baptist influence through extensive local preaching and occasional tours. As one historian has noted, the Baptist preachers "simply could not match the canvassing power of the Methodist itinerants who preached nearly every day." Still, the Baptist preachers did preach as often as they could, to move their hearers and to advance the cause.[38]

Most early Baptist preachers, however, likely thought little about their influence on the "destinies of the religious world." Yet to their minds, the sermons they preached locally dealt with matters of cosmic significance. The sermon resided at the center of the preacher's vocation in the same way that it served as the focal point of a Baptist meeting. In this regard, the movement participated in the larger Protestant practice of giving liturgical preeminence to the sermon. In early Kentucky Baptist life, it was not unusual for a sermon to fill an hour. This helps explain why some licentiates' first efforts were so painful in their brevity. Generally, the preacher chose a sermon to fit an occasion or to address a need or concern of the congregation. Over time, preachers built a stable of sermons from which they could draw at will and repeat if needed. With the bibliocentric nature of the Baptist movement, congregations expected to hear preaching based upon a biblical text. More often than not, preachers chose passages from the New Testament—again perhaps to be expected of an evangelistic sect rooted in the teachings of Jesus and the explications of the apostles. The Old Testament texts did receive attention, though roughly half as often as New Testament passages. Of the

nine sermons that veteran preacher John Taylor recalled in his memoirs, six drew upon the New Testament. In northern Kentucky, an associated group of churches opened their annual meetings with sermons from respected clergymen. In the first twenty years of the association's existence, seventeen of these introductory sermons were described by the appointed clerk. Of these seventeen, twelve used the New Testament as their source.[39]

Though a minister might begin with a biblical citation in mind, his sermon often strayed from simple exposition of the passage and delved into abstractions and "spiritualizations." For example, the sermons of Sugg Fort, who preached along the border of southwestern Kentucky and Tennessee in the 1820s, reveal the practice of "typing" that accompanied the spiritualization of texts. Fort drew several interesting conclusions in a sermon on Exodus 15:27, in which the Israelites fleeing from Egypt "came to Elim, where were twelve wells of water, and three score and ten palm trees; and they encamped there by the waters." According to Fort, not only did the verse describe the place where the Israelites camped, but the journey through the wilderness itself symbolized the "Christian's journey through the wilderness of this world." Further, the twelve wells figured the "twelve holy apostles, whose writings contain the waters of eternal life," and the seventy palms represent the "seventy [disciples] sent out by Christ, as recorded by Luke, to publish the glad tidings of salvation." By typing Old Testament stories to represent New Testament ideas and people, the Baptist preacher could entertain and instruct his hearers, who marveled at his insights.[40]

Some of the "spiritualizing" that occurred in early Baptist sermons had roots in the limited literacy of some preachers and in the fact that Baptists did not regard classical or theological education as necessary for an effective ministry. Most Baptists agreed with John Taylor's assessment that "a good motive to the work and the call of the church is all-sufficient as to a man's authority to preach the gospel." Thus literacy and education played limited roles at best. Daniel Drake, whose parents attended the Baptist church at Mayslick, recalled that most of the Baptist preachers he encountered near the turn of the century "were illiterate persons, but some were men of considerable natural talents." Drake's preference for literate people is clear in his memoirs. Of the three preachers he mentioned by name, each had an above-average level of literacy, but each represents a different aspect of early Kentucky Baptist preachers. William Wood, whom Drake knew as a child, had helped plan the nearby town of Washington. He had purchased an extensive tract of land and laid out the town on it in 1785. In 1788, Wood was in New Jersey encouraging families

like the Drakes to migrate to the frontier. After the Drakes settled in Mayslick, Wood often visited and gave young Daniel a catechism to study. The catechism had the opposite effect for which Wood intended it. It began with the doctrine of the Trinity, which so confused Daniel that he developed an aversion to catechisms of any kind. A few years later, Wood, the entrepreneur preacher, engaged in a questionable business transaction with another church member, for which he was excluded from the church at Washington, even though he was its pastor.[41]

A second preacher mentioned by Drake was John Gano, who also traveled to Kentucky in the late 1780s and praised the territory both to Drake's family and to Wood. Gano, a native of New Jersey, had gained a reputation for his preaching tours of the southern colonies in the 1750s. He had few equals in the pulpit, an above-average education, and was well-known for his mastery of the spiritualization of biblical texts. This was revealed in his first preaching in Kentucky. During his family's move there in 1788, his boat overturned on the Ohio River, resulting in heavy property loss but no fatalities. Upon arriving in Washington, Kentucky, he preached to his companions from Acts 27:44—"And so it came to pass, that they escaped all safe to land"—a passage referring to Paul's ship wreck on Malta. Later when his son Stephen, a pastor in Rhode Island, visited the family in Kentucky, the elder Gano preached from I Corinthians 16:17—"I am glad of the coming of *Stephanas*, Fortunatus, and Achaicus: for that which was lacking on your part they have supplied"—a passage in which Paul expresses his pleasure that these three preachers have visited the church at Corinth. Spiritualization of such biblical texts was part of Gano's style, as it was of many early preachers.

The third preacher mentioned by Drake, and the least remembered in the historical record, was Hiram Curry. This preacher taught the local school where Drake acquired a rudimentary education. Curry held a dishonorable position in Drake's recollection, because he strongly emphasized learning the catechism, much to the boy's chagrin, and because he seemed just as keen on hickory switches.[42] Each of these three—Wood, the entrepreneur who let business conflict with his ministry; Gano, the venerable and creative expositor; and Curry, the teacher-preacher unafraid of disciplining the mind and body—had above-average literacy skills.

One analyst of early Kentucky Baptist preachers determined that ministers with some common school education and average literacy constituted the largest percentage of preachers, perhaps the majority. This group included

teacher William Downs, whose education emboldened him in his theological debates with Catholic priests and Universalist preachers. It likewise included farmer Jacob Rogers, whose schooling of six months duration provided only enough literacy to read haltingly. A smaller group of preachers received no formal education of any kind. Warren Cash, a minister of this kind, converted in 1785 at age twenty-five, not knowing the letters of the alphabet. Still, he married the literate daughter of a Virginia preacher, and she taught him to read the Bible before he received ordination. Jacob Locke's church licensed him to preach knowing of his illiteracy. However, before his ordination almost two years later, he studied to learn to read. He was not alone in this pursuit of self-improvement. Wilson Thompson converted while illiterate, and when he felt the call to preach, he recalled later, his "mind became greatly enamored with the Scriptures. Every leisure moment I had I spent in their study." In this way he taught himself to read.[43]

The smallest group were the few preachers who had received a college education or formal theological training. As might be expected, opportunities for advanced education depended upon the resources of the family, both intellectual and financial. Silas Mercer Noel, one of the few well-educated early Baptist preachers, was himself the son of a venerated Baptist minister in Virginia. Noel received tutoring from his father, then advanced to receive a classical education and studied law before moving to Kentucky. Another native Virginian, James Fishback, attended Transylvania University in Lexington in 1793 before traveling abroad to obtain a degree in medicine. After his ordination in 1817, Fishback assumed the pastorate of the Baptist church in Lexington, where he would play a key role in the theological schisms of the 1820s and 1830s over the doctrines of Barton Stone and Alexander Campbell. Another early Baptist scholar and physician's son, William C. Warfield, graduated from Transylvania and worked in a Bardstown law office when he converted in 1817. A few years later, after his ordination, Warfield continued his education at Princeton Theological Seminary in New Jersey before returning for the duration of his career.[44]

Though literacy, or the lack of it, could constrain or expand the expository depth of early Baptist sermons, what often impressed a congregation most was the preacher's style in the pulpit. For many early preachers, manner of delivery was almost as important as the matter being delivered. The much emulated preacher John Taylor revealed himself in his memoirs as a keen observer of his

fellow preachers' doctrine and delivery. He noted how William Hickman, Sr. spoke so slowly that his hearers at times got ahead of him in the subject. His son, William Hickman, Jr., on the other hand, spoke "too fast as the old gentleman speaks too slow." To Taylor's lights, Lewis Craig seemed the epitome of the relational preacher whose voice "would make men tremble and rejoice." Taylor recalled, "The first time I heard him preach, I seemed to hear the sound of his voice for many months." Though Craig failed to exposit the Bible skillfully and did not dwell on doctrine in his sermons, he "dealt closely with the heart," and was "better acquainted with men than with books."[45]

Regardless of speed of delivery or tone of voice, the early preacher targeted the hearts of his hearers. Baptist preachers followed in the wide New Light wake in their enthusiastic preaching, which was aimed at pietism and conversion by grace. They preached extemporaneous sermons, charged with dramatic vigor, infused with emotional energy, and spoken in the language of the people. Baptist meetings generally ran the emotional gamut from somberness to excitement, from fear and sadness to joy, but in each respect the meeting house represented a haven for emotion and especially for tears. Weeping seemed to accompany every facet of the Baptist worship meeting. John Taylor noted the many "floods of tears" among church members celebrating communion, his own tears in prayer for a revival of religion, and the weeping associated with the agonies and joys of conversion. Wilson Thompson recalled the tears flowing at the water's edge during baptism. Preachers like William White Penney, Benjamin Keeling, and Enos Keith gained reputations for their tearful proclamations.[46]

Despite such an emphasis on emotionalism in preaching and in Baptist worship, the Kentucky Baptists tended towards balance between feeling and intellect. Baptists appreciated pathos in worship, but rejected emotional excesses of the kind demonstrated in some of the turn-of-the-century revivals. Baptists approved of the revivals' aim and certainly enjoyed tremendous numerical growth from them, but they denounced the means of the revival preachers, who seemed to encourage, or at least tolerate, the more controversial revival demonstrations, such as jerking, dancing, and barking. The Baptist belief in orderly worship moderated their understanding of enthusiasm in religious meetings, and each church looked to its pastor to set a tone in the congregation. Thus views about enthusiastic religious exercises, while typically more conservative than other religious groups, varied by occasion and location.

John Taylor, in his memoirs written in the 1820s, recalled a wintry baptismal service in 1788 at which he immersed twenty-six converts. To get to the water, a six-inch layer of ice was cut away, and after the service Taylor's clothes froze before he could put on dry ones. That he could experience such an event without suffering any "inconvenience," he claimed, could be "attributed to enthusiasm." He wrote then that he did not know "why enthusiasm may not be used in religion as any other laudable work."[47]

As enthusiastic religion existed in the late eighteenth and early nineteenth centuries, Taylor's brand ran rather mild. Another minister's approach reveals how a pastor could rein in an enthusiastic congregation. After preaching in Kentucky for twenty-five years, James Suggett moved to Missouri and in 1841 teamed with a young preacher, S. H. Ford, for a preaching appointment. While the younger minister preached and the elder looked on, a middle-aged man in the congregation fell to his knees, weeping loudly. Just then a woman, observing this emotional expression, leaped to her feet and piercingly proclaimed, "Jesus, Jesus, have mercy!" As quickly as she arose, she fell to the ground as if lifeless. The congregation was agitated with surprise and excitement. The young Ford, having never seen such an exhibition, was dumbfounded and sat down from the pulpit. Calmly, the experienced Suggett stood, struck up a hymn, then, having recaptured the attention of those assembled, concluded the meeting as if nothing had occurred. Sixteen years later, Samuel Ford, having become a well-educated Baptist intellectual, reflected upon enthusiasm in worship and still denounced revivalistic extremes as absurdities; but he would not deny the veracity of inexplicable enthusiasm. The rationalist Ford explained, "Our passions, our sympathies, the influence of the mind or the body—who can comprehend?" Quoting Shakespeare's *The Tempest*, Ford continued, "'We are such stuff as dreams are made of [sic].' Man is an unfathomable, mysterious being. A word brings moisture to his eye . . . or sends a chill through his whole frame. Who can account for it? I shall not make the attempt." Throughout the early nineteenth century, Baptist clergymen both guided and reflected the movement's opinions on enthusiasm as they did in other areas of Baptist thought.[48]

Though many elements of the Baptist ministry remained constant throughout the early nineteenth century, the tumultuous 1830s led Kentucky's Baptists to revise their assumptions and expectations about the ministry. Yet through it all, preachers remained at the forefront of the movement's growth.

Through their preaching appointments in homes, courthouses, schools, and fields, they won converts to the movement. By organizing believers into churches, they established networks of faith which would continue their individual work on a more expansive level. In their own communities, preachers laid down roots and formed kinship structures that could complicate their ministries at times, but which helped establish the preachers as relational and familiar community figures. Wherever the preacher's ministry took him—to the far end of their church's neighborhood or to distant fields destitute of preaching—Baptists recognized him as a figure of authority, but also a leader whose authority lay in the church, among the people whom he led. Ever without tenure, a pastor never stood beyond the discipline of his followers. His sermons purposefully and powerfully communicated images and ideas of eternal significance in commonplace terms and in familiar and emotional language. Pastors expected good-natured jesting. However, when they failed to satisfy an audience empowered by Baptist egalitarian principles, they faced ridicule and chastisement from their own.

In each of these conditions and qualities, Kentucky Baptist preachers anticipated, reflected, cultivated, and manifested the democratic ethos of the early national period, which rejected hierarchy, especially in religious life. Baptists had historically threatened traditional socio-religious orders. In seventeenth-century England, Baptist separatists faced sundry penalties for their dissent, including restriction of worship, confiscation of property, bodily harm, and imprisonment. Puritan New England offered no haven for persecuted Baptists, who found refuge in Rhode Island and further south in Pennsylvania. Many early Kentucky Baptists could personally recall the persecution they and their ministers encountered in colonial Anglican Virginia. In these situations, church members claimed their persecution as a badge of honor when they cited Jesus's last two beatitudes: "Blessed are they which are persecuted for righteousness' sake: for theirs is the kingdom of heaven. Blessed are ye, when men shall revile you, and persecute you, and shall say all manner of evil against you falsely, for my sake."[49] However, in the new American order, and especially in newly settled states such as Kentucky, Baptists experienced an unprecedented level of freedom to shape their own religious forms according to their own traditions, interpretations, and needs. That the democratic and egalitarian Baptist and American sensibilities existed together only helped propel the Baptists into a leading position in the

pluralistic religious marketplace. As the products and articulators of Baptist religious forms, Baptist preachers stood at the forefront of the movement's expansion, as first among equals and republican representatives, and as propagators of popularized religion.

3

Divine Channels of Democracy: Baptist Churches and Associations

In the dimness of early morning, under a dense verdant canopy, little Johnny Spencer struggled to keep pace with his parents as they strode through the unbroken forest. Though the long trek along an uncut path may have wearied the boy, the excitement of spending a summer Sunday away from the farm and with his grandfather certainly bore him up. Settlement in the Spencers' neighborhood in south-central Kentucky was sparse in the early 1830s. Young Johnny only saw two cabins, nestled in clearings of one or two acres, as he ambled along behind his parents. Johnny's mother sighted the family's destination, a third cabin just visible through the woods, and stayed her family as she sat down for a moment on a fallen tree trunk. She slipped off her cowskin shoes and put on her nicer pair made of prunella. Fixed with her finer footwear, Mrs. Spencer led her family into the clearing to join the crowd around the crude cabin which served as the meeting house for the Bethel Baptist Church. Though the Spencer's were not church members, like many of their neighbors who had migrated from South Carolina and Virginia,

they were "Baptists in sentiment." Johnny's paternal grandfather served as a lay leader in the Bethel church and was one of the few male church members in the Spencers' immediate neighborhood. In the clearing around the cabin, several rude benches had been supplied for the overflowing congregation and, as the meeting began, Johnny's parents sat there while the boy wandered off to play with some of the other children. After a while, he returned from his playing and stood just away from the congregants. He listened for a moment as the preacher delivered his message from the doorway of the cabin. The preacher stood in such a way as to address "both the people who filled the cabin and those who were seated on benches in the yard." Spying her son, Johnny's mother "stealthily glided out from among the people," captured the boy, and carried him back to her seat, where he remained restrained until the sermon concluded.[1]

At about the same time, in Boone County, Kentucky which was over 150 miles away from where Johnny and his parents sat as part of the Bethel congregation, seven men and seven women, including five slaves, met to establish the Sardis Baptist Church. They drew up a set of rules for the government of the church, the first of which stated, "It is the duty of church members to attend church meetings." They put in writing their own rules of discipline and conduct. They agreed to attend "appointed meetings as far as the Lord shall enable us, not neglecting any of them but on cases of necessity." Before their work had finished, however, they drafted an extensive "covenant," or statement of their core beliefs. This covenant included doctrinal pronouncements about God, the Trinity, divine justice, salvation, heaven and hell, as well as baptism and communion. The assembled Baptists agreed that before the beginning of time, God himself had made a covenant with his son Jesus, "in whom the church was chosen," and that the church "should be holy and without blame before him in love, having predestined them unto the adoption of children by Jesus Christ." As adopted children, "the church with all her grace and glory was placed in the hands of the Lord Jesus Christ and made his especial care and charge." Having asserted their key beliefs, and ordered their business, discipline, and relationships, placing the church at the center of each of them, the tiny church at Sardis came into existence on October 27, 1831.[2]

Five years later, in the western reaches of Kentucky, four churches revolted against an association of Baptist churches they had previously joined. In their explanation of the separation, the representatives of the four churches in the minority argued that the majority had imposed and infringed upon their rights

and had misused the powers of the association. In a list of grievances, the four churches contended first that the majority in the Highland Association had formed "illegal committees, investing them with power to hear and determine authoritatively on matters which rightfully belong to the churches alone." Second, the majority had nullified and voided decisions made by the churches in the minority. And third, the majority had published a document that the minority considered "a direct attack and an infringement upon the internal labor of the churches." The latter document also contained "charges against many baptist [sic] ministers of the best standing, propriety and usefulness in our Baptist Denomination, which statements and charges are grossly and glaringly false." With this testimony of injustice, the four churches declared their independence from the Highland Association and formed their own body, the Little Bethel Association.[3]

Each of these three tableaus, unconnected in time and place, presents images of early Baptist church life in Kentucky. They depict churches in their conception and self-conception, their eminent position in the life of the movement, and their actual unpolished existence, wherein congregants gathered in forest clearings to hear preaching. They also depict isolated, though certainly familiar, instances of social realities played out in individual churches. Young Johnny Spencer's family attended worship as part of the congregation and not as part of the church's membership, a division made clear in the conversion-relation process. Thus they could be adherents, or "Baptists in sentiment," remaining clear of the church's authority. While Mrs. Spencer may have kept church discipline at arm's length as part of the congregation, she was concerned enough about social expectations in the church to change shoes before the members could see her. Johnny's grandfather's status as one of the few male members also reflected the widespread pattern of gender disparity in church membership during the nineteenth century, a pattern not restricted to Baptists or the century by any means. The Sardis church's constitution and articulation of rules reveal the democratic ideal in the midst of inequalities. Seven men and seven women, nine whites and five black slaves, came together to create a new church. Despite gender and racial differences, they covenanted together, agreed upon a statement of doctrine, and placed their communal voice above themselves as individuals. Finally, the four churches that aligned themselves in the newly constituted Little Bethel Association reveal the passionate ideal of congregational independence. More reversionary than revolutionary, they strove to recover the

Old Stone Meeting House. Southern Baptist Historical Library and Archives, Nashville, Tennessee.

rights they perceived as inherent to the Baptist movement, particularly the rights of local churches. The vision and practice represented in these tableaus permeated the Baptist impulse in early Kentucky and indeed remained part of the Baptist denomination into the modern era. The congregational ethic distinguished the Baptists from all of their competitors in the Second Great Awakening.[4]

The Baptist dedication to congregational autonomy colored every aspect of the movement's thought and practice to a higher degree than their commitment to baptism of believers by immersion. More importantly, if populist religious movements require localized, institutional expressions of faith, then the early Baptists were preeminently populist. They also confronted the perils of such intense localism. The American socio-political landscape itself resonated with the Baptist democratic ethic. Baptists themselves recognized the commonalities between the expanding democratic populism of the early national period and their own historical commitment to congregationalism.

In their churches, the people selected their own leaders, including the pastors, deacons, clerks, and business-meeting moderators. The people determined who could join them—who had provided credible evidence of having gained citizenship in the redeemer's kingdom through conversion. The people evaluated the call of prospective ministers and approved their ordination. In their business meetings, the people determined who among them needed to be disciplined, suspended from membership, or even excluded, to protect the church's collective purity as a chosen people of God. Their deeply rooted and consistently practiced democratic ethic convinced the Baptists that they alone exemplified truly American religion. This attitude became even more apparent by the 1840s, as Baptists faced greater competition from without, as well as doubts inside the movement about localism. Assertions in this regard by Baptist groups and periodical editors included bold declarations such as, "The Scriptures plainly show that the form of all Church Government ought to be Democratic or Republican; and that the majority ought to rule to the exclusion of all privileged characters or orders of men"; and idealistic propositions like, "*Equal rights* is written in glowing capitals over the door of the 'house of God.'"[5]

Baptist claims of exceptionalism about their form of church polity could also contain acerbic barbs aimed at Catholics, or the preferred target, the Methodists. One influential Baptist writer, upon hearing a rumor that Methodism had entered a period of decline, saw the news as unsurprising, since "the despotic nature of their church government does not comport at all with our free republican institutions," and "in this land of religious light and liberty," Methodists should be unwilling to "submit to the dictation of their own priesthood." Methodist laity, he said, had no more authority over "who shall have the charge over them, than have the surfs [*sic*] of Russia." Likewise, in response to an assertion that the Baptist "congregational and democratic form of church government lacks strength and energy, and that the substitution of the Diocesan and Episcopal offices would be an improvement," one group of Baptists asserted that such "Papal usurpations" were part of an "old fashioned religious humbugery, brought into being, during the dark ages." These Baptists declared that all the Protestant denominations should follow them into the nineteenth century.[6]

Despite any claims to modernity that Kentucky Baptists made concerning their form of church government, they recognized that congregational polity had deep historical roots. Every populist religious movement of the Second

Great Awakening held at its core a primitivist impulse to restore the pure Christian church. To these populists, the Protestant Reformation had forever shattered the Roman Catholic monopoly on religion, but had not restored the ancient Christian order. Filling this vacuum in the free religious atmosphere of the post-revolutionary decades, several popular religious movements claimed that they alone were the "divine channel of purity for the primitive gospel." When Baptists read the New Testament, they perceived the earliest churches in Palestine, Asia Minor, Greece, and westward as independent local communities of believers connected only by tenuous threads of occasional cooperation. Though Baptists approved of the type of congregationalism practiced by seventeenth-century Puritans in England and in the colonies, they resisted the Puritan linking of church and state. Thus by the early nineteenth century, the Baptists stood almost alone as a populist movement completely dedicated to the intense localism of the primitivist ideal. By the mid-nineteenth century, a more forward-looking Baptist movement would conjoin their primitivism with modernism, claiming that congregationalism represented not only the ancient order, but also the future of Christianity in a free republic.[7]

With congregational theory playing such an important role in their connection with the past and their construction of the future, Kentucky Baptists applied the theory to their present in the conception, constitution, composition, and administration of their churches. Like many Christian movements, they conceived of the church in several ways. The most obvious and simple way was the individual church as the local gathering of believers. A higher usage of the term, however, was the abstract church, or the "church militant," which presumably incorporated all Christians who attended the visible local church. When a member of the visible church militant died, he became a member of the "church triumphant" in heaven. In Baptist life, only the converted could gain access to local church membership, and by default become part of the church militant and triumphant. Thus, when early Baptists spoke of the church, they often had the idea of a local church in mind, but might just as well have had the others in view. By linking conversion and church membership, the Baptists helped foster a more holistic faith. Beliefs, rituals, and procedures all flowed together to create a coherent church system. In this way, one group of Baptists in central Kentucky fashioned a list of prerequisites for participation in the church. When these Baptists read about the first-century churches in the New Testament, they saw a seven-fold delineation of "qualifications . . . for poor, dying, sinful mortals to possess, in order to prepare

them for the churches militant and triumphant." These seven requisites were conviction of sin, repentance, "embracing by faith the benefits flowing from the promise of the Savior," baptism, church membership, holding to biblical doctrines and good fellowship, and participation in communion. The list illustrates how the vision of Baptist churches involved converted and baptized members, the maintenance of discipline for the sake of piety and purity, and the role of communion in securing unity.[8]

As the movement expanded, views of what churches should be and what they should do derived solely from the experience of the individuals who joined together to form the local church. This purely populist maintenance of the movement magnified the opportunities and perils associated with localism. Early Kentucky Baptists could not rely upon efficient, coordinated religious coverage of a geographic area in the same way as the frontier Methodists or Presbyterians. These latter groups embraced centralized polity structures and managed preachers in networks, creating a greater homogeneity in practice and standards. The Baptist dedication to the autonomy of the local congregation did create regional distinctions and led to factional schism among Baptists, but the core elements of the Baptist impulse remained constant, preserved by the movement's adherents, who continually started new churches.[9]

Forming a Baptist church, as one Kentucky associational statement asserted in 1831, was "not a very difficult matter." The initiative for constituting a church could come from a minister in an area without a church or from a group of adherents in a region who wished to join together in a church. In other cases, members of one church amicably broke off and formed another nearer their homes. If they did not wish to form a completely separate church, they could exist as an "arm" of the mother church and act under its authority. This extension of the church could request its own constitution at any later date. In October 1811, for example, sixteen members of the Providence church in north-central Kentucky successfully petitioned for "liberty to convene and do business as an arm of the church." By February of the next year, they wished to be constituted separately. Likewise, in 1801, in the midst of the Great Revival, the Forks of Elkhorn church experienced unprecedented shuffling of membership. The church began January with a relatively large membership of 120. By the end of August, 199 new members had joined their number, three groups of members had left to start new churches, and one group of twenty-one members had asked permission to form an arm. Such fluidity of membership and the ease of

starting new churches helped the movement expand its territory swiftly and in a way suitable to the needs of Baptist adherents.[10]

Regardless of the reason why a group of adherents wanted a church, the process of forming it followed a general pattern that itself revealed Baptist priorities. Though the impetus for constitution might come from the people, they sought ordained ministers to oversee and evaluate their effort to create a new church. By convening a committee of ministers to approve their constitution and doctrinal statement, Baptists accorded ordained preachers a significant measure of authority. When the process ended, though, the balance of power returned to the church members. In some cases, adherents were discriminating about whom they requested to supervise the process. In 1801, the members of influential preacher John Taylor's church bruised his ego when they did not appoint him to a committee that would oversee a new church formation. About twenty members of the Bullittsburg church, of which Taylor was a member, had requested to form their own church to the south. Though the members of Bullittsburg agreed and selected five of their ordained ministers to oversee the constitution process, they chose not to appoint Taylor. He immediately thought the members wanted him to leave and join the new church. He later concluded that the members wished him no ill, but had worried that he might "not approve of what they considered a good work." They knew that four years earlier Taylor had refused to approve the constitution of a different church.[11]

Though a constitutional committee rarely refused approval, it was never a foregone conclusion. As could happen in ordination proceedings, the examination of prospective church constituents might end poorly. The experience at Dry Creek was just such an occasion. A number of Virginia Baptists who had settled along Dry Creek, approximately ten miles from the Bullittsburg church in northern Kentucky, asked nearby churches to send their ministers to help constitute the prospective Dry Creek church. Bullittsburg sent five representatives, including John Taylor, to assist the relocated Virginians. Taylor later recalled that the committee's initial impressions were favorable. The Dry Creek Baptists lived far enough away from other churches that to approve them would not detract from or overlap the efforts of the nearby churches. Also, since almost half of the prospective members were "respectable, free" men, their prospects for self-sufficiency and endurance seemed sure, according to the respectable and free Taylor. During the committee's examination of the constituents, however, the general opinion shifted. One of the chief concerns related to the very independence of the proposed church. Taylor inquired if

74   *Divine Channels of Democracy*

the church could meet to worship without requiring a preacher or exhorter to travel the distance to their church. The prospective members responded affirmatively, naming one of their own who could lead worship. However, this man immediately denied his ability for leadership and pointed to another man who could. This second man claimed he, too, was unable. This continued until Taylor asked if any of the men prayed with their families, with the understanding that if they did not, neither would they in public worship. None of the men did. After the examination, the committee withdrew to consider their ruling. Despite their initial favor, the committee declined to constitute the new church—much to the chagrin of the examined. Nevertheless, when the rejected constituents met the following week to discuss what to do next, they were joined by Moses Vickers, a nearby settler who led them in song and exhorted them to pray. They continued in this way for nearly three years before finally forming a church in July 1800, with Vickers as their pastor.[12]

Beyond such investigations and interrogations, committees also inspected the proposed church's documents of incorporation, which usually included articles of faith, a statement of communal covenant, and rules of decorum for self-governance. These documents followed the Baptist model of church constitution. While making a constitution may have posed a challenge to the newly independent American leaders after the revolution, Baptists had long used written foundations for church formation. European Anabaptists used written agreements as the foundation of their exclusivist communities. Likewise, English separatists used such documents to assure members of the level of piety expected of them and the community's duty to watch and to admonish the individual to meet such expectations. Colonial Baptists and Puritans in New England both used covenantal agreements, signifying the church as the enforcer of moral laws for the community, though the two groups differed about who should be the agent of this enforcement. Since church covenants often consisted of doctrinal assertions, many Kentucky churches blended their articles of faith, or confessions, with their covenant statements. As a document of a different nature, their rules of decorum were typically separate from the other documents.[13] Whether together or separate, however, these documents reveal the complicated nature of church formation, though the Baptists themselves considered it relatively simple. Baptists used their heritage to create their own future. Having borne the bruises of persecution on both sides of the Atlantic from both church and state, Baptists believed they could create New Testament communities of

believers, free from outside corruption and dedicated to institutional purity. To do this correctly, they needed written agreements delineating and advertising the beliefs they held in common; a statement affirming that the church and the individual existed for the benefit of each other; and a set of formal procedures for working together, which would maintain purity and harmony.

Early Kentucky Baptists who wished to constitute themselves as a church rarely had trained theologians among them to record their doctrinal profession for a committee's inspection. Thus they often borrowed the confession they had known in their former church. If they chose not to borrow what they had known previously, they had no reservations forming their own confession. They conceived of themselves as a church, the highest ecclesiastical body allowed by the Bible, and they were fully within their rights to borrow or create anew. Given the habitual borrowing and general agreement on theological fundamentals, most church doctrinal statements resembled each other. The confessions of Kentucky churches typically included eight to ten articles on core doctrinal matters. Invariably, the first or second article dealt with the doctrine of God, who was usually described as the one true and living God who created the universe. Often included in their statement on God, but just as often listed as a separate article, was the Baptist belief in the Trinity, or the triune nature of God. Churches frequently listed in the first two articles their view on the Bible, which Baptists described as their "only rule of faith and practice." Many churches specifically labeled their Scriptures "infallible." The Sardis church members wrote that the Old and New Testaments contained everything they needed "to know, believe, or do in the service of God." In a different vein, the Mayslick Baptists believed it contained "the whole mind of God respecting our salvation." The consistent listing of the doctrine of God reveals their commitment to the cosmic realities associated with a living, creator God who transcended time. Likewise, the constant presence at the beginning of Baptist confessions of their view of the Bible shows their faith that it was God's mode of revelation to his people. Not only did the Bible reveal the will of God, but it contained a record of his revelation in different points of history. This assertion imbued Baptists with the certainty that the God who worked through the ancient patriarchs could work through them in the early nineteenth century. Such a certainty carried with it the burden and responsibility of fulfilling divine mandates.[14]

The doctrines asserted and listed after the entries on God and the Bible were generally related to salvation: why it was necessary, how it was accomplished,

who was its agent, and what was its result. Here new churches could show the extent of their devotion to Calvinistic ideas, and most avowed a belief in human depravity. Some churches assumed a degree of background knowledge from those who would hear their covenants by simply stating they believed "in the doctrine of original sin." The terms of the union between Regular and Separate Baptists, which were adopted by many churches after their ratification in 1801, stated the same: "By nature we are fallen and depraved creatures." Other churches unfolded their views on depravity more explicitly. The articles of Buck Run Church, for example, explained that due to Adam's sin in the Garden of Eden, "All his posterity became guilty and sinful in every part and helpless as to any aid they can give in the great work of converting their own souls." Details in Baptist confessions likewise varied in their explication of salvation's accomplishment and agency, but each figured Jesus at the center of that work. Despite such variance, the statements reveal commonalities not only of substance but of word choice—a circumstance attributable both to widespread borrowing and to similar interpretations of the Pauline epistles. Some Kentucky Baptist confessions emphasized salvation and the work of Jesus as predestined. Many others noted salvation as determined by the grace of God alone. Quite a few declared that Jesus's atoning death and resurrection "imputed" an unearned righteousness upon depraved sinners, who accepted that imputation by an "effectual calling" from God himself. A great many Baptists professed the Calvinistic belief that saints would persevere, that is, that they could not lose their salvation.[15]

Baptists typically concluded their confession statements with references to the ordinances of baptism and communion and to the eternal destinies of saints and non-believers. Given the centrality and uniqueness of the movement's view of baptism, one might expect churches' assertions on the issue to have appeared earlier in the confessions. By placing the article on baptism near the end, Kentucky's Baptists continued an old tradition begun in the earliest of Baptist confessions, such as Thomas Helwys's 1611 "Declaration of Faith," which placed it fourteenth of twenty-two articles. Likewise, the influential London Confession of 1644 addressed baptism in articles thirty-nine through forty-one in a list of fifty-two. Though some early Kentucky Baptists accepted rituals such as foot washing and "laying on of hands" as ordinances, most recognized only baptism and communion. Their confessions stated that true baptism necessitated immersion of a believer and that only those thus baptized could partake of communion. This assertion, more than any other,

distinguished the Baptists from other popular movements. Baptist confessions agreed that believers (also labeled the "righteous" or the "just") could anticipate an eternity of joy, happiness, and life, while non-believers (or more commonly, the "wicked") were doomed to everlasting punishment.[16]

Though the covenants of Kentucky Baptist churches included these core elements, each church had the liberty to include whatever it considered necessary to educate, unify, or confirm those within the fold, or to explain, defend, or clarify their faith to outsiders. Some churches, like Buck Run, decided to include and articulate its view of the church. The fifth article of its confession asserts, "There is no higher ecclesiastical authority on earth than the congregated, worshiping church of Christ," who had the right "to govern themselves by their own voices [and] select their own officers." Some churches included duties belonging to church members, such as tenderly watching over one another for protective admonishment; diligently fulfilling obligations to God, church, and neighbor; and consistently promoting the general happiness of Christians and the honor of God. Other churches, like the Paris church, even noted their power to amend their confession and rules of order whenever they felt it necessary. Though the church at Stamping Ground did not make this power explicit at their 1795 founding, within five years they had reconsidered their covenant. They struck out the preamble and the last three articles that had addressed member duties. What remained dealt solely with doctrinal issues, and they retained these "as a Declaration for the Information of Strangers." Stamping Ground church members revised their confession again in 1801 to add an article stating their views on communion. When a layman asked if members of the church could commune with "any church not of the same faith and order," the church voted against the proposition. Though churches could settle matters early on by addressing them in their founding statements, the majority of churches still chose to include only core beliefs, or views they considered essential, and then let the rest be decided later as issues arose.[17]

The practice of borrowing covenants from other bodies connected churches with each other ideologically on a trans-Atlantic scale. Time-tested confessions, such as the well-known Philadelphia Confession of 1742, which some churches borrowed as their own, helped to establish and ingrain certain beliefs as essential. The Philadelphia Confession itself was a revised version of the Second London Confession of 1689. Even though a church might borrow a confession, as an autonomous entity it still had the option to revise, discontinue, or add to it as they saw fit. In 1801, the founding members of the Mount

Pleasant church borrowed the Philadelphia Confession as their own, recording it at the front of their church book. In important respects, the church contained its identity in the church book: the repository for its founding documents and monthly meeting records. When schisms arose in a church, an important issue was which party would retain the church book. In 1807, the Mount Pleasant church pondered what to do when the association of Baptists in Philadelphia (who gave their name to the original confession) revised it. The members at Mount Pleasant compared the old version that they had borrowed with the new revision, and chose to retain the old. Though no change occurred in that 1807 meeting, the church's deliberation on the subject reveals the larger significance of the democratic autonomous nature of Baptist congregations and their confessions, original or otherwise. With a primitivist ethos, early nineteenth-century Kentucky Baptists placed far less value on innovative religious practices and beliefs than they did on recovering what they viewed as eternal, essential truths. Even so, their belief in the democratic application and documentation of these truths allowed them to articulate truth in their own way. This autonomy and expressiveness encouraged diversity and led to more factionalism than there might have been otherwise. Baptists countered this centrifugal tendency primarily in their tendency to imitate the confessions of others, but also in their tradition of receiving the blessings of other churches. If a group of Baptists desired to form a church that would be in good fellowship with existing churches, they would invite ministers and lay leaders to evaluate their confession.[18]

A new church's rules for decorum also gave examination committees an opportunity to encourage uniformity, while also allowing the church to construct its own identity and order. These sets of rules also reveal the efforts of Baptists to balance the liberating impulse inherent in Baptist democracy with their appreciation of orderliness in all things. In effect, a church's rules of decorum served as the constitution upon which the citizens of Zion met for town meeting. Nathan Hatch claims in his study of the democratization of Christianity in the early republic that this phenomenon of egalitarianism had "less to do with the specifics of polity and governance and more with the incarnation of the church into popular cultures." While his latter assertion on the relationship between religion and culture enjoys an abundance of evidentiary support, Hatch's initial assertion about polity derives from his conflation of five diverse popular religious movements. Three of these groups—the Methodists, the Mormons, and the Christian Connection—had no democratic polity, but had

worked out their egalitarianism in other ways. Baptists alone established formal, democratic procedures to govern themselves. They also anticipated the license to which liberty could lead. Thus, Baptists created strict rules to govern their proceedings and debates, to assure order and harmony, and to protect the rights of the minority within the church. Even though early Kentucky Baptists constricted their own egalitarian theory based upon their cultural views of race, class, and gender at various times and places and to varying extents, they established a clear egalitarian legacy.[19]

As with covenants, the rules churches adopted for monthly business meetings and disciplinary hearings varied widely from church to church. Church members tended to establish rules based on their previous experiences, adapting and modifying the rules of their former churches. The common elements in the statements of rules reveal Baptists as deeply concerned with certain questions, including when majority rule sufficed, when unanimity was required, and how many times a member could speak on an issue before he had to receive permission. Another significant rule which appeared in many church books dealt with the biblical model for disciplining wayward saints. In addition, churches gave specific details of how they would be governed. Some rules stated that the meeting moderator alone could determine who would speak first if two rose to speak simultaneously, that members needed to apply for a letter of dismissal from the church before they moved away, and that visitors to the meeting could speak, but not vote. The churches even established behavioral standards for their meetings. The Buck Run church, like others, decreed, "There shall be no laughing, talking, or whispering in the time of a public speech, nor shall there be any ungenerous reflection on a brother who has spoken before." Likewise, the Mount Pleasant church pronounced that those who rose to speak should address the moderator and not anyone with whom they might disagree. They were also to speak "in a mild and Christian manner."[20] These written rules and guidelines not only served the practical purpose of implementing order in necessary meetings, but demonstrated to the examining committee that a prospective church wanted to preserve the Baptist devotion to order.

By submitting their confessions and rules to constitutional examination committees, churches bridged the precarious line between self-determination and participation in a larger movement. But in the end, the examination committee only made sure the church had ordered itself according to time-tested principles that fostered congregational success. The committee would

expect general consonance, but not strict conformity. In this way, the Baptists anticipated secular American notions. In the late eighteenth and early nineteenth centuries, post-revolutionary Americans constituted themselves into independent (but united) states, weaving their own image into the national tapestry. The American self-conception was of a nation of independent states cooperating under one banner, and the Baptists had pursued the same ideal in their grassroots churches. Baptists negotiated a delicate harmony between the individual and the community in their ritual. They asserted their republican democracy through their leadership. And they fashioned independent congregations as part of a larger movement. By doing so, the Baptists not only participated in the national devotion to "freedom *from* government as well as freedom *under* government," but they also incorporated government "of, by, and for" the people into American religion, long before the articulation of those values at Gettysburg.[21]

A Baptist church, once constituted, needed leaders to organize church efforts, to preach and lead in worship meetings, and to keep records. Chief among these was the pastor. Many churches did not have their own pastor at the time of their founding, so any licensed or ordained preacher could fill the pulpit until the church secured one. When the Bethel church formed in July 1810, it had no regular pastor, but received preaching at its monthly meetings from Isham Burnett, a pastor from nearby Sinking Creek church. In April of the following year, the church voted to ordain one of their own, John Smith, to serve as pastor. Even with regular labor from Smith, who was one of the nine charter members, the Bethel church experienced a situation common among the congregationalist Baptist churches. The members of a church could select or dismiss their own pastor as they wished. Likewise, a minister could accept or reject a church call as he wished, and even after becoming a church's pastor he could resign whenever he chose. In Methodist and Presbyterian churches, only ecclesiastical authorities could make such decisions. Presbyterian and Methodist ministers served at the will of their synods and bishops, which organized church efforts and assigned parishes and itinerant circuits. The very freedom the Baptists cherished—the freedom of congregations and ministers to choose each other—often disordered their work, and at times made them ineffectual. Thus the Bethel church endured inconsistent pastoral leadership because of its commitment to this freedom. After John Smith assumed the pastorate in April 1811, he continued there only until October 1814, when he and his wife left the church. After this, another local pastor, Richard Barrier,

performed the monthly preaching duties until the church called John Smith again in November 1816. Eleven months later Smith resigned again, and Isham Burnett filled in once more. The next pastor, Henry Tuggle, who was called in February 1819, continued longer than any other, but still resigned sometime before the summer of 1825, when George Dodson became pastor. Dodson himself resigned two years later. The pastoral turnover took its toll on the church. Bethel had grown in numbers under the popular and witty preaching of John Smith in his first term, but in the tumultuous years afterward it faltered, losing a third of its membership between 1815 and 1822.[22]

Democratic polity did not necessitate such pastoral transience. Whereas the Bethel church endured seven pastorates by five different men in its first seventeen years, the Mount Pleasant church enjoyed a far different experience. When 100 members of the South Elkhorn church separated to form Mount Pleasant in August 1801, they temporarily obtained preaching services from their former pastor at South Elkhorn, John Shackleford, who was at the beginning of a thirty-seven year tenure at that church. In January 1803, the members of Mount Pleasant called George S. Smith as their first pastor. Smith continued with the church until his death in 1810 and was succeeded by Edmund Waller, who also pastored the church until his death, in 1843. Such extended pastorates did much to unite Baptist churches and endeared the preachers in the churches' memories. For example, in 1836, the members of Mayslick church in northern Kentucky were shocked to hear news of the death of their pastor of twenty-two years, Walter Warder. The pastor had died while in Missouri visiting his children, and had been buried there. Seven years later, while the Mayslick church suffered tremendous factionalism due to disagreements with Warder's successor, the members arranged with Warder's family to have their beloved pastor's remains "removed from the state of Missouri and interred in the graveyard attached to the church." A year later, they collected money to erect a monument over his grave. In the Baptist democratic ecclesiastical climate, where pastors and congregations chose each other and could dedicate themselves to each other (or not), churches made their own opportunities for the stability.[23]

A pastor's remuneration, an inconsistent element of early Kentucky Baptist life, was seldom cited as important by pastors, but could affect their work. Certainly the humility expected from preachers muted their thoughts on the subject, but when Baptist men "felt the call" to preach, they had no reasonable expectation of reaping financial benefit from the pursuit. The Baptists

themselves were conflicted over the issue of salaried ministers. Whether or not a church chose to support its pastor financially varied by its principles and affluence, but a consistent thread binding their ambivalent thoughts on the subject was twofold. First, they feared that payment could corrupt the ministry, because young men might enter the clergy for love of money. James Pendleton recalled that before the 1830s many Kentucky Baptist preachers feared discussing the idea of financial support lest they be characterized as advocating "preaching for money." When Pendleton himself entered the ministry, his father joked that the Baptist policy seemed to be, "The Lord keep our preachers humble, and we will keep them poor."[24] Though John Taylor received financial rewards for his preaching both as an itinerant and as a settled pastor, in his memoirs he wrote, "It never sat well on my feelings to receive pay from the people for preaching. I, therefore, preferred my own exertions to supply my own wants." Part of Taylor's reticence derived from his antipathy to the type of corruption that Protestants perceived in the Catholic Church and that American separatists had seen in the established colonial churches. In Taylor's influential tract of 1820, *Thoughts on Missions*, the preacher articulated the connection between money and power as he perceived it in the machinations of the General Missionary Convention, the first nationally oriented Baptist organization, which formed in 1814. Railing against the new body, Taylor asserted that "a false teacher always loves money, or popularity, or both, more than the religion he professes." Taylor decried what he saw as a scheme to drain money from the church to usurp the power entrusted to it. Calling the ministers who governed the convention "horse leeches," Taylor claimed, "These great men are verging close on an aristocracy, with an object to sap the foundation of Baptist republican government." The key to preserving ecclesiastical virtue was to keep power and money close to the people, meaning the church members. The first small step down the treacherous path to clerical aristocracy was a salaried ministry.[25]

Despite this fear, Baptists expressed a dedication to a second idea: dutiful church members should seek ways to attend to their minister's material needs. They usually stipulated, though, that no member should ever be required to contribute to the pastor's needs. Baptists did compensate their pastors, sometimes with money and on other occasions with goods and services. When John Taylor began his pastorate at Clear Creek church in 1786, the members agreed to pay him seventy dollars annually and the next year raised it to a hundred. Members of Mayslick church appropriated forty dollars for their minister

Donald Holmes, "As a compensation for his services in the following year." Many preachers, Holmes among them, served the church for terms of one year at a time, and their churches budgeted accordingly. Holmes's "contract" obliged him to commit "the whole of his time except for one Lord's Day in each month" to the church. Reuben Ross's parishioners, being poor, aided their pastor in times of planting and harvest. Some female members would spend weeks with the Ross family, helping when the pastor's wife was ill. Ross accommodated his congregation's poverty by traveling to perform weddings and funeral sermons, for which he often received small sums. Churches often spelled out plainly what efforts would be required to aid their pastors. Members of many churches raised the issue in business meetings, compelling a response. At the Stamping Ground church, one member bluntly asked, "Is it not the duty of every free male member to contribute to the support of the gospel?" To which they responded, "We think it is." In 1811, the Mount Pleasant church met in a specially called meeting to discuss their responsibility to support ministers. They declared that it was their "indispensable duty to administer to the necessities" of their preachers, but, like many other churches, they left it up to each member to decide how much to give. This same issue garnered the attention of the churches in west-central Kentucky in 1825 when their association issued a letter exhorting the churches to "pay particular attention to the temporal support" of their pastors, but to employ no other means but voluntary contributions. For Baptists who still recalled or had heard the tales of religious persecution in colonial Virginia or New England, any other means would smack of a religious tax.[26]

Such a commitment to support on a voluntary basis suited the ethic of the early movement in Kentucky and resonated in the climate of voluntarism that permeated the early national period. But it did, as James Pendleton's father quipped, "keep the preachers poor." Ministry was not a road to financial stability. Of the one hundred and seventy dollars promised in money and goods to John Taylor for his first two years at Clear Creek church, he received only about forty dollars. The corruption from luxury and power that many Baptists feared was neatly kept at bay. Though the Baptist hesitance to professionalize the ministry did not restrict the movement's growth, it hindered its efficiency by compelling the Baptist's front-line warriors to spread themselves thin in bi-vocationalism. By the late-nineteenth century, Baptist leaders would in one breath nostalgically praise the bi-vocational preacher who led despite adversity and, in the next, condemn his lack of professional efficiency. In 1887, looking

back on the period his father had criticized, James Pendleton indicted those on both sides of the pulpit, saying, "Pastors and churches [before the 1830s] were mutually blamable. They both made a lamentable mistake." Pendleton's perspective devalued the cultural milieu of the Kentucky Baptists, whose congregational emphasis was part of a broader republican ethic. Baptists revealed their sympathy with republicanism in their beliefs, practices, fear of clerical aristocracy, ministerial support, and voluntarism. The Baptist impulse perpetuated old republican ideals in its fear of corruption and of the loss of virtue caused by luxury, in its preservation of the common good, and in its devotion to protecting tender congregational liberty from the ravenous forces of power.[27]

Since lack of financial support could encourage ministerial transience, lay leadership provided continuity when pastors came and went. As in other areas of their faith and practice, Kentucky Baptists looked to the New Testament for guidance in how to conduct their church life and who should handle church work. Beyond the position of pastor, Baptists attempted to reconstruct a first-century deacon ministry. The Greek word "diakonos," from which the term "deacon" is derived, means "servant" or "waiter." Its verb form, "diakoneo," means simply "to minister or serve." While these terms are used dozens of times in the New Testament, Baptists tended to focus on two passages for their understandings of the deacon ministry. The first of these, the sixth chapter of Acts, records how the early church selected "seven men of good reputation" to "serve tables," that is, to make sure the church's needy received daily food distributions so that Jesus's apostles could focus on the spiritual ministry of the church. The need for these servers arose when some of the needy complained that the food was being distributed unfairly. Once the issue was settled, the author of Acts notes that the church grew even more. The second passage Baptists relied upon was the third chapter of the first book of Timothy, wherein Paul lists the qualities for deacons: reverence, sobriety, honesty, generosity, a tested faith, a faithful wife, and tractable children.[28]

Scriptural guidance about the qualifications and work of deacons did not necessarily make the selection of deacons an easy task, nor did it make the specific duties of Baptist deacons any clearer. Churches typically elected deacons from among themselves within the first months of their founding. In 1818, the church at Paris, just two months after their constitution, elected Nicholas Talbott and George Bryan as deacons by private ballot, and then two more deacons by voice vote five months after that. When a need arose for another

deacon in the Mayslick church in 1795, members took the task seriously and proclaimed their next business meeting as "a day of fasting and prayer for the purpose of choosing." Other churches, like the Forks at Elkhorn, were less structured in selecting deacons. In April 1804, to fill the vacancy left by a deacon who had died, a member nominated Isaac Palmer. But by July, the church had its misgivings about Palmer and rescinded his nomination, selecting three brethren named Peak, Gregory, and Price as nominees. The next month Price withdrew his name from consideration, and the church selected Gregory and dismissed Peak. At the same time it opened a second round of nominations, naming brethren Haden Edwards and Jesse Cole. During September's meeting the church selected Cole, and so in November both Gregory and Cole were finally ordained as deacons, after an eight-month process. The deacons themselves often took their roles and the ordination process very seriously. William Allen quit the deaconship because his wife was not a "professor of religion." His church only grudgingly accepted his resignation and agreed with his reasoning despite its "high opinion of him as being as near the character of a deacon as we could expect in this imperfect state." Deacon Thomas Longley resigned from his position when a large majority of his church's membership voted that "laying on of hands" was unnecessary to the ordination ceremony. Five years later, his church changed its mind on this subject when another deacon threatened to resign.[29]

The question of the deacon's work caused confusion for some early Baptists because churches varied considerably in their opinion. Baptist statements on the diaconate followed the nebulous directions from the book of Acts. One associational letter dealing with the duties of all those in the church invited deacons to remember they were "called to serve tables,—the table of the Lord, the table of the poor and the table of [the] ministers." The Mayslick church came to the same conclusion in 1821, but nineteen years previously they could not be as certain when a member asked the question, "What is the work of a deacon?" They conversed upon the question of the deacon's work for four months in 1802 before finally dropping the question. When they returned to it in 1821, they agreed deacons should "serve tables" and "visit the sick and pray for them." Making this confusion in Mayslick more interesting was the fact that the church had given the deacons other duties. Like many other churches, Mayslick deacons collected and expended funds raised by subscription in the church to pay the pastor or meet other members' needs. In 1817, the deacons had overseen such a collection for Brother Ned, an indigent free man of color.[30]

Such confusion revealed the dilemma inherent in the Baptist devotion to first-century primitivism in post-revolutionary America, a dilemma faced by many of the popular religious movements seeking to harmonize principle with practice.[31] The primitivist impulse compelled Baptists to include the position of deacon in their churches, but the vagueness of the Bible regarding his duties encouraged creativity in assigning him work to do. Such innovation, by definition, contrasted with pure primitivism and caused contention in some churches. Given the relative insignificance of this confusion over what to do with the deacons, the issue is easily overlooked. Still, the dilemma of primitivism, innovation, and Baptist identity would strike at the heart of the movement's culture in the 1830s and 1840s, when other, more significant challenges confronted the Baptists.

Church life among Kentucky Baptists throughout the early nineteenth century, however, did not depend upon pastors and deacons or covenants and

Cedar Creek Baptist Church, Bardstown, Kentucky. Southern Baptist Historical Library and Archives, Nashville, Tennessee.

rules. Certainly, these fundamental elements revealed the importance of the congregational theory and practice that guided the democratic congregations in their work of worship, in ritual, and in the expansion of their corner of Christendom. But these structural components undergirded their significant understanding of the *church*: defined as the local gathering of believers and manifested in its many meetings. Though churches varied in the frequency, type, and style of their meetings, certain patterns of liturgy and practice did occur—patterns largely attributable to popular transmission, since Baptists had no uniform discipline to shape practice and since church manuals were rare. The most significant meetings occurred in the typical church one week-end per month. On Saturday, church members would convene for their business meeting in the early part of the day and gather again for preaching that night, fellowshipping throughout the day. On Sunday, they met for their worship service, which was followed by a baptismal service at a nearby pond or creek. Then they might gather once more on Sunday evening for a brief service before heading home. Most early churches only met once a month in this way, though a few met every other week for worship, coinciding their monthly business meeting with one of these weekends.[32]

The weekend events offered opportunities both for social communion and contention, as the work of a church involved not only worship but also discipline of the flock's wayward members. Like other early American religious groups, the Baptists believed the pursuit of holiness should characterize the Christian life, but they did not extend this notion of pursuit to a belief in "perfectionism." Baptists held holiness to be the continuing work of God's Holy Spirit in the Christian life. When Baptists exercised formative and corrective discipline among the membership, they acted as God's representatives. They viewed themselves individually as Christ's representatives on earth, and the church collectively as the bride of Christ; thus individual and institutional purity were paramount to a church's reputation in the secular community. With the movement's emphasis on order, the church set down its rules for discipline in their constitution. The Mount Pleasant church of northern Kentucky, founded in 1801, was typical in this regard. In their exercise of discipline, they differentiated between private sins that defiled the church from within and public sins that soiled the church's good name. To correct the former, they followed the three-step pattern mandated by Jesus in the eighteenth chapter of Matthew. According to this method, anyone offended by a sinning Christian confronted the sinner privately. If he did not repent, then a committee of two

or three were to confront the sinner more boldly, but still privately. If this did not work, the whole church would hear the matter and expel him from the membership if he refused to obey their decision. Public sins, on the other hand, could be brought before the church directly.[33]

Baptists kept detailed records of actions taken by the church in their business meetings. A great majority of these notes, recorded in church books, kept track of disciplinary measures and the status of cases where such were required. Baptists exercised patience in meting out discipline, and the church record books proved their usefulness, as several cases might be pending at any one time. In his study of early Kentucky Baptist discipline, James E. Humphrey noted that in five representative churches, 71 percent of cases took two or more meetings to decide. Such meticulous record keeping also helped churches maintain accountability. Often, when a member was charged with a sin, a few members would be appointed to "cite," or subpoena, that member to appear before the church and defend himself, and to present witnesses to that end. Detailed meeting minutes allowed a record of who was cited and whom the church held responsible for bringing the indictment. Once the indicted appeared, heard the evidence of guilt, and presented a defense, he faced one of several outcomes. The defendant might be acquitted and cleared of all charges, or admonished by the church—a minor slap on the wrist for minor offenses. The members could also suspend the defendant from church privileges. Suspension meant that defendants would remain church members, but could not partake in the communion ritual or vote in church meetings. Finally, the church might exclude the defendant from membership entirely. Later, if the excluded sinner evidenced appropriate repentance to the church, he could be restored to his previous membership status. The infractions necessitating discipline fell into three categories. Social sins included drunkenness, profanity, lying, theft, and dancing. Sexual sins included adultery, fornication, seduction, and extra-marital pregnancy. A third category of transgressions were sins against the church, such as non-attendance at meetings, non-compliance with church directives, preaching without the church's license, holding the church or its ministers in contempt, or joining a church of a different faith.[34]

The type of infraction for which one might face a penalty, especially the highest penalty of exclusion from a church, varied according to a member's race and gender. In this regard, as in many others, Kentucky churches participated in a larger, national pattern among Baptists. One of the stark trends of Baptist exclusion was the far greater number of excluded men. Baptists excluded twice

as many white men than white women, while the ratio of black men to women was closer, at roughly five to four. Another obvious contrast along these lines was the nature of the transgression. White men and black church members were far more likely to be excluded for sins against society. Roughly 60 percent of all male offenses worthy of exclusion dealt with social transgressions. Chief among these were drunkenness and profanity. Black men, though, were excluded disproportionately for drunkenness and theft, as well as for sins peculiar to slaves, such as running away and disobeying their masters. Social sins also accounted for over 50 percent of exclusions of black women, who also endured the highest percentage of exclusions for sexual offenses. More white than black members, and more white women than men, were excluded for sins against the church; almost three-fourths of these exclusions were for leaving the Baptist church and joining another denomination.[35]

As studies of Baptist discipline have shown, these representative figures suggest not only a disparity in activity—men were more likely to get drunk and swear than were women—but they also reveal social expectations of race and gender in the church. Among the clearest of these was that Baptists expected Christian slaves to fulfill their duties to their masters. Running away, disobedience, and theft from a master were each clear violations of the racial hierarchy. They also violated biblical precepts that many Baptists interpreted as not only condoning slavery but as putting obligations on both slave and master. Likewise, white women were disproportionately excluded for nonattendance and joining other denominations, indicating that they were expected to be the moral backbone of the local church. The discipline cases of black slaves and white women show that when either group acted against social expectations, they received the harshest possible punishment.[36]

Scholars have studied the profusion of discipline cases recorded in Baptist church books and used them to highlight varying facets of early American life, from the Turnerian frontier to the demonization of women.[37] One historian, highlighting this aspect of the movement, asserts that some Baptists "placed discipline at the center of church life," and that "not even preaching the gospel was more important to them than the exercise of discipline."[38] Such a contention certainly does not apply to Kentucky Baptists and, as a key to understanding Baptists generally, the argument is analogous to seeing an apple's skin as the "center" of the apple. Clearly, discipline was an important element in Baptist business meetings and in their social interactions, but only as it served as a tool to promote more important goals. Discipline was to begin individually. One Baptist writer

reminded his fellow adherents that it was their "duty to watch against the evils" in their own hearts, words, and deeds, and admonished them "to support a strict discipline between God" and their own souls. That accomplished, they should then "watch over one another, not for evil but for good." Exercising such care and observing and maintaining "that discipline and ... order, peace, harmony, and brotherly love, which should characterize every christian church ... is more than human power, wisdom or skill can accomplish," contended one group of Baptists. "It can only be effected by *almighty* power."[39]

Baptists saw themselves as conduits of God in the continuous sanctification of his chosen people. Thus when periods of apparent spiritual declension or torpor occurred, Baptists often looked to their disciplinary processes for correction. In addition, like many other early American Christians, Baptists perceived themselves as participating in the third act of an ancient religious drama. They saw the interaction between God and man as beginning in the Old Testament, continuing afresh in the New Testament, and even affecting American history. By neglecting discipline, the tool for promoting piety, Baptists risked losing their role in the drama. Thus when the Bracken Association met during a period of spiritual stagnation in September 1823, their work combined these beliefs. The association agreed to urge the churches to observe a day of fasting and prayer to God, "that he would revive his work among us." Later the same day, they resolved to encourage churches and their fellow citizens to "celebrate the fourth day of July, annually, as a day of public praise and thanksgiving to Almighty God, for the independence of the United States; and as a day of prayer . . . that tyranny and despotism be put under foot; and, that the mild institutions dictated by the spirit of the Gospel, be embraced and cherished by every tongue and people under heaven." At the same meeting, the group approved a letter to their churches lamenting a "general gloom" prevalent among them, and concluding, "Sin, doubtless, is the cause." To encourage "a time of refreshing," they admonished their holy compatriots to resist sin and pursue holiness, specifically by preserving a "well regulated system of discipline" in the church, attending to parents' obligation to nurture their children, and respecting the sanctity of the Lord's Day.[40] Each of these duties had been neglected and, spiritual declension was the result. These Baptists perceived God at work in their nation, their churches, their families, and in themselves as individuals. Church discipline was an important tool in allowing this work to progress smoothly, but it was only a conduit and a catalyst for the larger goals of propagating the gospel in their communities, of

pursuing holiness in their churches and families, and by so doing, of expanding the "mild institutions" of the Baptist movement.

While studies of Baptist discipline tend to focus on the sins committed, the virtues extolled through the discipline process are just as significant, if not more so. Though early Kentucky Baptists did not condemn drinking alcohol, they demanded sobriety among their members. Likewise, discipline records show that they expected honesty in business and speech, control both of the tongue and sexual appetite, avoidance of frivolous and scandalous pursuits such as dancing and gambling, attendance at church meetings (and orderliness therein), and respect for recognized authorities civil or ecclesiastical. Though members of Baptist churches might fail to live up to these expectations and bring upon themselves the rebuke of the church, they accepted the expectations in their voluntary confession and application for church membership. Those adherents who chose to remain on the periphery as mere congregants were under no official obligation to adhere to the members' standards. Voluntary submission to such strict discipline reveals the individual Baptist's broad commitment to self-improvement and a more specific devotion to sobriety and self-control, honesty, earnestness, orderliness, and respectfulness—qualities and values that would bring success in the increasingly market-driven society of the early republic. Pursuit of success in the market revolution did not conflict with religious practice. Indeed, devotion was expected to contribute to a member's financial prosperity. The Bracken Association's circular letter of 1823 asserted that when a "humble Christian" gathered with others to worship on Sunday, he left "refreshed" and "better prepared to pursue the laudable business that may require his attention through the week."[41] The practice of discipline undergirded valuation of those qualities that would foster pecuniary success, yet it also indicates Baptists' devotion to the republican value of placing the common good (the church) above their own.[42] The Baptist practice of discipline, like so many aspects of the movement, also clearly illustrates the unparalleled emphasis Baptists placed on the local church. There was no appeals process—the church's word was final. But despite such intense congregationalism, Baptist life did not begin and end at the local level.

Even as Kentucky Baptists in local churches saw themselves as small parts of the larger Christian community and as isolated manifestations of the larger Baptist movement, the associational principle, dating back to seventeenth-century England, encouraged a process of relationship-building between churches that lingered on even after some of the initial reasons for these ties no longer existed. This practice of churches associating together promoted the development

and expansion of the Baptist movement, acted as a unifying force for incipient denominationalism, and forced Baptists to continually define and defend their devotion to localism. Associations of Baptist churches, in their earliest form, offered a mechanism whereby adherents could more easily defend themselves against external theological challenges and civil persecution. They also offered the benefits of inter-congregational fellowship among like-minded adherents, as well as intra-church fellowship between scattered congregations, or "arms."[43] In post-revolutionary America, as Baptists ceased to be a persecuted sect, they retained the associational principle.

Baptists formed their associations in one of two ways. First, a group of churches already part of one association might, for reasons of geographic expediency or theological conflict, withdraw and form their own association. Second, a group of churches in a newly settled region might agree to band together to create a completely new association. As representatives, or "messengers," from the churches met and formed the association, they constituted themselves as they would a church, establishing a statement of common beliefs and rules of decorum. One of the most important elements in an associational constitution was the restriction on the body's authority. Baptist churches were to hold the power, and the association existed solely as an advisory body, having no authority over the churches. If this idea was not made clear in the constitution, discussion during associational business meetings soon made it apparent. Any church had the freedom to withdraw, and the association could vote to dismiss a church if it broke its agreement to abide by the association's constitution.[44]

Though Baptists created their own associations, church members continually and carefully monitored the work performed by the gathered representatives at the association's annual meeting. Messengers ceaselessly brought questions before the association about the nature of its authority. In 1793, the Elkhorn Association received a query from the Town Fork church about the use and extent of the association's power. The association deferred the question one year, then appointed a committee of three members to prepare an answer. Finally, they responded in 1795 that the association should use its power "for mutual edification and assistance to cultivate uniformity of sentiments in principles and practice and that its power is to regulate and govern itself as a body and give such advice to the churches as may be for their peace." Baptists worried constantly that their association, their own creation, might turn on its churches, a threat they warned against in vehement terms. One Baptist messenger queried his association about their practice of advising churches on

how to ordain ministers; he asked, "Is it not Popery for a counsel to advise the churches to such measures?" Likewise, John Taylor, ever a popular preacher at associational meetings, declared, "If associations are to have more power than mere advisory [*sic*] counsel, I wish them all dead at once."[45]

Regardless of how an association began, as a separation or a new creation, it only existed as an idea—an understood alliance—except when the churches held their annual or semi-annual meetings. Typically held in late summer or early fall, the associational gathering extended over a long weekend and offered early Baptists one of the most exciting religious and social events of the year. Not only did the occasion gather together Baptists from the many allied churches, but also Baptists from churches outside the association, and even some non-Baptists. In 1838, when the Long Run Association could claim less than three thousand members in its two dozen churches, over five thousand people attended its association meeting.[46]

Each year a different church in an association hosted the meeting, and the host church went to great lengths to create an orderly setting for the assembly. When the lot fell to the Stamping Ground church in 1822, the members selected three men to construct a platform, or a stand, for the use of the associational preachers, and also unanimously agreed to house and accommodate any associational visitor who wished it. They further hired two "trusty servants" to furnish ample supplies of water. Disorder at a meeting could bring dishonor to the host church. Because of this threat, the Paris church in 1826 appointed one of its deacons and two other men to "suppress any disorder that may appear on the ground near the association." The myriad adherents drawn to the social and religious aspects of the association meeting drew other, more undesirable elements. Particularly irksome were the vendors who fed off such events and sold their wares to those visiting. Host churches sought to suppress this activity since it was their own duty to provide for their guests. By the 1840s, especially as Baptists increasingly committed themselves to temperance efforts, some Baptists labeled the vending of "cakes, beer, cider, melons, liquors" and other provisions a "growing and alarming evil," and they sought diligently to expel such "hucksters" who might "interrupt us in the worship of God," or at least to keep them a sufficient distance from the assembly "to secure good order."[47]

Association meetings typically included outdoor preaching at a stand, or in multiple locations in a large area, as well as a formal business meeting for the messengers from the churches. Each association determined how many

delegates a church could send, but each church usually sent its pastor, any licensed ministers it had, one or two deacons, and any laymen who had the interest and the time. Though many other adherents probably attended the assembly, it was the messengers who carried the church's letter—a record of the church's condition in the intervening year. The messengers also spoke for their church if it had business for the association. If the association had a question for the church, the messengers had to return to the church, let the church vote on the issue, and then respond the following year at the next associational meeting. Thus, each business session began (after an introductory sermon and election of officers) by hearing each church's letter read by one of its messengers. New churches that applied for admission to the association were questioned and received or denied at this time. If a member church had experienced a schism in the intervening year and both factions submitted letters to the association, all the gathered messengers voted on which faction truly represented the church. Typically the basis for such a decision was not which faction represented the majority, but which could declare their theology and practice more in line with the other association members. This system worked well until association-wide disputes brought the very identity of the association into question.[48]

After the validity of the participants had been verified in the business meeting and their church letters had been read, the association heard letters from the representatives of other "corresponding" associations. Unless a reason was offered to the contrary, the association members appointed delegates to write and present a letter of correspondence to these sister associations. Though some historians have suggested that this kind of correspondence between associations, which dated back to the mid-1700s, was the first stage of a national consciousness among the locally oriented Baptists, the associations in early Kentucky fail to bear out the claim. Even by the mid-nineteenth century, Kentucky Baptists tended to correspond only with their sister associations within the state or with those that straddled the state's borders. This kind of communication did provide an ephemeral but important connective tissue among the churches and associations; nevertheless, the Baptist dedication to the democratic integrity and moral purity of the local church compelled resistance to alliances beyond the associational level.[49]

Once the extra-associational visitors read their letters and gained an honorary seat in the meeting, the elected moderator of the session typically called for the reading of the circular letter, which they would forward to the churches

within the association. This letter—often a brief theological or ecclesiological treatise, admonition to piety, or lament of declension—offered to those who could not attend the meeting a window into the important religious issues of the day. Often written by an individual or committee, reported and revised in the business session, then approved by the messengers, the circular letter represented a portrait of the collective mind of the Baptists in a region. These expressions of thought, attitude, and feeling did not represent just the clergy's opinion, but also that of the laity, who made up the majority of associational messengers. Throughout the early and mid-nineteenth century, laymen were approximately three-fourths of the voting members of an association. In some instances, laity made up 90 percent of an association's messengers.[50]

Prior to the 1850s, Kentucky Baptist associational letters very rarely addressed political issues or those issues relevant to society as a whole. Historically, Baptists had seen a clear distinction between church and state, as well as between the "world" and the "community of the saints." At the same time, they saw history providentially, with God's hand guiding and protecting America. Even in the 1840s and 1850s, as churches and associations addressed social issues, it was always on moral terms. For example, temperance in general was advocated due to its emphasis on self-control. The Know-Nothing Party was often denounced because of its secretiveness, which smacked of a church and state alliance. Antebellum Kentucky Baptists, however, did not see slavery or abolition in strictly moral terms. Instead they saw shades of gray that allowed for the existence of the institution.

An ever-present item of business in the associational meeting was the response to questions, or "queries," brought by individual churches. Usually, these queries dealt with significant issues that the church passed on to the association. In a church's local business meeting, members wrestled with questions posed by individuals. The subjects of these queries were typically ethics, church polity, or church business. When a church could not reach a satisfactory answer, or if they desired the advice of other churches, they brought the query to the association. When the gathered messengers rendered their advice, they expected that advice to be followed. Should the association's advice not be followed as it was passed down, they could vote to expel the church from their ranks. More often than not, however, associations expelled churches not for differences in polity, but for heresy. In 1803, for example, the Elkhorn Association excluded the Coopers Run church "for denying the doctrine of the Trinity and holding that Jesus Christ is not truly God."[51] Though hostility could emerge between an association and a church, the goal of associational advice was to secure the peace of the churches

generally. The "faceless" association was actually a large committee of church men, both clergy and laity, ardently interested in uniformity about important doctrines and practices, but also accepting differences in non-essentials.[52]

The query system could accomplish the association's goal of uniformity in essentials, but the association also recognized its limits regarding non-essentials. Two practices often deemed optional were the rituals of "laying on of hands" and foot washing. Both customs were brought into Kentucky by Separate Baptist migrants. The former involved church members simply placing their hands on the head of a newly baptized convert and praying a blessing. Some churches considered washing feet, however, to be an ordinance on par with baptism and communion. Taking their example from the thirteenth chapter of the gospel of John, wherein Jesus washes the feet of his disciples, some Baptists believed cleansing each other's feet to be a commanded rite of humility. Historian Charles Sellers cites these Baptist customs as evidence of a sacralization of touching, which completed the adherent's mental flight from the "estranging competition" of the world generally and the market revolution specifically. The mere fact that so many Baptist ministers proclaimed the gospel while also attending to their secular trades seems to call Seller's argument into question, but the rituals were in any case falling out of practice when the market revolution began. Between the 1780s and the 1820s, many Baptist churches dropped them from their liturgy. Baptist associations likewise refused to deem them essential Baptist practices.[53]

Since the members of the association issued their advice and opinions to the specific queries of the churches and then issued a general admonition or encouragement to the churches in the circular letter, there was little else to do in the actual business session but coordinate future meetings throughout the year in which association members could take part. Baptists enjoyed large gatherings like the association meetings. Thus at the end of the annual meeting they organized smaller quarterly or "union" meetings of the association at member churches of the association. These three-day weekend gatherings included opportunities to hear preaching and exhortation, as well as to contribute in prayer and singing. In the era before religious newspapers, these fellowship and worship meetings provided adherents with the chance to hear news, spiritual and otherwise, from around the region on a regular basis. Association members might also assign individuals to publicize or take care of unsavory matters on behalf of the churches collectively. For example, the Salem Association ended their meeting of 1823 by appointing two members to visit a third, James Haycraft, who had left the movement. The association charged the appointed ministers with demanding Haycraft forfeit his

preaching credentials. Haycraft refused, and the association labeled him a "disorderly preacher"—a brand that helped the churches recognize a minister who did not have the movement's interests at heart.[54]

By issuing cautions, offering messages of encouragement and admonition, advising on controversial questions, and coordinating the goals of the churches, the associations served their primary duties of establishing and protecting unity among the churches and helping to define the movement generally. Such definition helped the Baptists retain a collective consciousness, especially important since they were one of the most decentralized religious groups in early America. Though an organization devoted to foreign missionary activity, formed in 1814, was the first Baptist institution with a national scope, few church members saw themselves as defined by a national denomination.[55] They defined themselves locally, church by church, and hesitantly on a regional level through their associations.

This intense localism advanced the scattering of Baptist churches across the country. Yet the churches remained tied together. When one church gave birth to another (or many others), it often transmitted its tradition, theology, and polity. During the early republic, when migration westward took on epic proportions, "mother churches" spawned rapidly. Certainly real kinship networks existed in these early churches, but just as real was the informal kinship between churches birthed from the same mother. Over time, a nation-wide movement developed, unified only by the DNA of the Baptist impulse. Though associations brought the Baptist family together region by region, supralocal union was no virtue by itself. If anything, it could threaten the virtue of the Kingdom of Christ manifested not just in the church, but in the *people* of the church. These people voluntarily bound themselves together in churches that they perceived as tiny, unicameral democracies. These democracies allied into associations, but they did not entangle themselves in such alliances. This structure satisfied Kentucky Baptists until the late 1820s. By then, new ideas had filtered in to challenge old assumptions of Calvinism, a reformer had forced the movement to define what it meant to be a Baptist, and Methodist success compelled Baptists to question their previous optimism about dominating America's religious future. In this turmoil, Baptists' commitment to virtue in polity took second place to mere survival.

4

Reforming the Impulse, 1825-1845

"This is an age of invention and speculation," wrote Baptist preacher John Holland for the 1832 meeting of the Long Run Association. The minister's letter for the association would prove him an acute observer of his times and of his denomination. The 1830s offered Americans a dizzying mixture of technological changes, economic opportunities, social dislocations, political skirmishes, class stratification, and cultural reforms. The Canal Age and steam power began the process of sewing together the national economic fabric. The market revolution brought new ways of viewing work and family. An energized nationalism burdened political decision makers, whose differing visions of progress and liberty helped define the age. Visions of moral improvement compelled the formation of reform movements, the targets of which ranged from dietary indulgence to the inhumanity of slavery. And in American religion, the age of invention and speculation encouraged the visionary innovations of Joseph Smith and John Humphrey Noyes, the revivalism of Charles Finney, and the theology of reason and reform promoted

by Alexander Campbell. In the midst of an era of religious invention, John Holland saw this age as no boon. Rather, he perceived a "crisis of serious importance," wherein "the spirit of emendation and schism has gone forth and is stalking like the unclean spirit of old, through the churches, seeking its unhallowed rest in the banishment of peace and union from the house of God." What specifically troubled the perspicacious Holland was the so-called Reformation begun by Alexander Campbell and his followers among the Baptists. Due to the Reformers' efforts, roughly 25 percent of Kentucky's Baptists had joined the new sect. Campbell's Reformation was not the only "spirit of emendation." Other stressors included the influence of British Baptist Andrew Fuller's ideas on Calvinism, the advent of religious higher education in Kentucky, anti-institutionalism within the Baptist movement, and the intense competition offered by Methodists in the religious marketplace. Each worked to alter John Holland's religious world and re-orient his role as a minister. Like many others of his era, Holland saw this crisis as spiritual. In the age of invention, he asserted, "Zion has been bleeding, her gates solitary, her beauties shadowed." However, with spiritual reinvigoration, "She begins to arise and look forth as the morning, and we trust will soon shine."[1]

The roots of the Baptist struggle with the Campbell Reformation ran deep. When Alexander Campbell rode into Kentucky for the first time in 1823, he himself had been a work in progress. Born a Scotch-Irish Presbyterian, Campbell immigrated to America in 1808 having already rejected Christian sectarianism. His father Thomas was of similar mind as the twenty year-old Alexander and united other disaffected Presbyterians into an independent congregation in Pennsylvania. A few years later, Alexander rejected the doctrine of infant baptism after the birth of his first child, and he convinced his wife and parents to undergo immersion by a Baptist minister. In 1813, as pastor of his father's church and a believer in congregational autonomy and immersive baptism of the adult believer, Alexander led his church to join the Redstone Baptist Association of Pennsylvania. His antisectarian sentiments, however, kept the alliance tenuous. Alexander's individualistic religious temperament, as well as his study of Francis Bacon's inductive method, John Locke's epistemology, and Scottish "common sense" philosophy, fueled a solitary pursuit of biblical truth on his own terms. By 1816, his revised theology started to take shape. He began to believe in the authority of the New Testament alone, not the Old. By the early 1820s, his antisectarianism had nurtured an antipathy to the doctrinal statements typically used by Baptist churches. In each of his formative stages,

however, Campbell remained inside the margins of the Baptist impulse. Thus, when he arrived in Washington, Kentucky, on October 11, 1823, to debate with Presbyterian minister William McCalla, many local Baptists regarded him as their champion of democratic congregationalism and the chief antagonist of the Pedobaptists.[2]

Though the debate brought him into Kentucky for the first time, Campbell knew the flavor of the state and the Baptist movement there from his father's recent western travels. Thomas Campbell had toured the northern counties in 1817 and, as his son later recorded, found the Baptists there a "free, candid, and hospitable people, of liberal religious views, but not well read in the Scriptures." Thomas blamed this deficiency on the emotionalism that Baptists learned from their preachers. Their ministers seemed to be "eloquent in tears," but "not mighty in the Scriptures." The elder Campbell's assessment of the Baptist view of the Bible reflected his son's perception. Even though the Baptists attempted to model their faith and practice on the Bible, and particularly on the New Testament, the Campbells believed Baptists had not taken the scriptures seriously or as literally as they should have.[3]

Alexander's conviction about what the Bible really said evidenced itself in his 1823 debate with William McCalla. Hundreds of such religious debates occurred in the early nineteenth century throughout the country, although they were more commonly staged in settled agricultural locales in the South and Midwest. Religious disputation had long been a forum for both academic debate among scholars and theological wrangling between common folk in the colonial period. In the early nineteenth century, with the outgrowth of competition in the religious marketplace, the debates involved many groups, from Catholics to Native Americans. But they particularly appealed to the more populist movements like the Methodists and Baptists.[4]

Like most of the common religious debates, the focus of the Campbell-McCalla dispute dealt with infant baptism. Campbell took the opportunity to announce publically his innovative, yet allegedly primitive, views on the significance of baptism. Highlighting biblical texts, such as Acts 2:38, that encouraged baptism "for the remission of sins," Campbell stressed immersion as the act that "*formally* washes away our sins," while agreeing that it was faith in Christ that "*really* cleanses us who believe from all sin."[5] Such a nuanced argument allowed Campbell to explain why the Presbyterians and others baptized their infant children: they had misunderstood this New Testament command and applied it to the sinful *nature* of infants when it only applied to sins

Alexander Campbell. (Frontispiece, Robert Richardson, *Memoirs of Alexander Campbell*, 1868).

actually *committed*. Campbell clearly recognized the revolutionary nature of his interpretation of baptism since, in his prefatory remarks, he claimed that "neither Baptists nor Pedobaptists" understood the significance of the ordinance. Campbell's logic appealed to many of his fellow Baptists since he emphasized the centrality of the Bible and the significance of immersion baptism. Since public debates also served as venues of entertainment, his masterful skills in debate and eloquent preaching made his arguments more entrancing. Most Baptists gave the win to Campbell over McCalla. Before Campbell returned to Pennsylvania, he preached by invitation to Lexington's Baptists, in churches pastored by his admirers Jeremiah Vardeman and James Fishback. Both of these men were respected preachers in the area and they, too, enhanced the innovator's appeal.[6]

The McCalla debate and the brief preaching tour, combined with published accounts of his prior debates in Ohio, not only spread Campbell's renown, but his reforms. His most powerful intellectual ingress came from the wide circulation of his publication, the *Christian Baptist,* begun in 1823. Campbell's excursions into publishing were part of the explosion of popular printed material, and particularly religious material, in the early republic. Through this monthly periodical, Campbell delineated and promulgated his many thoughts on reforming religion. His views on faith tended to emphasize its intellectual aspects. Since faith came from the individual's encounter with the written word, the Holy Spirit did not personally engage the convert. Instead, the Spirit worked through the Bible, which he had already inspired. In addition to his views on faith, Campbell also publicized his antisectarianism in the *Christian Baptist.* Campbell envisioned a new Christian era wherein denominational boundaries fell away and the kingdom of Christ united around certain essential, fundamental truths in the New Testament. He warned, however, the task of creating such unity would challenge true Christians. The barriers to this grand union included all varieties of creeds, missionary organizations, Bible and tract societies, Sabbath schools, and unbiblical forms of church hierarchy. Even the existence of Baptist associations would hinder unification. In short, Campbell condemned any agency or entity which restricted local churches or individuals. And his own role in the grand design of creating a new order was that of prophetic visionary. He saw himself as an iconoclastic revolutionary on par with Washington and Jefferson, as he advocated a "declaration of independence of the Kingdom of Jesus."[7]

Campbell's anti-institutionalism reflected his participation in a much larger primitivist movement that rebelled against the alleged new missionary menace. The transatlantic missionary movement that coalesced at the turn of the nineteenth century enthralled many Anglo-American Christians, but it also provoked resistance. Seldom was the inherent goodness of spreading the "good news" challenged. Practically every Christian movement took seriously Jesus's instruction for his disciples to make more disciples by teaching them his commandments and baptizing them. The book of Acts takes its very name from the fact that it chronicles the efforts of Paul, Peter, and others to carry out this charge. From the 1790s onward, however, evangelical Protestants conceived of new ways to accomplish the goal. The most controversial mode involved formal denominational or inter-denominational organizations commissioning missionaries to proclaim the gospel overseas and throughout the American continent. The first organization of this kind in America was the American Board of Commissioners for Foreign Missions, formed by Massachusetts Congregationalist leaders in 1810. When two of the board's leading missionaries, Adoniram Judson and Luther Rice, embraced Baptist views in 1812 while on mission tours to India, their defection provided the decentralized Baptist churches and associations an occasion to join in common cause. Some Baptist individuals, churches, and associations already supported the Congregationalist endeavor, thus Rice toured the seaboard cities to secure and filter that Baptist support for Judson, who remained in India and was now deprived of Congregationalist funding. Rice's efforts proved fruitful when, in 1814, thirty-three delegates from local and regional mission societies met in Philadelphia and formed the General Missionary Convention of the Baptist Denomination in the United States for Foreign Mission. The unwieldy appellation quickly encouraged a nickname, the Triennial Convention, because it met every three years. Among its first decisions was to offer Rice a key role as an American itinerant official. He would promote the mission cause professionally. In the summer and fall of 1815 and 1816, Rice visited northern and central Kentucky to promote the cause at several associational meetings. Typically, he presented a letter of correspondence as if from another association, only his was a request for correspondence from the mission board. Most associations agreed with this novel procedure and early on Rice was successful in his attempts. By 1816, six missionary societies had affiliated with the Philadelphia-based Baptist Board, and Rice had received hundreds

of dollars in donations from churches, associations, and individual Baptists in Kentucky.[8]

From the beginning, however, some of Luther Rice's audiences heard in his speeches, and saw in his method, innovations that seemed to contradict the localist, Baptist model—a standard they further connected to the democratic American ethos. The elderly preacher John Taylor, long a fixture in western Baptist life by this time, attended Rice's introductory meeting with Kentuckians at the 1815 Elkhorn Association. Though they were both in the Baptist fold, Taylor viewed Rice's methods with vicious contempt. To Taylor's eyes, this missionary seemed more interested in getting into the Baptists' purse than in pursuing Baptist evangelical aims. Taylor poetically asserted that Rice's "motive was thro' sophistry and Yankee art, to get money for the Mission, of which himself was to have a part." According to Taylor, Rice and the board—which he called "the great machine"—were out to establish an ecclesiastical aristocracy whereby their acquisition of money and power could "sap the foundation of Baptist republican government." For four years, Taylor perceived Rice and other eastern missionaries insulting the state of religion in the West. This led Taylor to publish his opposing views on the subject. He characterized the easterners as lecherous beggers and gluttonous hucksters no better than the vendors who marketed their wares at associational meetings. He also condemned their encouragement of "patrimonial, theological education." Apparently, wrote Taylor facetiously, the call of God and the church failed to produce truly equipped preachers. The missionaries "would have us think that our homespun preachers have only been converting the vulgar part of the community," Taylor mocked, "but by a more refined kind of preaching, the rich and wise will become converted." One of Taylor's favorite targets was John Mason Peck, a New York native. Peck's missionary journals reveal that many Kentucky Baptists shared Taylor's opinions. On Peck's first tour of the state in 1817, he found some congregations in favor, and financially supportive, of his missions cause. Others, though, tended toward tepid reception or outright opposition.[9]

The initial Baptist response to the age of missions was generally ambivalent, but their primary concerns dealt with loss of piety and local autonomy. As acerbic as Taylor's treatise on missionaries was, he personally supported the work they did. The preacher had devoted his entire ministry to preaching evangelistically to the converted and unconverted alike. His popularity

among western Baptists signals the acceptance his preaching and his ideas received among the membership. Any opposition he offered to mission agents, though, stemmed from a fourfold concern. First, he feared mission societies would encourage extra-local control of the churches. Second, he disdained the agents' constant preaching aimed at gathering collections for missions. Such moneygrubbing violated Christian ethics in Taylor's opinion. Third, he condemned the missionaries' suggestion that pastors needed more formal theological education. And fourth, he tired of the missionaries' constant complaints of privation and suffering in the cause of Christ.[10]

Other preachers imitated Taylor's brand of opposition. Since the opposition was to the mission societies' motives and methods and not their goals, it allowed both preachers and churches to support evangelism and still reject innovations that threatened their principles. Many churches took rather pronounced stands in favor of or in opposition to the board. The Providence Church in Clark County proclaimed their position during the spring of 1817. In their March business meeting, one member asked to know if the church were "willing to correspond with the board of Foreign Missions." A month later, as the church convened, they voted that they were "not willing" to embrace the board as they would another church. That fall, missionary John Peck traveled through the area and stopped at a different Providence Church in nearby Jessamine County during their October meeting. After the church concluded its business, Peck preached to a rather stoic audience. The following day, however, he preached the Sunday sermon and left with over twenty-five dollars for the mission cause. Some churches could not agree what stand to take due to differing opinions among the membership. Peck preached to the Friendship Church in the village of Winchester. This group had established correspondence with the board, then later withdrew it. The members of the church divided on the issue of missions and apparently not because of method. Peck noted that he knew many who opposed the board's efforts as "unwise in manner," but he claimed that the unfriendly members of the Friendship church were different. These, he said, "Hoped they should never hear more of missionaries." Nevertheless he did collect almost nine dollars from those few church members in favor.[11]

If Alexander Campbell's anti-institutional, "anti-mission" message resonated among some Baptists because of their own localist and primitivist priorities, his anti-creedal rhetoric appealed for similar reasons. Baptists, like many Protestants, revered the idea of "no creed but the Bible." From Lutherans and Wesleyans to

Calvinists and Universalists, the claim of the Bible as the only necessary creed book signaled them as elevating the authority of the Bible above all other possible sources, including tradition, clergy, and other texts. Given the atomistic tendency of anti-creedalism, Alexander Campbell's quest for Christian unity under the anti-creedal banner is particularly ironic.[12] It appealed to Baptists, however, because they had actually already come as close to implementing his vision as was possible, but many were disappointed with the results. The factionalism that seemed to plague Baptist attempts at anti-creedalism propelled many Baptists to hope that Campbell could perfect it in a new order.

In short, Campbell's reforms enjoyed success because his theological innovations came from within, from no less than a Baptist champion, and sounded the timbre of widely held Protestant biblicism. But conflict emerged in the 1820s as other Baptists heard heresy in the heralds of the new order. For better or worse, the decentralized nature of the Baptist movement restricted a wholesale acceptance or rejection of Campbell's reformation. By design, such decentralization determined that any contestation would begin locally, in the hundreds of churches and dozens of associations. In many churches, pastors accepted the reforms and preached them to their congregations. Baptist hearers, though, encouraged by their polity, were free to accept or reject pastoral proclamations. Often, factions developed in such cases; some in support of the pastor and his views, others opposed. Since Baptist churches in the 1820s largely met once a month, and their preachers were bi-vocational and preached to multiple churches within a given month, the effect of any one pastor accepting the innovations could be vast. Lawyer-preacher Samuel Carpenter led reforming factions in both of the churches he pastored. Likewise, carpenter-preacher Benjamin Allen introduced the new doctrines to the congregations at two of the churches he pastored. He persuaded a large majority of members at the Flat Rock Church and then seven out of every eight members at his Harrod's Creek Church. In some churches, factionalism developed slowly over time, largely due to the confusion and ambiguity of certain innovations as well as the language used to express them. Informal theological discussions and formal debates could easily become debates over meaning and definition. Dealing with abstruse concepts such as Christian obedience, baptism, salvation, biblical authority, the agency of the Holy Spirit, and the connections between them, led to heady exercises in semantics and hermeneutics. In seeking out order in the confusion, some pastors, like Walter Warder at Mayslick Church, sought harmony and unity, thinking it

better "to agree with Mr. Campbell as far as he could conscientiously than cause a rupture."[13]

The divisions within churches due to Campbell's reformation tested the Kentucky Baptist devotion to congregational autonomy. The schism of the Mayslick Church, while likely atypical in its duration, highlights the problematic issues of intense Baptist strife. As in most churches, reformation sentiments entered the church in the 1820s and spread among the congregation partly due to pastor Warder's vacillation on the issues. Warder was no neophyte. Born in 1787 and ordained around 1811, he gained a reputation in the state for his powerful preaching and his abilities in church growth. When he accepted the pastorate of Mayslick in 1814, it had fewer than seventy members and had been in decline since the turn of the century. Growth came slowly, but spiked in 1828 when over 400 converts joined the church and Warder baptized them all. The preacher met Alexander Campbell in 1824 during the reformer's second tour of Kentucky and, like many others, mulled over Campbell's innovations for the next few years and did not dissuade his church members from accepting them. During that revival of religion in 1828—a revival that involved thousands of converts throughout the state—many of the new church members adopted reformation principles. In the fall of 1828, Warder's friend and fellow preacher William Vaughan returned to the area after a year's absence in Ohio. Vaughan persuaded the pastor and many congregants of the errors of "Campbellism." Warder's new-found certitude led him to protest against the doctrines in his sermons. This, in turn, encouraged the factionalism he had worked so hard to avoid. That the 1828 revival had multiplied church membership to around 800—not counting non-member adherents—made resolution all the more difficult. As the controversy raged over the next eighteen months, Warder had the dubious distinction of pastoring one of the largest churches in the state and one of the many contentious congregations.[14]

With so many new converts in the Mayslick church, and so many of them supporters of Campbell's reformation, the very identity of the church came into question. The church members had very little prior experience in dealing with discipline over purely doctrinal matters. In 1806, they had excluded fifteen members after a lengthy disagreement on slavery. The fifteen believed slavery to be a sin and had already left the church prior to their official exclusion. Thus their exclusion could have easily been classified as contempt for the church. The only other possible exclusion over doctrine occurred in January 1829, when Patsy, a slave, suffered expulsion after joining the Presbyterians. Here

again, the exclusion was a *de jure* response to a *de facto* reality. Thus, from the church's founding in 1789, it had no clear precedent upon which to rely. By 1830, inter-factional relations in the church grew less civil, with some ridiculing the beliefs of others and tempers easily lost. The breaking point came in May when, in the absence of the anti-Reformation faction, Alexander Campbell himself and several other Reformation leaders administered communion in the meeting house with the pro-Campbell faction only. Celebrating one of the two revered ordinances outside of a regular meeting was scandalous enough, but by choosing the one ritual most representative of the church's collective unity, the Reformers inflicted a more personal wound upon their opponents. After a failed attempt in June by a joint committee to resolve the disputes, the anti-reformers made an offer that they separate peaceably and form two separate churches. The offer stipulated that they would co-own the meeting house and grounds (and the debt) and also have co-equal access to the church record book and rights to the graveyard. Their proposal reveals that contentious issues extended beyond academic matters of theology and polity. The issues also dealt with the finances and assets of the church, and the equally important ownership of identity. Possession of the church book, the only written record of a church's founding, constitution, elections, business decisions, and disciplinary actions, connoted connection with the church's history and also its true identity, and thus became particularly significant in times of schism. Graveyard access, of course, signified the familiar connections to the past. With so much at stake and uncertain, the Reformers rejected the proposal.[15]

Faced with few options, the anti-Campbell faction in the Mayslick church drew up a resolution to force a vote in their August meeting on the divisive issues. The document denounced Campbell's doctrines on baptism and conversion. It affirmed the "original constitution and covenant" of the church and claimed that only those who signed the document (or had someone sign for them) would be considered members. At the meeting, 189 voted in favor of the resolution and 100 voted against. Many who might have agreed with the document's sentiment and proposals resisted signing; it smacked too much of coercion. However, since its only evident purpose was to determine which faction held the majority, it served its intent both at the first vote and later, when it ultimately received 385 signatures. The proposal's timing proved propitious. Less than a month later, the Mayslick Church had two contingents of messengers representing them to their associational meeting. Each party claimed

to be the original church. Since the majority of the association opposed Campbell's Reformation, it received the Mayslick anti-Reformation party. The decision clearly turned on theology, since the association simultaneously acknowledged the *minority* delegation from the Bethel Church, which had also suffered a schism that year. Once the association accepted the Mayslick majority as the real delegation of the church, the minority had no recourse but to establish themselves as another church. This did not conclude the difficulties, however, since the minority still had a legal right to the meeting house. Neither group needed the meeting house every week, and they agreed to share it. The two factions worked with this arrangement fairly peaceably for eight years until the Baptists began to engage in "protracted meetings," revival services that could last days or weeks. One particular meeting commenced in early February and lasted over twenty days. Such extensive use of the meeting house drove a critical wedge between the two bodies. By year's end, the Reformers prepared to file a claim to the property. Disputes and negotiation to settle the matter out of court continued for three more years. Finally, in October 1841, the Baptists agreed that over the next year they would pay the Reformers $900 to compensate them for the amount their members had paid to construct the meeting house. After full payment was made, the Reformers would relinquish their claims and build a new meeting house elsewhere. Thus, strife begun in the mid 1820s ended by the fall of 1842.[16]

Many Kentucky Baptist leaders anticipated the new challenge that Campbell would offer the movement and tried to warn the churches. As Campbell's innovations became more clearly understood by the mid-1820s, some associations drafted circular letters to their churches informing them of the dangerous Reformation. One of the earliest concerns for the associations was the Reformers' intense anti-creedalism. In their advisory role, some associations urged churches to reject this idea. Others could not take a position on creeds without first inquiring of the churches. In 1825, the Long Run Association received the following query from the Louisville Church: "Is there any authority in the New Testament for religious bodies to make human creeds and confessions of faith the constitutions or directories of such bodies in matters of faith or practice?" The collected messengers decided to solicit the wisdom of the churches individually; the following year, seventeen out of the twenty-two associated churches asserted that the Bible was "the only directory of our faith and practice," but also agreed it necessary for "unity and purity in the churches, that we have a written declaration of our faith." A few

associations that disavowed creeds of any kind, like Bracken and Tate's Creek, had already fallen under the Reformation's influence.[17]

The study of the Kentucky Baptist relationship with creeds easily results in confusion, since their rhetoric often seemed to contrast with historical Baptist commitments. Denominational historians have highlighted the important distinction between creeds and confessions. One such historian, H. Leon McBeth, describes Baptists as historically "confessional but not *creedal*" (emphasis in the original). McBeth explains, "A confession designates what people *do* believe; a creed what they *must* believe." Acknowledging that creeds "are the natural and normal expression of the religious life," influential Baptist theologian E. Y. Mullins also asserts that Christians "have no right to enforce them upon men against their wills." This dichotomy and the tendency to formalize statements of faith have led Baptists, in the words of Baptist historian H. Wheeler Robinson, "to hold a very detached position in regard to creeds and formal confessions of faith as such."[18]

An analysis of the creedalism issue in the context of the Campbell controversy reveals another strand of the thematic thread under consideration here: that the Baptist democratic impulse made the movement flexible, and thus better able to survive periods of conflict. Reformers claimed to be the true Baptists, and their opponents had to demarcate what it meant to be truly "Baptist." In the end, anti-Reformation Baptists blurred the line between confessions and creeds and developed purposefully inclusive doctrinal statements that would allow for disagreement among the faithful while culling out the vilest of heretics—which included the "Campbellite" Reformers. The issue became not whether to *have* a doctrinal statement, but what could be included in it without violating the conscience of the believing individual. The Baptists of Kentucky drew up statements of doctrinal fundamentals to weed out the traitors in their midst while still preserving their treasured liberties.

The controversy over the use of such doctrinal statements struck deeply because early Kentucky Baptists were products of their past. As legatees of the New Light tradition, eighteenth-century Separate Baptists preferred "covenants" and disavowed confessions, then denounced the Regular Baptists' theological documents as creeds. Both Separates and Regulars agreed on the core beliefs of the Baptist impulse, yet the "covenant" emphasized relationship over theology and allowed for greater doctrinal flexibility. When the factions fused in Kentucky in 1801, their rhetoric also tended to meld, and churches founded after the merger combined the ideas. For example, when the church at Williamstown formed in

1826, it labeled its ten-point doctrinal statement a "church covenant." Not only did Kentucky Baptists blend covenant and confession, they made few distinctions between confessions and creeds. The terms of union adopted by Regulars and Separates in 1801 avoided the words "confession" and "creed" entirely, opting instead for the generic word "plan." John Taylor used the terms interchangeably in his memoirs, since, to him, both confessions and creeds were systematic listings of beliefs gleaned from the Bible. When Campbell and his fellow reformers denounced all such lists as creeds, Baptists responded on his terms. Defending the faith was more important than playing semantic games. One central Kentucky association resolved to oppose the Reformation, and in the hope of curtailing further conflict, it created an "abstract of principles (or creed if you please)" wherein it stated its beliefs "in an undisguised and unreserved manner." Following an 1830 schism, the anti-Reformation minority of the North District Association appointed a committee to research historical Baptist customs. They hoped they might hold these historical truths in common and avoid further schism. The section of the report on "constituting churches" reflected the ambiguity of the movement's language. The report observed that, historically, "a constitution, Covenant or creed, (whichever you please,) being a compendium of Gospel principles and duties, is unanimously assented to."[19]

The clearest early Kentucky Baptist statement on the role of creeds in response to Campbell came from the lawyer-preacher Silas Mercer Noel. Writing a circular letter for the 1826 Franklin Association, Noel clarified the questions facing Baptist churches. He asked, "Is it lawful and expedient, to adhere to a Creed," for admitting prospective members and for electing church officers? For Noel and his fellow Baptists in north-central Kentucky, the question necessitated an affirmative response. He defined "creed" along Taylor's lines, as "an epitome, or summary exhibition of what the scriptures teach," but he also spoke of creeds and confessions as the same. Creeds formed by civil authorities, Noel argued, led to despotism, while "those formed by voluntary Associations of Christians" were "not only lawful, but necessary." Without a creed, no distinction whatsoever could be made as to who could commune under the banner of Christ. In a creedless church, those who denied the divinity of Jesus could not be excluded by those who saw him as God in the flesh. Trinitarians would have to fellowship with Unitarians, and those who believed the non-elect spent eternity in hell had to acknowledge Universalism as an equally justifiable doctrine for a fellow church member. Far from an ecumenical utopia, the messengers at the Franklin Association

saw such possible extremes in a non-creedal congregation as a "Babel confederacy," referencing the confusion which afflicted the builders of the Tower of Babel in the book of Genesis. Such extreme diversity violated "the unity, purity, and peace" as well as the "symmetry of the Church of Jesus Christ as described by the pen of inspiration," referring to the Bible. The association did affirm the right of every individual to interpret the Bible for himself; to do otherwise "would be tyranny." But as congregationalists, they privileged the interpretation of the church, that is, the collective opinion of the members, and affirmed the church's right to examine, approve, or exclude members or officers based on this collected wisdom. Noel did not "propose to enquire" how long a church covenant or creed should be, or even whether or not it should be written down. He set out only to persuade his fellow Baptists, who were struggling with their religious identity and at a loss over how to repel anti-creedal attacks, that "to erase [confessions] from our books, our memory and our practice, is to make a tremendous leap, a leap into chaos." The Franklin Association's counsel to maintain a systematic list of beliefs reflected other associations' previous opinions. In 1819, the Salem Association's letter to its churches proposed several ways of creating unity, purity, and discipline among congregations. First among these was the "maintenance of a system of sound doctrine" by which heresy could be distinguished. Likewise, two years later, the Long Run Association argued for the necessity of "a well digested system of doctrines" for both associations and churches.[20]

In Noel's urgent letter, in associational admonishments, and in many other instances when creeds, covenants, and confessions were defended, the arguments were accompanied by a sample list of doctrines considered fundamental to the Baptist impulse. Such an emphasis upon essential points of doctrine did not reflect a restrictiveness in Kentucky Baptist creeds. On the contrary, it was a purposeful effort to accept differences of interpretation, as long as there was agreement on certain basics. Thus, Baptists aimed at democracy and tolerance far more than their creeds might suggest at first glance.

If Baptists agreed upon one truth in the 1820s and 1830s, it was that healthy disagreement on non-essential points often characterized their churches. Even in doctrine, difference of opinion was not anathema. For example, Silas Mercer Noel's staunch defense of creeds also clearly explained that the interpretations of the Bible that a church used to admit or exclude were those touching "upon fundamental points." When a church refused an individual's interpretation, he said, it was because its basic doctrines had already been settled. The letter in

which the Long Run Association advised churches to create "a well digested system of doctrines" also included a brief list of what the association considered "essential truths of Christianity." Before the tumult of Campbell's Reformation, Salem Association members recognized doctrinal diversity. They observed, "We know that differences do exist amongst the most affectionate brethren, but not in cardinal points." They agreed that "a spirit of peace is desirable, and ought to be cultivated when consistent with unity of faith in the great fundamentals of Christianity." After the Reformation divided the Bracken Association, the Baptist remnant noted "that there is in this Association, as well as in every other, some shades of difference on some doctrinal questions, yet none that should produce any unpleasantness." The Green River Association of south-central Kentucky commented on the futility of trying to achieve perfect agreement in doctrine: "It cannot be a matter of surprise that differences of opinion should exist even among those who equally desire deliverance from it." Though each of these associational enumerations of essential doctrines differed, the common elements included: the sovereignty and triunity of God; the divinity of Jesus and his atoning work; the depravity and dependency of humanity; and the influence of the Holy Spirit in regeneration and sanctification. Though not as frequently, some lists included the Bible as sole authority on faith and practice, the perseverance of the saints, and the nature and design of immersion baptism and the Lord's Supper among the cardinal truths.[21]

Though the Baptists of Kentucky shared many of their core doctrines with other Christian groups, they strove to highlight several points of difference. These included their disavowal of perceived heresies both ancient and modern, their participation in the theological legacy of John Calvin, and their distinctive view of baptism. Alexander Campbell's reformative vision had helped Baptists clarify their view on the necessity of doctrinal statements: that they were only valid when approved by the people, and when they allowed for diversity of opinion on a multitude of lesser doctrines and practices. This valuation of individual difference did not cause the widespread division of churches and associations between 1828 and 1832, but it did help push the Reformers away. In 1830, Campbell himself began his final separation from the Baptists and united his Reformers with Barton Stone's Christian Connection. By 1832, Campbell had persuaded approximately 25 percent of the Baptists in Kentucky to join his movement. The impact of the defections was significant. It drew away those from the Baptist fold who denied the value of doctrinal statements, the value of missionary societies, and the mere symbolism of baptism. Campbell also drew out many who favored the popular nineteenth-century rejection of strict Calvinism.[22]

If Alexander Campbell was, as Nathan Hatch calls him, one of the "profaners of the Calvinist temple," then he cast his aspersions in a timely manner; much of the American religious world joined him, and Kentucky Baptists themselves were redecorating the temple. Into the nineteenth century, the inclusive Baptist impulse had proven a fertile ground for staunch Calvinism, variations on Calvinism, and even outright rejection. Calvin's controversial doctrines were clarified at the 1618–1619 Synod of Dort, and they included five essential points: the total depravity of man's nature, the unearned election of those predestined to be saved, the redemptive and atoning work of Christ as particularly for and exclusively limited to the elect, the irresistibility of God's grace, and the perseverance of the saints. The majority of colonial Baptists were inclined toward Calvinism. After the American Revolution, however, new religious movements following the intriguing ideas of Jacob Arminius began to prosper. Arminius, a Dutch reformer and a strict Calvinist in his training, concluded that Calvin had misunderstood biblical predestination. Arminius's followers, who were called the "Remonstrants," saw ambiguity in how God's omniscience affected predestination and election. They believed that while Christ's atonement was available to all, it was applicable only to believers. They asserted that God's grace alone allowed true goodness and that man can actually resist the grace of God if he chooses. Finally, as a group, the Remonstrants were undecided on whether salvation could be lost.[23]

Often considered the antithesis of Calvinism, Arminianism actually only contradicts it in one of five points: the level of resistance man has against God's grace. On the issues of predestination and perseverance, the Remonstrants simply could not be as dogmatic as the Calvinists. Arminius's followers saw atonement as universal in availability, yet limited only in its application. In a similar vein, they qualified man's depraved state, asserting that man "can of and by himself, neither think, will, nor do any thing that is truly good." The word "truly" barely, but effectively, distinguished the doctrine from the Calvinist belief that depravity hinders goodness of all sorts, spiritual or otherwise. Despite these differences, the Arminianism professed by religious groups such as the Methodists, in their rejection of Calvinist predestination, emphasized the pragmatism of man's free will to seek salvation: an emphasis that surpassed the doctrine's seventeenth-century articulations.[24]

Eighteenth-century American Baptists were divided over these issues. Regular Baptists favored staunch Calvinism. Meanwhile, the Separate Baptists varied amongst themselves because of their aversion to confessions of faith and the patchwork influence of the Calvinistic Great Awakening in the mid-Atlantic

and southern states. Following post-revolutionary trans-Appalachian expansion, however, the differences between the two groups began to break down in the western lands. Scarcity of preachers compelled pulpit sharing between churches of differing emphasis, encouraging broader understanding and relationship building. In 1801, after the Kentucky revivals, the two leading Baptist associations, Elkhorn (comprised of Regular churches) and South Kentucky (comprised of Separates), agreed to an eleven-point plan of union whereby they would drop their former labels and call themselves "United Baptists." By 1803, all other associations and churches in the state joined in correspondence under the same terms. The significance of the agreement lay in their willingness to moderate their Calvinism to accommodate union. Eight of the eleven terms were solely theological, affirming standards such as the infallible authority of the Bible, the Trinity, baptism by immersion and as a condition for communion, and so forth. Point three emphasized human depravity and point five asserted final perseverance of the saints, each Calvinist mainstays. The terms did not list grace's irresistibility or predestination, and the union was accomplished by practically rejecting the idea of limited atonement. Point nine stated that communion would not be denied because of disagreement over whether "Christ tasted death for every man." Such an admission still acknowledged God's sovereignty over salvation, but allowed the kind of evangelistic preaching that had occurred in the revival inferno.[25]

This simple idea of preaching repentance to sinners, based upon the theological reassessment of the extent of the atonement, revolutionized the Baptist movement in the early nineteenth century. Still another source of the change lay in the late eighteenth-century writings of the British Baptist pastor Andrew Fuller. Like Arminius, Fuller (1754–1815) was reared in the high Calvinist tradition, but had his doubts. By the 1780s, however, he had been introduced to the thoughts of Abraham Taylor, Robert Hall, John Sutcliff, John Ryland, Jr., and Jonathan Edwards. All these preachers were evangelical Calvinists, and they impelled Fuller to review his understanding of atonement. The result encouraged him to publish in 1785 the earliest and clearest explication of revisionary Calvinist thinking, *The Gospel Worthy of All Acceptation*. Fuller's work particularly placed him in opposition to the earlier works of Englishmen John Gill and John Brine. Gill and Brine upheld the doctrine of limited atonement, and they denounced evangelical preaching and open invitations for sinners to believe. By the 1810s, this British debate had produced schisms among American Baptists. Staunchly Calvinist Gillites accused the Fullerites of Arminianism. For their

part, the modified Calvinist Fullerites blasted the Gillites as Hyper-Calvinists (that is, those who took Calvin's ideas to paralytic extremes).[26]

Despite the attacks, Andrew Fuller was no Arminian. Indeed, he drew fire from English Arminian Baptists who disagreed with his Calvinism. Arminian Baptists, like Wesleyans, emphasized human freedom to choose to believe a gospel universally offered. The same divine grace that enabled the belief could also be resisted and the convert could fall away. This insecurity led to constant striving for conversion and holiness. Fuller, on the other hand, asserted the Calvinist doctrine of predestination, which de-emphasized individual choice. But he denied the doctrine of limited atonement, thus making salvation open to anyone who heard the preaching of the gospel. Once the sinner converted, Fuller contended in Calvinistic fashion, her soul was secure and her salvation perseverant. The significance of Fuller's revisions was in the mandate it placed on preaching the gospel. The preacher's job was not to persuade. That was the role of God's grace. The preacher's task was to fervently and frequently proclaim an available atonement. Firmly entrenched Calvinists, like Gill, saw this as presumptuous at best and sinful at worst. In the end, however, the armies of Baptist preachers who accepted "Fullerism" believed much like Calvinists, but acted much like Arminians.[27]

The Fullerites gradually gained ground in the West. Throughout Kentucky, Baptists studied Fuller's ideas. In northern Mason County, preacher William Vaughan studied both Gill's and Fuller's works in the mid-1810s and adopted the latter's views as his own. In 1817, after he preached Fuller's ideas in his church (Lee's Creek), some members took offense and requested that a second minister, William Grinstead, be called to preach to them once a month. Rather than split the church or resign, Vaughan capitulated, and for a few months the congregation heard preaching alternately from two ministers: one Fullerite, one Gillite. After a few months, though, Grinstead quit when the congregation refused to remunerate him. That same year, the Red River Association in southwest Kentucky also struggled over this modified Calvinism. The association, comprised of churches in Kentucky and Tennessee, found itself divided over the implications of rejecting limited atonement. Preacher Reuben Ross, a staunch Calvinist who had migrated from North Carolina, desired to study both sides of the dispute. Like Vaughan, he read Gill first, then Fuller. After lengthy introspection, he sided with Fuller; but his association continued to debate the issue for seven more years. In another instance of Fuller's impact, the twenty-four

churches in the Red River Association sent delegates to a specially called convention in 1824 to resolve their theological disagreement. The delegates unanimously agreed to "live together in peace and harmony," though "some little difference of sentiments" existed among them. Many churches within the association, however, apparently rejected their delegates' agreement. At the associational meeting in 1825, sixteen churches declared their opposition to moderating limited atonement. The association agreed to divide, and the Fullerite minority formed the Bethel Association in October. The "Abstract of Principles" of the new association affirmed depravity, predestined election, and perseverance, but did not mention views of the atonement as among their twelve principles. In 1836, however, they produced a new statement of faith that, while again affirming depravity, emphasized election after repentance, affirmed unlimited atonement clearly, and highlighted the need for proclaiming the gospel message. Lest there be any doubt of the association's stance, the annual circular letter to the churches focused on and affirmed the doctrine that "Christ tasted death for every man."[28]

The influence of Andrew Fuller's ideas in Kentucky became more apparent in the 1830s. In 1831, when Campbell's Reformers in the Tate's Creek Association appealed for the restoration of the simpler, ancient order, they claimed that the first-century church "knew nothing of the modern gospels—such as *Calvinism, Armenianism* [sic], or *Fullerism*" (emphasis in the original). When Baptist newspaper editor John L. Waller attacked both the Reformers and the anti-mission faction in 1835, he asserted that each was "an uncompromising enemy of the United Baptists, and both violent opposers of Mr. Fuller." A year later, Waller predicted that churches which adhered to "ultra-Calvinism" and decried Fullerism would be "doomed to barrenness." The triumph of Fullerism in Baptist life by the mid-1830s seemed clear to the members of the Nolynn Association. As long-time advocates of Fuller's ideas, in 1834 they wrote that "we have seen the doctrines of Calvinism and Predestination rise to awful heights, at different times and in different places." But, they continued, "We have also seen them decline. And we now feel ourselves authorized to say, that the Heavenly truths of a free and unbounded grace in God to save all who will seek him, are almost universally acknowledged."[29]

The impact of Fuller on Kentucky Baptists reveals not only the importance of theology and the finer points of doctrine to both clergy and laity, but also how such doctrines could compel behavior. Broadening their view of atonement put a burden of duty on the Baptists. If Christ died for all and sinners

were duty-bound to repent, then it fell upon Christians to announce that fact and invite that repentance in mission fields both foreign and domestic. This practical conclusion produced its own controversy. Already Campbell's Reformation had drawn off a significant percentage of anti-institutional, anti-mission board Baptists. Fuller's general atonement began a new kind of division. Between 1833 and 1841, a second schism drew off those Baptists who rejected both Fuller and Campbell. Fuller's ideas had already encouraged the British mission movement, which in turn inspired similar local ventures in America. In 1813, lawyer-preacher Silas Mercer Noel tried to initiate a state-wide meeting of correspondence to organize local mission societies in Kentucky. Noel's efforts foundered, especially after Luther Rice focused the local societies on supporting the national Baptist Board. In 1827, preachers Spencer Clack and George Waller tried to resuscitate Noel's idea, but by that time, the Reformation controversy commanded Baptist attention. Following this turmoil, Noel tried again in 1831 and gathered 153 friends of state missions. They organized the Kentucky Baptist Convention in 1832, but the effort held out little promise, as only nine of the state's six hundred Baptist churches sent delegates. Between 1832 and 1836, the convention ran into a variety of setbacks. Several of the key organizers and agents of the convention died—many of these in the cholera epidemic of 1833. The organization was continually restructured. The very word "convention" heightened many Baptists' suspicions, since they associated the term with political gatherings. Finally, though the convention's charter had been specifically worded to include "anti-mission" Baptists, their opposition kept the organization controversial and marginalized in Baptist life. By 1836, the convention's leaders had accepted failure.[30]

On the grass roots level, however, Fuller's ideas encouraged Baptists to pursue innovations during this period that would help them counter their steadily advancing Methodist rivals. In the first third of the nineteenth century, Methodism had proven to be one of the wonders of the early republic, growing from a small marginalized sect at the time of the American Revolution to a commanding religious presence nationwide. Methodist numbers doubled between 1820 and 1830 (from a quarter- to a half-million) and tripled again before the Civil War. The proportions of growth for Kentucky Methodists matched the national patterns. Travelers through the state found Methodists wherever they found Baptists. Francois Andre Michaux found the two sects the most prolific in the state as early as 1802. In their abundance, tension easily arose between the groups, and the resulting conflicts typically

involved their ministers. The rivalry could be bitter, as when Baptist preachers attacked the Methodist Arminian doctrines or structure of church government. Sometimes their competition could be more good-natured. One Baptist minister, likely Jeremiah Vardeman, joked that he was fairly successful at proselytizing Methodist minister Valentine Cook's converts. Wishing to get Cook's Methodists into the water for immersion baptism, Vardeman jested that he had been fortunate in transforming Cook's "fine flock of chickens into ducks."[31]

By the mid-1830s, the Baptists lamented losing the numerical advantage they had enjoyed earlier in the century, and they proved more open to Fullerite principles and to coopting Methodist practices. W. C. Buck wrote, "Other denominations have increased in a much greater ratio, and sometimes by inroads made upon the very families of Baptists." In the midst of apparently declining fortunes, the Baptists adapted, in fits and starts, a new and overtly evangelical (and conspicuously Methodist) method in their churches. They called the method "protracted meetings," though some labeled it "meeting of days"; in many respects it resembled a Methodist camp meeting without much camping. Ironically, and perhaps importantly, Baptists appropriated the revivalistic practice at the same time it was losing its meaning among the Methodists. Just as Methodist camp meetings had developed out of their quarterly conference meetings, Baptists in the early 1830s used protracted meetings in lieu of the less-formal quarterly associational gatherings. These quarterly meetings, often called "union meetings," offered three days of worship and preaching and excluded formal associational business. As the name might indicate, the protracted meetings established a date of commencement, but left open the possibility that the meeting could extend past the third day.[32] The innovators of this practice in Kentucky were a handful of preachers in the Gaspar River Association in the Green River valley. In 1835, their association resolved to replace the union meetings of the following year with three protracted meetings. All the ministers agreed to attend the meetings. Again the next year, they appointed three more meetings for October 1836, and May and July 1837, with the preaching duties specifically allotted to seven ministers. Because so many of the region's older ministers had died between 1834 and 1835, largely from typhoid fever, the mantle of movement fell to their younger colleagues, whose ages ranged from twenty-nine to forty. Their openness to new methods, in line with a new theology, helped to standardize the protracted meeting as a fixture of their associational religious life. More than this, their success in the meetings, measured in terms of

converts added to the church, helped to popularize protracted meetings first across the southern and western reaches, then in the northern Bluegrass.[33]

As the popularity and success of the protracted meetings spread across the state, the Baptists proved willing to adapt the Methodist pattern into their own tradition. Meetings, such as the one held outside Glasgow in 1837, often incorporated an anxious seat for those congregants who felt anxiety for the state of their souls. The protracted meetings extended over two to four weeks, depending on the indications of fervency, and were often described as emotionally moving experiences. They welcomed weeping, but conspicuously absent were the gyrating, falling, and jerking physical expressions associated with exorbitant Methodist revivalism. Protracted meetings drew hundreds of converts into the Baptist movement. In one instance, the sixty-eight converts produced at an 1837 Shepherdsville meeting were all baptized and then constituted into a new church on the final day of that revival. But despite Baptist efforts, converts from the protracted meetings did not always join the Baptist churches. More often than not, preachers either baptized the new believers or saw many of them join nearby Methodist and Presbyterian churches. This likely occurred because the meetings became interdenominational gatherings and often moved from place to place over the several weeks of their duration. An 1840 meeting that began in a Presbyterian church outside Louisville had to relocate to a Baptist church when the crowds grew too large. A few months later, a hundred miles away in Burkesville, organizers held their two-week meeting at the courthouse because they lacked sufficiently large meeting houses. Of the twenty-five to thirty converts in that meeting, eight joined the Baptists, twelve affiliated with the Cumberland Presbyterians, and the rest had not decided when the preacher reported the revival to the state Baptist newspaper.[34]

By late 1837, Kentucky Baptists reveled in the new wave of revival that seemed to engulf the entire state, and which brought in converts by the hundreds. The reports of the revivals, however, indicated that the movement's leaders were tracking not just the numbers, but the social status of the new believers. Reporting the almost forty conversions in a nearby protracted meeting, lay-man W. R. McFerron noted, "Most of them I believe were heads of families and of the most respectable class of our citizens." Likewise, preacher Thomas J. Fisher announced the success of his meeting, observing, "There were about twelve colored persons, all the rest were influential, and some the most wealthy persons in the county." Another letter, from an eyewitness of Fisher's revival, pointedly noted that the converts "were the very flower of society, embracing

the oldest and most influential citizens." Later in the missive he called them the "substantial and respectable class." Four years later, Rice Maxey, himself a prominent lawyer in Albany, reported that the courthouse revival in his home town yielded over twenty converts, and "amongst them were some of our very best and most influential citizens." The appreciation of social success even extended to the "respectable" of all ages. The converts at the 1841 meeting in Lawrenceburg were "all young people from the best families."[35]

This emphasis on respectable converts reflected a subtle shift in the religious identity of Baptists and their relationship to what historian Richard L. Bushman labels "the refinement of America." This study accepts Bushman's definition of refined religion as tasteful, ornamented, polite, and appealing to the cultivated. While they acknowledged that the proverbial fields of humanity were ripe for harvest, the Baptists, like many other groups during the 1830s, expressed evident satisfaction in drawing in those who had proven successful in worldly ventures. New infusions of wealth into the church encouraged a heightened sense of decorousness in the once spartan Baptist meeting houses. Some changes reflected only interest in cosmetic refurbishment, as when the Mayslick church members desired to stain or paint their previously unfinished pews and to "furnish a suitable carpet for the pulpit." The Mount Zion Baptist Church, likewise, voted to make their meeting house as "comfortable" as they could. One of the boldest statements of the Baptist search for refinement involved the construction of the church at Georgetown in 1842. When completed, the new meeting house ran seventy-five feet in length and forty-five feet in width. It contained seventy pews on the lower floor and a three-sided gallery. The exterior of the church had a Grecian facade with four large, white pillars. Within a year of the new building's dedication, the church members would add a fifty-foot steeple to accommodate a bell and a clock. Such imposing edifices might have startled early preachers like William Hickman who traveled the state preaching in forts, barns, and private homes.[36]

The lurching Baptist drive toward refinement also deeply affected the movement's understanding and expectations of their ministers. In the early national period, the few Baptists calling for full-time, salaried ministers were hooted down by republican fears of corruption. Bi-vocationalism, critics said, had kept the movement free of despotism. Working a trade had kept the preachers independent of their congregation and, at the same time, helped them maintain an understanding of their hearers through their work life. However, many wanted a professional ministry supported solely by the congregation. Even

before the 1830s, some Baptists saw in the New Testament an admonition to pay their pastors. In 1825, the Goshen Association advised its churches to follow the apostle Paul's words in I Corinthians 9:14, that "they which preach the gospel should live of the gospel" in the same way that Jewish priests had lived on sacrifices brought to the temple. Advocates of professionalization held high Paul's words as their banner. By the late 1830s, the choir of voices crying out for professionalization of the Baptist clergy grew to a swell.[37]

After the Kentucky Baptist Convention failed in 1836, some of the original organizers re-grouped in 1837 and established the General Association of Baptists in Kentucky, with a bolder, more forthright platform that included ministerial support. In their initial meeting, the fifty-seven delegates from around the state (including thirty-six lay members) resolved "that one of the primary objects" of their association would be "to effect this important measure upon the part of the churches." Likewise, in their circular letter to the churches, they condemned Baptists who were "cradled in affluence and munificently blessed with every temporal good," and who had "starved into exile many of the most useful ministers." Interestingly, they also blasted the numerous bi-vocational ministers who encouraged such faithlessness. "Unwilling to trust the Lord and their brethren for a support, or too ambitious of wealth to be content with a bare competence," the association asserted, "these men usually devote a part of one day in seven to the work of the ministry, employing the remainder of their time in the field, in the school house, on the shop-board, or in some other way, to amass in abundance, the glittering dust of earth." W. C. Buck, writing the Long Run Association's circular letter in 1838, labeled the lack of professional ministers "our great denominational error, and the fruitful cause of all our distresses." Noting that "other denominations have been crowding their preachers upon us," he chided his fellow Baptists, saying, "We neglect to employ, as we should do, the very instrumentality . . . which God has ordained to build up and perpetuate his church." In the decade following these pronouncements, ten other Baptist associations came out in favor of professionalization.[38]

With the drive for professional efficiency came a new appetite for an educated ministry. Part of the movement's early appeal had been the vernacular preaching of unlearned men. Kentucky Baptists, like many other Christians and Americans in general, saw virtue in the common touch. As pietists, they also placed supreme value upon the preacher's conduct rather than his fluency in theological nuance. By the late 1820s, however, Alexander Campbell's subtle

alterations of Baptist theological basics challenged the capacities of many of the unschooled preachers. Walter Warder, for example, received little education when he was young. After he began preaching at the age of twenty-two, his mentors included some of the best-known ministers in the state. With little other than this practical training, he accepted the pastorate of the Mayslick Church in 1814. When he met Campbell ten years later, the reformer's ideas challenged the uneducated preacher, and Warder asked his church to relieve him of his pastoral duties because he had "some difficulties of the mind." He was willing to continue as a teacher, but he doubted his role as pastor. To lawyer-preacher Silas Mercer Noel, ever an opponent of Campbell's nuanced innovations, ministerial training seemed the best way to prevent institutional rot from within. With endowments from wealthy laymen and support from like-minded preachers, Noel arranged the formation of a Baptist college to be located in Georgetown.[39]

Located along the thoroughfare connecting Lexington to Cincinnati, and as the home to a great many Baptists, Georgetown offered a propitious venue for the first Baptist college west of the Alleghenies. However, a decade of ideological division, amorphous mission statements, and Baptist skepticism in the effort nearly doomed the college. While Silas Noel saw benefits in ministerial education, he also believed in the efficacy of the education reform movement generally. While working to establish Georgetown College, Noel also led the movement for free public education in Kentucky. To succeed, the college needed not only the support of interested Baptist clergy and laity, but the assistance of the citizens of Georgetown. To secure this support, college advocates advertised the benefits of higher education generally and Christian education broadly. Thus, by the time the school enrolled its first students in 1830, its curriculum was more literary than theological. Complicating the school's mission further was the fact that just as the Baptist churches and associations divided in the early 1830s over Campbell's Reformation, so too did Georgetown's board of trustees. Because of this split, the college had no president from 1832 to 1836. Further, a few of the college's trustees in the 1830s also allied with the small Baptist "anti-mission" movement and were suspicious of extra-ecclesiastical institutions—like colleges. Conflict within the campus community filled the county courthouse with lawsuits between the bitter trustees and the college's administration. Not surprisingly, the majority of Kentucky's Baptists doubted whether the college truly represented their interests and they held back their support. In 1837, a new college president tried to emphasize the Baptist identity

of the school. In response, the college's mathematics professor lured five out at every six Georgetown students to a new Reformationist school nearby. Had that Reformation college not relocated to Harrodsburg in 1839, Georgetown likely would have folded.[40]

The eventual success of Georgetown College depended not only on the absence of their rival, but the approval and financial support of the state's Baptists, gained in large part by the tactics of the college's next two presidents, Rockwood Giddings and Howard Malcom. Giddings, a twenty-six year old New Hampshire native and recent migrant to Kentucky, persuaded the Primitivist trustees to surrender their seats, but his broader contribution lay in traveling the state and persuading Baptists of the importance of an educated ministry. After his unexpected death in 1839, Giddings was replaced with Philadelphian Howard Malcom. For ten years, Malcom continued his

Esteria Butler Farnam, *Georgetown College 1848*. The church with the highest spire and Grecian façade is the refined structure that Georgetown Baptist Church built in 1842. Oil on panel, 22¼" x 29⅓". Courtesy of Georgetown College, Fine Art Galleries, 2000.70.

predecessor's course, fleshing out the idea that piety and intellect need not oppose one another. He advertised Georgetown as a college where moral influence pervaded the curriculum. Even so, Malcom noted to potential benefactors that the school's goals included general education as well as theology, and that training future school masters was as much a necessity as creating a learned ministry. Malcom's direction for the school matched the priorities of other antebellum Baptist colleges in the nation. The graduates of these Baptist colleges were as likely to take up law as they were the ministry. Slightly less numerous were those who pursued medicine or teaching.[41]

Kentucky Baptists gradually accepted the broad priorities of Giddings and Malcom and saw their college as conducive for educating ministers and other professionals, as necessary for the movement to keep pace with the age of progress, and even as an aid to national progress. The college presidents recognized the need to maintain denominational support, and toured the state's association meetings to keep channels of dialogue open. Visits to associational meetings offered the most efficient means of addressing church leaders, including both laity and clergy. Giddings's visit to the Bethel Association in 1839 prompted it to dissolve its own Bethel Education Society and to donate its funds to Georgetown's endowment. The association also called on the local churches to recommend their licentiates to the college. In a similar statement of support from the Franklin Association, church leaders recognized the college's broad mission, asserting that "all who love Baptist doctrines, and desire the spread of intelligence and sound learning" should support it. Baptists in the northern Bracken Association, not wishing there to be "any shadow of ground for reproaching us as not being a reading people," resolved that "as Americans we regard such institutions as of the highest importance to our national welfare." They added, "As Baptists, we would cherish this institution . . . that our young ministers may there acquire such a measure of intellectual cultivation as may fit them, under God, for the great exigencies of the times."[42]

Both the institutional mission of the Baptists' college and the tone of their approval signaled the movement's accommodation to social expectations, their broader quest for institutional refinement, and their reevaluation of the ministry. Few expressions of this negotiated identity capture the extent of the change as fully as the Middle District Association's 1842 advisory letter to its churches. This northern association's lengthy message focused solely on ministerial education. In establishing the grounds for their argument, the association disclosed their altered conception of the minister's status within

the church. Where formerly Baptists took pride in their preacher's role as first among equals, here they noted the minister's duties as "more important and responsible than any other that has been committed to the hands of men . . . . No other known to men can be compared with it." They saw the ministry as elevated, a position "awful and important," and even "the most difficult work in which man was ever called to engage." They posited, "As a denomination, we have ever been accustomed to look . . . for the signs of personal piety in those who have been candidates for the ministerial office." Yet that piety, as important as it was, was incomplete without a "most vigorous and cultivated" intellect. Churches, the association recommended, should not only consider a candidate's zeal, but ensure "that he is possessed of intelligence suited to the performance" of such a high calling. The association gave four reasons for the importance of ministerial education. The first, and the only reason that related to scriptural mandate, was that a pastor should "be apt to teach." Second, though the Bible contained obvious fundamental truths, "We must not deny, that in the sacred writings there are many obscurities." Adequate and successful elucidation of these obscurities, the Baptists contended, required not only the revealing spirit of Christ, but education. Third, they asserted that the "most enlightened ministers" were "generally the most humble," and the most likely to avoid temptations. Lastly, the need for an educated ministry was demanded by "the general progress of society to a higher state of intellectual culture." With the ever-widening wave of publication, the pervasive "spirit of inquiry," and the new and cheaper sources of information satiating the thirst for knowledge, an educated ministry would "attract public attention" and "inspire the community with confidence in its ability to feed their minds." After presenting these revelatory arguments, the Baptists specified their intent. Because many ministers were "called when young, and from among those who are neither wealthy nor well-educated," they urged churches to provide for the licentiate's education so that he would not fall into the bi-vocational rut and lack in "usefulness."[43]

The increased support and demand for an educated, professionalized ministry and the adoption of protracted meetings between 1835 and 1845 showed a self-renovated religious movement. Instead of emphasizing the past, Baptists now focused on the future by evaluating their relationship to the present. But a small minority of Baptists, both clergy and laity, denounced the reappraisal as simply a rejection of biblical Christianity and their own noble Baptist heritage. These Primitivists focused their protest on the innovative, extra-local mission

organizations, giving them the sobriquet "anti-mission Baptists." While some Baptists whose staunch Calvinism disinclined them to preach repentance were truly against missions, most opposed the extra-biblical (or in their words, unscriptural) innovations. In Kentucky, such innovations gained widespread acceptance in the late 1830s and 1840s. The bold creation in 1837 of the General Association, seemingly founded upon these new measures, pushed the Primitivists further to the movement's margins. For the Primitivists, the Baptists' willingness to participate in and institutionalize Sabbath schools, temperance and benevolence efforts derived largely from faddishness. More importantly, it demonstrated to the Primativists an irreparable inner corruption within the Baptist movement. With few options, the Primitivists resolved to separate themselves from their reprobate cohorts.[44]

Coinciding with the growing swell of Primitivist discontent, some "mainstream" Baptists grew skeptical of protracted meetings. For some, the practice went stale through overuse or seemed to overshadow regularly scheduled church activities, such as the weekly gathering for prayer. One association condemned the "fearful wrecklessness [sic]" that churches used in holding too many useless protracted meetings. This association feared that such meetings stoked spiritual fires for the sake of stoking. It warned that the church would "be quite sure to decline soon after the meeting closes." Other critics condemned the "managed" nature of the meetings. The coopted Methodist practice seemed too much method and too little meaning. "The effort was nothing but *mere* effort," wrote one opponent. "The excitement is no sooner over . . . than the church falls into a state of collapse." Following this criticism, some Kentucky Baptists began moderating their usage of protracted meetings. The Ten Mile Association, after years of coordinating meetings and seeing little benefit, ceased the habit in 1851. However, many Baptist churches continued the practice with regularity because it helped win converts.[45]

For Primitivists, any mainstream dissatisfaction with protracted meetings only bolstered their claims and amplified their broad antipathy to innovation. Some Primitivist protests blended Jacksonian rhetoric with antipapalism to damn the new, emboldened General Association. When John L. Waller, the Baptist newspaper editor in Louisville, traveled the rural byways, he heard first-hand the Primitivist stories of the General Association "monster—'the beast'—a priestly contrivance—a money institution—a machine of discord and destruction to the churches—a sink of heterodoxy—a device of the devil—a new fangled concern, etc." When the Sulpher Fork

Association split over innovation in 1840, the Primitivist minority lambasted "modern Theological schools . . . missionary societies . . . Bible, Tract, and Sunday School societies . . . regular bred revival preachers, with all their apparatus for convert-making, Protracted (or rather *distracted*) meetings, Anxious Benches, &c.," as "the abominations of the great mother of harlots." Controversy between Primitivists and innovators within a church could grow just as malevolent. In one such division, each faction claimed possession of the church's meeting house. To force out the innovators, some of the Primitivists put primer on the church pews to stain their opponents' clothes when they held their meeting. But such bitter disputes over innovation came to an end by the mid-1840s as the Primitivist minority—about 10 percent of all Kentucky Baptists—separated to form their own churches and associations. The "modernist" mainstream saw the division as beneficial, and John Waller's comments upon the Primitivist exodus suggest there was little love lost. "I am happy to say that the number of these is rapidly diminishing," the editor wrote. "They are weights upon our prosperity. They are as a dead tied to a living man; their putrescence is painfully nauseating and unhealthy; they may cause sickness and death to a live person. Their own body will soon be consumed by corruption and rottenness."[46]

While the Baptist movement would seldom be free of controversies and schisms, once the Primitivist fire-brands had purged themselves from those in the culturally conscious mainstream, the movement could devote itself to ever-increasing professionalism, bureaucratization, and efficiency. Certainly, these developments took hold gradually and in patchwork fashion, given the ever-present Baptist commitment to localism. Moreover, not all innovations caught on quickly or easily. "This is an age of progress, but all progress is not improvement," cried "Vido," an anonymous Baptist commentator in 1856. Acceptance of innovation in the late 1830s had opened the floodgate for varieties of new measures and practices. Churches and associations, in their freedom, explored the boundaries of acceptable practice, and each experiment created a reactive worry that the change was too great. In response to "Vido's" concern, even S. H. Ford, the voice of urbane Kentucky Baptists, observed the "general wakening up among Baptists, in regard to our conformity to and imitation of other denominations," as well as the "deep-felt desire to return to the simplicity of our forefathers." The tension between future and past affected the movement to varying degrees throughout the nineteenth century. The significance of the tension that flavored the Baptist movement after 1845 was captured in

the opening sentence of the Concord Association's 1857 circular letter. "Permit us," they enjoined, "in this age of progress and development of mind, to direct you to the importance of always adhering to the Bible as the only true and legitimate test in all matters of faith and practice."[47] In the space of twenty years, the Baptists weathered two potentially devastating schisms, renovated their Calvinism, elevated the status of their clergy, and reconceived the role of education, all while (and partly because they were) engaging in break-neck competition with the Methodist juggernaut. These innovations revised the Baptist image, but not the Baptist impulse. Indeed, the democratic spirit and the fluid institutional structure at the core of the Baptist impulse helped the movement weather these early nineteenth-century storms and helped Baptists secure their status among the most popular of American religious movements of the age.

5

Sisters, Friends, and Proprietors: Women and Baptist Identity

When Mary Beckley Bristow sat down in August 1857 near Covington, Kentucky, to compile and transcribe many of her compositions and letters into one volume, she chose to include an untitled poem that began, "Oh tell me—What is Truth?" Her poetic question did not represent a sentimentalist's epistemological query, but the sorrowful quandary of a devout Baptist. She had written the poem just after a church meeting in which she had heard two of her favorite Baptist preachers proclaiming doctrines from the pulpit that she viewed as unorthodox. Her doleful poem continued,

> *I on the waves am tost [sic]*
> *So many errors are afloat*
> *I fear the truth is lost.*[1]

Mary Bristow's fears certainly reflected those of many antebellum Baptists in Kentucky, given the factionalism that seemed to pervade the movement.

But her question of truth also shows the perils of deciphering truth among the democratic Baptists, and the fact that Baptist women were not marginalized consumers of religion, but active producers of the movement's identity. Concluding her poetic catharsis affirmatively, she asserted that her faith was not tied to any clerical interpretations.

> Poor simple soul, can truth be lost
> Though error's waves roll high
> They lift themselves awhile and foam
> Then roll away and die.
> But Truth shall live through endless years
> Forever still the same
> It is immortal and it bears
> The Savior's glorious name.

Reflecting upon her poem after she transcribed it into her journal, Bristow noted that at the time of its composition she "had not then learned a very important lesson, that is, not to trust too much in man, whose breath is in his nostrils."[2] Beyond this single poem, Mary Bristow's diary and letters point to the ways she and other Baptist women found in their churches comfort, belonging, a platform for self-expression, and a source of frustration. Few women held leadership positions, such as preacher or deacon, among seventeenth-century English Baptists, and fewer still in colonial America. Indeed, the sweeping majority of women who filled the Baptist churches left little evidence that they sought more than lay status. However, the fluid structure of the Baptist movement and its democratic localism—that is, the Baptist impulse—provided them opportunities to influence the direction of the movement. Far from seeing themselves as "strangers and pilgrims" among the faithful, Baptist women seem to have embraced and taken advantage of their position as sisters in Christ, friends of the church, and proprietors of Baptist identity.[3]

The prominent presence of women in Baptist churches was a critical part of the tremendous numerical growth of the Baptist movement in the early nineteenth century, and can be seen as a paradox. It seems obvious that a religious movement that often restricted or rejected the involvement of the majority of its membership would not prosper. Indeed, it should not find the foundation of its growth among a class it oppresses. Official leadership positions such as

pastor, deacon, moderator, clerk, and associational delegate were limited to white men in the vast majority of white-controlled churches. The resolution to this apparent paradox is complex, but the answer runs throughout the democratic current of the movement and the theological distinctions that upheld the institutional structures: that women found meaning in their lives as Baptists, despite the restrictions and limitations. This held true even when other, sometimes more "liberating," religious alternatives were available. When examined in total, the depth of their faith was demonstrated in the intense fervor of their faith expressions, their zeal in introducing their faith to others, their support of church functions and leadership, and in their willing activity where doors were open and their pursuit of opportunity where doors seemed closed.

An often-analyzed truism of American religious history is that there were many more women than men in America's Christian churches. That fact, and the connection between women and religion, has led one historian to claim that "women's history *is* American religious history."[4] Membership rates for women in Kentucky during the early republic and antebellum years mirrored the national pattern. In her study of Kentucky Baptist women, Blair A. Pogue notes that only four of the thirty-two churches she examined had a male majority—and those four were slim majorities.[5] During the 1860 meeting of the Goshen Association in west-central Kentucky, many of the thirty affiliated churches categorized their membership by race and sex. All of the churches (thirteen) that provided the number of white women in their membership had a female majority.[6] This pattern held true throughout the period. In the 1820s, pastor John Taylor, having seen and preached in most of the western Baptist churches, echoed George Whitefield's claim that "whoever goes to heaven will see seven women for one man." As late as the 1850s, most churches resembled the one at Stamping Ground which reported having 203 women and 142 men among their membership in 1859.[7]

The presence of so many women in the democratic Baptist churches logically should correlate to their use of power in church affairs. Morgan Edwards pointed this out after he toured the Baptist churches of New England and the Middle Colonies in the 1760s. "Women," he noted, "who are always the most numerous, have in their power any time to decide everything against the men."[8] Nevertheless, on the whole, Baptist women accepted the patriarchal leadership patterns of the church. Of course, the decentralized nature of early Baptist life brought deviation. The practice of ordaining women as preachers or deacons fluctuated by time, place, and theology.

Seventeenth-century English Baptists, for instance, tended to approve of female deacons and only occasionally ordained women preachers. This trend in England diminished over time to statistical insignificance by the mid-nineteenth century. In America, meanwhile, Regular Baptists in the northern and mid-Atlantic states tended to restrict women's roles, even debating if they had the right to vote in church affairs. In the South, the predominant New Light Separate Baptists offered more opportunities for female ordination, especially as deacons. As the Regular and Separate branches of the larger movement merged in the late eighteenth-century South, the interests of unity gradually drowned out the issue of female ordination to any position. Thus, the practice largely faded away in the nineteenth century.[9]

Despite the widespread rejection of female preachers and deacons among early Kentucky Baptists, women still enjoyed voting rights in business sessions—though even this idea came under scrutiny at times. One of the earliest churches in the territory had to clarify its position on members' rights four years after being constituted. In 1788, the Providence church addressed the query "whether all members of the church male and female have a privilege to speak to any subject that comes before the church, petition for relief of any grievance or difficulty." The church agreed that all members held these rights equally.[10] The freedom to offer opinion and vote on debated topics, the ability to petition the church for redress of grievance, the right to give testimony in ecclesiastical trials, all provided women opportunities they seldom, if ever, enjoyed in secular society. But the opportunities also carried responsibilities, and women were brought before the church for discipline as well.

Though Baptist women in early Kentucky influenced the churches' activities through their voices and votes in the business and discipline meetings, to focus only on these monthly events would not give a full picture of the female influence, particularly given the patriarchal timbre of those gatherings. In the nineteenth century, when the position of pastoral leadership and the diaconate had been largely denied to Baptist women, they expressed their faith in less regulated forums, such as in their conversion narratives, at prayer meetings, in giving impromptu feedback to leadership, and in their family.

The first voice a Baptist woman had in the church came as she related her conversion experience to the membership. Men and women alike had to proffer the story of their conversion to gain entrance to church membership and baptism. Most converts approached the task hesitantly because of the personal subject matter, the general fear of public speaking, and the scrutiny

from the members. Many members of the church at Bryant's Station asked to hear Mary Bristow's experience at an informal religious meeting in 1836. She recalled, "It was a miserable day for me." She was willing, but her nervousness and ineloquence embarrassed her. Mistaking the congregation's response as criticism, Bristow wrote that she was "perfectly astonished to see the brethren and Sisters shedding tears," and concluded, "They either thought me a hypocrite or a poor deceived creature." Understandably, congregational weeping often accompanied the convert's narrative in the same way it occurred during a pastor's sermon. In many respects, narratives *were* powerful sermons that related spiritual concepts to a congregation and showed how they were applied in an intensely personal way. Since historically, more women joined the evangelical churches than men, the conversion narrative became the religious ritual most open to female influence in its tone and structure. Such public pronouncements of faith also gave women a chance to see the effect of their words on others. Thus, relating their conversion narrative gave women opportunity to experience and share the preacher's sensation in expounding upon the power of God and the ecstasy of his grace. Betsy Collier and Cynthia Coulman spoke as boldly as experienced preachers when they related their conversions for the Corn Creek church in 1822. Unlike Mary Bristow, who said her "tongue clove to the roof of [her] mouth," Collier and Coulman spoke so loudly "as to be heard all over the house." John Taylor recollected that the two women "gave such evidence that God was in them in truth that joyful tears flowed profusely from the old disciples of Christ." A convert's narrative became a landmark of her life and memorable enough to be recorded or recalled much later. It could even be used as a tool of religious instruction. The evening after Mary Bristow gave her experience on that "miserable day," her elderly aunt revived her spirits by recounting her own conversion as a child in colonial Virginia. As if remembering a great sermon, Mary later noted, "Nothing I had ever heard had so great an effect on my mind. My faith was greatly increased; my hope was brightened."[11]

While the relation of the conversion experience was perhaps the least regulated form of religious expression in the Baptist church meeting, in the prayer meeting women and men enjoyed similar opportunities to express freely and regularly their religious ideas, opinions, and experiences. Prayer meetings, by nature, were amorphous. They were sometimes instigated by the church membership as a whole and other times begun by a few members in one part of the church's territory. Participants saw the prayer meetings more as social

meetings of the saved than as formal gatherings of the body of Christ. Thus, the members assembled on varying days of the week depending on the local need. The popularity of such gatherings seems to have coincided with periods of religious revival. In some cases, given the high level of religious feeling generated by these worshipful gatherings, preachers credited the prayer meetings with starting the revival. A typical meeting could include scripture readings, singing of hymns, readings from popular religious authors (printed sermons or commentaries), and prayer. It might also involve exhortations and brief homilies delivered by laity. In substance, the exhortation was indistinguishable from a preacher's sermon, but the difference would have been understood by the Baptists, who cherished the right of the congregation to approve both ordination and the right to preach. In a social prayer meeting, the participants might also discuss the meaning of a passage of scripture. Lay involvement among men and women in the prayer meetings provided a unique bonding experience as well. Preacher Wilson Thompson treasured such meetings when he was a layman, observing, "I have ever been as much edified by the exercises of the members as by any sermons I ever heard." Nineteenth-century Kentucky Baptist preacher and historian J. H. Spencer saw manifold benefits in the meetings. In his opinion, they provided people an opportunity to speak and promoted piety in regions with few ministers. As popular and beneficial as social prayer meetings might have been, with their inherent fluidity, they easily disbanded and could not offer laywomen and laymen a consistent arena for religious self-expression.[12]

Whereas the conversion-relation ceremony enabled women to influence the meaning of religious experience, and the prayer meeting afforded similar opportunities in a less institutional format, one underappreciated area of influence was the Baptist woman's personal and private interactions with church leadership. In the congregationally centered Baptist churches, approval or disapproval of a pastor, his preaching, and his theology took on greater significance than it would in a more hierarchical denomination. In this regard the female members of a church, who often formed its majority, were a significant constituency and their support or criticism could affect a preacher's ministry. The memoirs of widely traveled preacher John Taylor, which were first published in 1823, are replete with references to the many women he knew. Notably, he not only recalled those women who supported him and the faith, but those who challenged him as well. One of those who

supported him was Elizabeth Arnold. Taylor's farm adjoined the Arnolds' land near the Clear Creek church, and the preacher was a close friend of the Arnold family.[13] Taylor described Elizabeth as having a "masculine fortitude," a "great aptitude to converse on things of religion," and a "zeal for the blessed cause." For the preacher, this Baptist "mother in Israel" represented the ideal which other women should strive to imitate. He even compared Arnold to the Hebrew prophetess Deborah, the only female leader mentioned in the Old Testament book of Judges. For Elizabeth Arnold, the preacher was a colleague in the Christian ministry. Elizabeth and her husband John had opened their home to Taylor's preaching appointments, and she continued to do so after her husband died. Following one such meeting, the elderly widow's son Thomas came forward to relate his conversion to those assembled in the house. The unexpected conversion elated the widow Arnold and, as the preacher recalled, she "reached out her hand" to him, "exclaiming loud enough to be heard all over the house, 'O Brother Taylor, God has answered our prayers.'" Though the widow and the preacher attributed Thomas Arnold's salvation to the grace of God, they also saw it as being facilitated through their cooperative efforts of prayer, preaching, and hospitality.[14]

Not all interactions between clergymen and congregant were as obviously supportive and collaborative. Some female members felt at liberty to offer their preachers pointed, though usually constructive, criticism. Another significant figure in John Taylor's career was Hannah Cave Graves, who, like Elizabeth Arnold, had a "warm attachment to the cause of religion," exhibited "much shrewdness of mind," and a "considerable understanding in the Scriptures." Beyond this, she was a perceptive "critic of preaching and a good judge of Christian experience." However, unlike the widow Arnold, Graves gained a reputation for her "blunt dealings with preachers," which, in Taylor's opinion, bordered on insulting God's specially called laborers. When Graves's long-time pastor refused to serve her church any longer, "She asked him if he was going to prove that he was only a hireling, seeing he fled when the wolf came and seemed not to care for the sheep." Taylor's basis for criticizing Sister Graves's candor came not from his expectations of her gender, but from his reading of David's song recorded in I Chronicles 16. David's admonition notes God's special relationship with Israel, with his anointed, and his prophets. In his memoir, John Taylor chastised Graves for seeming to violate this biblical and divine command to "do my prophet's no harm." Even so, Taylor recognized that Graves's

reproaches aimed to improve the ministers with whom she worked. After all, he recalled, she believed her accused hireling was "among the best of preachers."[15]

Critical evaluations of pastors from female church members suffused nineteenth-century Kentucky Baptist life. It pervaded the antebellum experiences of Mary Bristow just as it had Hannah Graves's in the early 1800s. Like Graves, Bristow was a strong supporter of her ministers and was free with her praise and criticism. One of the highlights of her religious calendar was the annual association meeting. She often suffered from debilitating health problems, but at association meetings, she said "I never give up when at meeting. Excitement always keeps me going." These gatherings not only allowed her social opportunities to see family and friends and to meet new friends, but also to hear the variety of preachers. As her letters indicate, she paid careful attention to who preached and what they said so that she could report it to those unable to attend. Bristow took particular satisfaction from the preaching at the 1844 Licking Association meeting, especially when her favorite preachers were in the stand. She took pleasure from the preaching of the elderly William Hume, who was her pastor and the minister who baptized her. She wrote to her aunt, "He preached better than I ever heard him. I was proud of my preacher." Likewise, she praised her friend Thomas P. Dudley's stint in the stand, writing, "It would be useless to tell you he preached well. He always does." Her evaluations focused not only on style but on the preachers' logic. Even though Wilson Thompson's Sunday sermon was one of the briefest she had ever heard, she commented, "In deep sound reasoning, making things so plain that anyone of common sense can understand them, he is ahead of any preacher."[16] Bristow did not always dispense compliments to the ministers she heard. On another occasion, she heard a sermon from an "old favorite" preacher and "watched him very closely." She noticed a change in him. He had "quit fighting arminians," but she did not "find fault in him for that," as she had "always thought he went farther than was profitable in his crusade against other denominations." Bristow declared in her diary that she had always felt that the satisfaction this minister took in his pugnacious efforts were not driven by "the religion or the spirit of our Lord Jesus Christ which is gentle and easy to be entreated."[17] Whether Baptist women showed praise and approbation or skepticism and condemnation, they demonstrated their concern over the message presented to them, both in terms of content, technique, and argument. As members of a democratic, congregational movement, they exhibited a proprietary interest in their faith that affected the nature and direction of the movement.

Since Baptist women rarely exerted influence from official positions of leadership, the institution most likely to see their direct impact was the family. Baptist wives and mothers propelled and directed the movement from their homes even before piety became popular in the cult of True Womanhood.[18] As was the case for women like Elizabeth Arnold, a Baptist woman's home *was* the church meeting place. This was particularly true in a church's formative stage, when members did not have the resources to construct a meeting house. But beyond the occasional meeting of the church in their homes, Baptist women took their faith seriously among their families. Since early Baptist churches received new converts into the fold at their monthly meeting, church records sometimes reveal patterns of household conversion. In one month, a church would record the conversion of a wife, then her husband would join the following month. Preacher Robert Kirtley, for instance, grew up in a Baptist family. His father, Jeremiah, was actively involved in the church and was licensed to preach when Robert was a teen. Nevertheless, Robert resisted any religious influence from his parents. When he was twenty-four, within five years of his marriage to Mary Thompson, his wife converted and joined the Bullittsburg church. One month later, the religious impressions of his youth and influences from his newly converted wife resulted in his conversion.[19] A church did not consider the conversion of a wife as a token of her husband's purity or piety, or as evidence of the efficacy of his alleged repentance. Men still had to stand before the church alone and submit to evaluation. In the midst of a revival at the Buck Run church in 1826, Thomas Casey's wife gave evidence of her conversion and the church accepted her. Shortly afterward, Thomas came before the church, but the members rejected him. They claimed he appeared to think too well of himself and his own goodness. This sent Casey into a brief depression wherein he ate and slept little. Only later, when he could "talk of the guilt of his sin and his just condemnation under the law," did the church allow him baptism and membership.[20]

A woman's influence in the home exceeded simply adding to the movement's membership. Some Baptist wives in early Kentucky also helped educate their preacher husbands. Though literacy was not necessary for ordination, in a biblically driven religious movement like the Baptists, the ability to read the Bible increased the depth of a preacher's religious knowledge and theological arguments. Susannah Cash and Sally Baker were critical figures in both the faith and education of their husbands. Susannah, herself a daughter of a Baptist preacher, did not convert until shortly after her 1783 marriage to Warren Cash.

His conversion followed immediately after hers in 1785. As was the case with other converts and those who felt the call to preach, Warren Cash expressed interest in learning to read. Susannah tutored him over the next few years; by the 1790s Warren had begun preaching, and was ordained in Shelby County in 1799.[21] Much farther south, in Barren County, John H. Baker married Sally Buford in 1804. John, the son of Baptist parents, had converted in 1784 at thirteen, but shortly afterward fell away from the religious duties expected of the pious. Sally Buford, meanwhile, came from a wealthy family and embraced Deism. Many years after they married, John grew troubled by his irreligion. He resolved to kill himself, but claimed that the grace of God prevented him. He told his wife about his rediscovered conviction and belief, and she converted as well. They both joined the church at Glasgow. Just as Warren Cash had, John found a new willingness to read after his conversion. His well-educated wife tutored him not only in Bible reading but in general literature as well. In 1821, John received ordination to the ministry.[22]

Beyond aiding conversions and educating preaching husbands, Baptist women in early Kentucky also served as sources and interpreters of theological truth for their family members. In this regard, women acted out their expected roles as moral guardians of the home, responsible republican mothers, and domestic apostles of the Baptist faith.[23] In 1849, W. C. Buck, editor of the *Baptist Banner and Western Pioneer*, reprinted an exhortation on the topic of a "Woman's Proper Sphere." The essay had been extracted from an address given by E. P. Rogers on "The Obligations and Duties of the Female Sex to Christianity." What Rogers had said to a Presbyterian audience at Washington Female Seminary in Georgia a few months previously, the Baptist editor thought fitting for his Kentucky readership. Rogers targeted those women "whose precious time is lavished only upon dress, and gaity, and fashionable visiting . . . whose conversation finds no higher or improving subject than the idle gossip of the day . . . whose reading is the miserable trash which is inundating every community . . . whose whole life seems to be an aimless, frivolous life." Rather, Rogers continued, the truly beautiful woman, worthy and noble, was she "whose refinement of thought and feeling, whose depth and richness of affection, and whose powerful influence on human hearts, are all consecrated to the cause of truth and holiness." Signs of this "powerful influence" from Baptist wives and mothers fill the biographies of many of early Kentucky's Baptist preachers and the conversion narratives of the brethren throughout the early nineteenth century.[24]

The "truth and holiness" of the Baptist way affected noted physician Daniel Drake, who grew up in Mayslick in the 1790s surrounded by Baptists. His parents and many of his extended family members belonged to the Mayslick church. In his memoirs, Drake admitted that while his parents were pious people, he tended to listen to and respect more highly the opinions of his Aunt Lydia and Uncle Cornelius Drake. Both, he said, were "staid & sober minded theologians—more deeply read in the Bible & theological works than Father & Mother." Using the gendered compliment of the nineteenth century, Drake noted that his Aunt Lydia had rather "a masculine cast of mind." His parents, aunt, and uncle spent a considerable amount of time together in their social life, and Drake said he "heard a great deal of religious, or at least, theological conversation" between them. Most of the themes of the conversations he heard dealt with a Calvinist Baptist's favorite topics of election, reprobation, predestination, and baptism. Young Drake respected the theology of his family members, male and female, more than that which he heard from ministers. He thought Baptist preachers often "lacked dignity & solemnity, and some of them now & then uttered very droll expressions in the pulpit." By Drake's own admission, the influence of Baptist family was undeniable. Being surrounded by Baptist conversation and debate "had given a cast of that kind to my own mind."[25]

Likewise, the Baptist women in Wilson Thompson's family affected his teen years and his sense of calling. His mother and aunt frequently discussed doctrine in the home. Their casual conversations about the line of accountability affected him for over a year. He heard them discussing that line, which Baptists saw as the time when a child crosses from innocent to culpable in God's eyes, and he determined that he would pursue as much vice as possible before crossing it. A few years later, when Thompson endured the frustrations and fears over his calling to the ministry, it was his aunt whom he turned to and trusted to give enlightenment. He feared his pastor as a stern man, but his aunt was a source of serenity for him. Her advice carried a divine impulsion for young Wilson, and she advised him, "Fight against the call no longer, for God intends you to go and preach His gospel, and you may as well yield at once, for He will not be disappointed."[26] Whether through their doctrinal advice, assurances of calling, or theological persuasion, Baptist women took their faith into their homes and blurred the boundaries of sacred and secular. By doing so, they propelled the Baptist movement forward on a much broader scale than could be accomplished institutionally.

Kentucky Baptist women in the early nineteenth century often saw their church as a source of refuge and protection from abuse, financial hardship, and even from the corrupting stain of sin that would infect themselves and the church. Most early church records from the period deal largely with disciplinary issues as the churches strove to pursue and maintain the purity of their fellowship. In this context, women were held accountable for their actions and held others accountable as well. At times, their protection ironically came while they were being accused. In 1831, for example, Parmelia Noe applied for a letter of dismissal from her church in Williamstown. Her letter would have proven her status as a member in good standing to any other Baptist church. But her fellow believers objected to issuing the letter because she had left her husband. Months later, Noe appeared before the church to defend herself and explain that "her husband was such that she could not live with him in any kind of satisfaction." In their reconsideration of the case, the church members understood her plight and made clear that while they could not condone a wife leaving her husband, they condemned such abusive relationships. Thus, they sided with Sister Noe and, by doing so, issued a lesson to all members and congregants on the church's standards for marital conduct.[27]

Protection provided by the church in the context of discipline could also extend to female slaves. The Stamping Ground church, for instance, agreed in the early 1800s that slavery was acceptable, but sexual immorality with slave women was not. In August 1801, Brother Wiley was accused by another male member of "improper conduct" with two slave women. In another episode, the church cited Daniel, a slave owned by Thomas Herndon, because Esther, owned by John Scott, accused him of "proposing to her to commit the sin of adultery." The church's stance remained consistently that the chastity of slave women should be protected. They also condemned specific abuse of slaves by church members. The Mayslick church cited Lucy Hughes for "barbarity to a female slave." After an investigation of Sister Hughes's conduct, the members found that the instance of barbarity was part of a larger pattern. They concluded that she was "given to the intemperate use of ardent spirits and unchristian conduct to her servants."[28] The significance of these decisions for the early nineteenth-century Baptist movement was that churches could offer a sort of haven for women, black and white, slave and free. Among the faithful, they would find respite from and redress for ill treatment. Behaviors sometimes accepted in society were not supposed to have a place among the people of God. Given the absence of protective services in secular society, the protective

nature of the church—as limited as it may have been—contrasted with a heart-less world.

Even the social realities of poverty that affected women came before the Baptist churches' attention. Though Baptists embraced the fundamental structure of the early American merchant economy, they also tried to implement the New Testament injunction to protect the social welfare of those who could not take care of themselves. In many church covenants, members agreed not "to live in the neglect of any known duty to God," their neighbor, or one another.[29] What actions individual members took on their own to seek the social welfare of their neighbors is more unclear than the churches' collective efforts, which were recorded in their minutes. Though occasionally male church members needed their church's help, more often it was women who found relief in the benevolence of their fellow Baptists. The church, however, typically granted such aid only in the short term. In the case of Sister Cornish, the Mount Pleasant church collected a one-time, free-will contribution in March 1821 to aid in her unrecorded necessity. Likewise, the Mayslick church agreed to supply the needs of one of their young members, Sister Polly, for a period of one month. Three months later, they also took up money for Sister Dothage, a poor widow, as "a maintenance for herself and family."[30] On other occasions, white church members volunteered to board black female members who were destitute of means or prospects. In June 1847, the Stamping Ground church determined to find a "place of safe keeping" for Dinah, "a deranged colored girl." In response, a white sister took her in and the church paid for the anticipated costs. By December, though, the situation had changed, and the members voted to have two men "carry Sister Dinah to the poor house when the order is obtained from court."[31]

When women poured into the Baptist churches in the first third of the nineteenth century, many found relief in their churches, found meaning in their beliefs, and accepted the patriarchal structure of the institutions. However, the twin denominational crises of the 1830s and 1840s—Alexander Campbell's Reformation and the anti-institutional schism—reveal how deeply important the movement, its theology, and its direction were to both the women who embraced the new groups and those who fought to save the old one. One remarkable fact about these faith migrations is that the women who left the Baptists to become part of Campbell's new order or the Primitivist Baptists joined more restrictive congregations than they had known previously. The Reformation churches endorsed local autonomy, so practices varied, but in

general they denied women more faith expressions than the Baptists had. Most Reformation churches eschewed women deacons or preachers, but more importantly, they refused women the right to vote in congregational business meetings. Like some colonial Baptist churches, the typical church of Campbell's Reformation took literally Paul's admonition to the early church at Corinth to "let your women keep silence in the churches: for it is not permitted unto them to speak." For early followers of Campbell, the church was outside of a woman's sphere of activity, or at least her influence. Unlike the Primitivist Baptists, Reformers believed in female education and constructed schools for that purpose. But their goal was to prepare young female Reformers for their rightful mission: encouraging the moral government of the world from the domestic circle. A women's academy established for any other reason, in their opinion, promoted something unnatural, and any school not based on Christianity was, in Campbell's mind, "a wild freak of uncultivated reason."[32]

Another restrictive aspect of the Reformers and Primitivist Baptists was their rejection of missionary and benevolence organizations, a restriction that grew out of their ultra-localism. Baptist localism colored the movement's identity, but part of the attraction of the Reformation and the Primitivist movement arose from the increasing Baptist acceptance of extra-local mission enterprises and benevolence activities. Campbell made his boldest and earliest denunciation of this Baptist acceptance in 1823, on the cusp of gaining popularity in Kentucky. He noted that the earliest Christian churches "were not fractured into missionary societies, Bible societies, education societies; nor did they dream of organizing such in the world." On the contrary, these entities, he said, were mere "hobbies of modern times." When the Primitivist Baptist schism occurred in the Sulpher Fork Association meeting of 1840, the Primitivist minority seemed to echo Campbell's condemnation from years before. They argued in a circular letter that "modern Theological schools set up for the purpose of qualifying men to preach; Missionary societies, spreading a spurious Gospel; Bible, Tract, and Sunday School Societies," and other modern innovations were "the abominations of the great mother of harlots"—a common Protestant reference the Catholic Church which they saw as corrupt and unfaithful.[33]

Such harsh denunciations of extra-ecclesiastical societies indicates that Reformationist and Primitivist women who participated in these organizations could expect to face corrective discipline from their church. As many historians have observed, the existence of these societies gave women throughout

early national America opportunities to engage society outside the domestic sphere. Women's historian Nancy Cott contends that womens' participation in benevolence associations was an extension of the Second Great Awakening and was part of the broad effort "to create an enduring and moral social order." Involvement in such groups "flowed naturally from church membership" and was a bond of womanhood. Likewise, Mary P. Ryan's work on the period demonstrates how this associative involvement came full circle in the Awakening. Such extra-domestic and extra-ecclesiastical activity could embolden women to bring the revival to their neighbors and extended families. It expanded their horizons and their faith.[34]

Yet when the restrictive Reformationist and Primitivist message spread through Kentucky's Baptist churches and the congregational separations began, women left in great numbers, forcing their churches to exclude them. When church members voted to exclude one of their own, according to the biblical rule of discipline, the violator had refused to "hear the church," or heed the church's condemnation of an action and repent. The rule Baptists and Reformers followed, from Matthew 18:15–17, stipulated that if the guilty member did not hear the church, "Let him be unto thee as an heathen man and a publican [tax collector]." Thus, if a church followed the biblical mandate, the exclusion was total. All Christian fellowship and privileges were cut off. In unavoidable social interactions, the excluded and "included" were not to be so familiar that the former might construe support from the latter.[35] Exclusion fractured not only church relationships but social ones as well. For a woman like Mary Bristow, an exclusion could ravage her social circle. In 1845, in her diary, Bristow criticized her own lack of interactions with non-Christians, or even non-Baptists. For that, she rebuked herself, saying, "It is a task for you to visit a neighbor unless they are a baptist and you are very soon weary of the company of near relations at times because they are not baptist." In a likely exaggeration, she added that she had "kept no other company for years."[36] Exclusion for joining a different religious sect would have decimated her social life. Of course, exclusions were *de jure* votes subsequent to a *de facto* separation by the dissenting member. Therefore, a woman who left a church for a different one without proper dismissal would have known and understood the cost, but would have chosen her fate purposefully.

Despite any social price they might pay, many women pursued and embraced these new restrictive religious groups. Blair Pogue's analysis of Baptist discipline in eight representative churches shows that, between 1780 and 1860,

21 percent of all women cited for their sins were charged with joining another denomination. Pogue notes that this percentage is actually a low estimate because many churches who cited members for joining the Reformers often recorded the offense in a non-specific way, such as "joining a society not in union with the church," or "joining a society in disorder." An analysis of the exclusions of five other churches demonstrates that 41 percent of all female exclusions were for the same. In stark contrast, only 7 percent of the men in these churches faced the charge of leaving the church without authorization in small numbers. In Pogue's study, only 3 percent of the total number of citations given to men were for leaving the church this way. These statistics spark interest for the disproportions of gender, but take on greater meaning given when they occurred and the denominations the women preferred.[37]

Between 1780 and 1860, most women excluded from the local Baptist churches for joining a different religious group left between 1830 and 1850, with some defections into the 1850s. The vast majority of them joined the Reformers and, to a lesser extent, the Primitivist Baptists. In the records of five representative Baptist churches between 1820 and 1860, at least 33 percent of the female defectors joined the Reformers. The percentage is likely higher since another 45 percent were cited more vaguely as joining a society not in order or fellowship. This 45 percent probably included some who joined the Reformers, as well as many others who affiliated with the Primitivists. The Methodists and Presbyterians were far less likely to inherit gain from the Baptists' loss. Each received less than 9 percent of the total. This small percentage might seem unexpected given the Methodist's historical reputation for allowing women more opportunities in class meetings to express their faith and shape their movement's identity. The Methodists, Presbyterians, and Baptists had established their own identities far before the middle of the nineteenth century. In contrast, the Reformers, Primitivists, and "typical" Baptists in the late 1820s could often only show differences of degree and shade. When these differences became clearer, many women chose the more restrictive groups. The exclusions of men, though fewer in number, match the same pattern. In the same decades, Methodists gained less than 5 percent of male defectors, while the Reformers received over 44 percent. Church records show over half the total left for churches not in fellowship or order.[38]

Masses of Baptist women left their churches during schisms. When a church's membership found itself significantly divided beyond reconciliation, each faction typically saw itself as the true legatees of the church's heritage. But

after this phase of contention passed, the factions typically resolved to dissolve their church and fashion two churches out of one—sometimes with both sharing the same meeting house. When the Providence church split in 1830 during the Reformation, women represented the vast majority of secessionists. Factionalism had brewed for some time in the church and, in August, a party of sixty-five members announced that they were "displeased with the rules and regulations" of the church and wished to withdraw. Of these sixty-five, forty-seven were women, including two free black women. The church members who stayed with their Baptist identity were able to keep the church afloat for another twenty years before it dissolved.[39] The Mayslick and Paris churches followed this pattern in the early 1830s on a larger scale, but their numbers were not broken down by sex. The Mayslick church reported having 685 members in 1829, but by the next summer had divided with almost 300 members following Campbell. Their entire association diminished as well. In 1829, the Bracken Association reported 2,303 Baptists among its affiliated churches. That number declined to 890 by 1831.[40] In a similar, but more devastating way, the Paris church divided in 1833, with over 400 members departing, leaving 48 Baptists.[41] In neither case were the hundreds who left reflected as exclusions in the church records. This pattern of formal schism repeated itself in the Primitivist separation that occurred largely in the 1840s. There, too, mass migrations were not included in the disciplinary record. Based on available statistics, it is reasonable to surmise that most of the defectors in the many mass migrations were women.[42]

Whether Baptist women separated from their churches in formal schisms or in isolation, many played influential roles in the conflict. During the factional tensions at the Mount Pleasant church in 1833, the members excluded Lucinda Deane and her husband Peter, as well as Polly Moseley, for breaking into the meeting house and inviting in a Reformation preacher. Later that year, Amanda Wilson, Judith Sallee, Edward Moseley, and his wife Lucy sued the church's trustees in a suit related to the ongoing Reformation factionalism. In December 1833, they all were excluded. In the church at Williamstown, Sister Landrum came before the church in January 1842 because she had attended "Campbellite meetings." She argued with the members and insisted that there was nothing sinful in merely attending meetings. The church refused to take any action against her. At the next monthly meeting, she *requested* exclusion. Her church had never dealt with such requests, so the members deferred the matter to give it thought. They convened the next month and denied that they

could honor such a request. In time, though, Sister Landrum forced the issues by joining the Reformers—for which she was excluded in May 1842.[43]

As many women as there were who fought the churches in the name of the Reformation, there were more who defended them and their traditional doctrines. Some Baptist women literally saved their churches from extinction in the midst of factional turmoil. In the late 1820s, the McCormack's church in Lincoln County had roughly fifty members on its rolls, but failed to send a representative to the 1830 South District Association meeting. After the association made an inquiry into the state of the church in 1832, the inquiry committee reported that almost everyone had "gone into the modern miscalled reformation," and that only five members remained. According to the committee, these stalwarts said they "intended to hold to the United Baptist doctrines and practices." The five hardy Baptists were Patsey McCormack, Elizabeth Jones, Nancy Alcorn, Susannah, and Syntha Kelly.[44] In another instance, at the Mount Pleasant church of Adair County in southern Kentucky, a group of women not only had to resist the Reformers but also the few remaining male members. A report on the church delivered to the Russell's Creek Association noted that after the formal Reformation schism, the three or four remaining male members "proposed to dissolve and attach themselves to sister Churches, which probably would have been the case had it not been, that some female members, MOTHERS IN ISRAEL, felt determined not to give up the *ship*, but still protract the war, fighting under the Banner of the Cross."[45]

When the factionalism had died down and after the revilers of extra-ecclesiastical benevolent effort left the larger Baptist movement, the majority who stayed behind pursued such societies and institutions with abandon. By the middle of the 1850s, almost every Kentucky Baptist association had resolved to promote Sunday school societies, Bible and tract societies, missionary efforts, temperance societies, and educational institutions. Each of these offered opportunities for Baptist women to extend their influence beyond the home and the church. Even within the church, women seemed to take on more independent, yet still supportive roles. The Mayslick church, for example, appointed a committee of four women in 1853 to solicit donations for the purchase of new communion trays. In previous decades, this task might have been assigned to the deacons. Such a collection also shows the prosperity of the church. The women's collection was one of many collections for a variety of causes as well as improving the meeting house and its accouterments. A more independent body of women connected with the church at Paris used

its fund-raising abilities to support and influence the church. Fashioning themselves as a sewing circle, they had raised enough money in 1856 to purchase a house to use as a parsonage for their pastor. In 1857, they purchased a melodeon, or an organ, for the church. In 1860, when the church decided to sell the parsonage, it appointed two men to "confer with the ladies of the sewing circle in relation to the proceeds of the sale of the parsonage and ascertain if they are willing for it to be appropriated toward building a new church edifice." These actions of the church and the group of women show a more affluent membership increasingly interested in the refinement of the church, a group of women committed to asserting their role in the church's well-being, and a church receptive of such influence for the sake of prosperity.[46]

The expectations of and the message sent to antebellum Baptist women in Kentucky appear to be two-fold and almost ambiguous. The Baptist ethic held that, in the home and church, women reigned as pious and gentle moral guardians and faithful supporters of the patriarchal leadership. Their role in the church was integral, but secondary to the increasingly professionalized ministry. However, in dealing with enemies of the Baptist movement, they were expected to fight as fierce warriors of the faith. The message tended to fuse together the archetypal Old Testament figures of Ruth and Jael. The character of Ruth exhibited a "whither thou goest, I will go" brand of faithfulness. Ruth also held a position of status in the genealogies of David and Jesus. As an archetype, Ruth was the maternal preserver of the faith. In contrast, Jael defended the armies of Israel by hammering a tent nail through the brain of Sisera, the Canaanite general. Her heroism, according to the author of the book of Judges, was God's means of subduing Israel's enemies. By her bravery, "the children of Israel prospered."[47] Baptist women were to exhibit Ruth's faithful submission within ecclesiastical and domestic circles, then fight Jael's good fight against Baptist foes within and without those circles.

While both sides of this ethic came through in Baptist literature, some male-dominated forums plainly reinforced the cult of True Womanhood, or the "Ruth" side of Baptist expectations. Denominational periodicals and magazines flowed from religious presses as part of the antebellum print revolution, and they found a market in the increasingly prosperous Baptist homes. In Kentucky, the *Baptist Banner and Western Pioneer* was the primary resource for printed denominational thought. The newspaper's editor, John L. Waller, sometimes commented personally on gender issues, but also included related clippings from other papers. From the *National Preacher*, Waller

reprinted such an article, entitled "A Good Wife," which advised that the good wife had common sense and self-command, exhibited industry, affection, a domestic disposition, and piety.[48] Waller elaborated on these pronouncements in one of his own editorials, in which he asserted that "ladies" should avoid contradicting their husbands and occupy themselves with their household. They should not nag their husband, but teach him by example. Further, a lady should pay attention to her husband and attend to his "vanity." If a husband is wrong in a matter, a good wife should lead him to the "rational way" only by steps, never by force. Finally, ladies should "cherish neatness without luxury."[49] That Waller saw the need to give such advice suggests that Baptist women were more aggressive in the home than he would prefer them to be.

In a telling 1840 editorial, Waller commented upon the schism that occurred in that year's meeting of the American Anti-Slavery Society. The abolitionist group divided over gender issues when Abby Kelley and others conjoined the human rights grievances of the slaves and of women. Kelley's agitation upset Waller's expectations of gender decorum, leading him to observe mockingly that she "must be a rare character." In Waller's eye, Kelley's abolitionist split signaled an "insurrection of the ladies," and the newspaperman's cultural chauvinism flavored his editorializing. "Some of the fair sex 'down east'" he wrote, "have, for several years, been clamorous (as women can be when they are so disposed,) for their *rights*." Even more pointedly, the Baptist editor continued, "They maintain that they should have all the rights and privileges of citizenship—of voting, of being lawyers, judges, legislators, governors, presidents—in short of being *men!*"[50] The doctrine Baptist men and women received from the most widely read western Baptist newspaper was the gospel of True Womanhood.

Both sides of the Baptist message for women were presented in the female-oriented portion of the *Christian Repository*, entitled the *Family Visitant*. The periodical began monthly publication in 1845, under the title *Western Baptist Review* and the editorship of John L. Waller. In 1849, Waller changed the name to the *Christian Repository*. S. H. Ford joined as co-editor of the monthly in 1853, just before Waller's death. Finding himself alone at the helm, Ford called upon his wife to edit the journal's women's section. In her family-oriented section, Sallie Rochester Ford included advice columns, doctrinal essays, letters and contributions from readers, as well as serials of religious fiction. One scholar has noted that Sallie Ford's contribution as co-editor increased the popularity of the journal by including a woman's viewpoint and by catering to a new

readership of educated Baptist women.[51] Subscriber lists for the journal tend to support this conclusion. Each monthly issue included a record of subscription fees received that month. An analysis of the subscriber lists in 1858 reveals that women paid 20 to 25 percent of all subscriptions. Many women assuredly received the magazine through their husband's or father's name, but the fact that so many women sought out a subscription of their own indicates the journal's popularity among Baptist women.[52] Throughout the West, women also helped advertise the journal to those in their churches. As far as needing agents to sell the monthly to local pockets of Baptists, Samuel Ford noted that "pastor's wives are among the most efficient agents" in encouraging new subscribers.[53]

Waller's newspaper expressed the expectation of wifely submission, and Sallie Ford's *Family Visitant* reflected similar expectations of Baptist women in antebellum society. The articles, essays, sermons, and serials that addressed gender issues signaled the preeminence of piety over power, submission over supremacy, and maternalism over "manliness." In one pointed commentary, simply entitled "Woman," a frequent contributor, Mrs. A. O. Smith, articulated this vision clearly. Men, she wrote, were naturally stronger for the protection of women. The human brain was the same in organization regardless of sex, but the man's had a greater vascular system, making him "more intellectual." If a man and woman's roles were reversed, "Man becomes ridiculous, and woman disgusting." Female education beyond the domestic arts tended to grant too much freedom, "which is unnecessary for her happiness." Instead, Smith added, a women should discover "the sublime simplicity of her sex," and enjoy that arena where her influence is "omnipotent." This sphere, her home, was where she nurtured the "statesman in embryo, the future king and minister . . . in her plastic hand." After all, Smith concluded, the gentle woman is never lovelier than when "dignifying and adorning her abode—thus obeying the command of St. Paul." In another, more didactic commentary, Sallie Ford listed the duties of a mother charged with "training and educating a soul for eternity," lest there be any doubt about how the plastic hand should work. Here, too, Ford reflected popular Victorian sentiments to her Baptist audience. The nurturing mother was "firm—gentle—kind—always ready to attend to her child." She should be patient and "never laugh at" her child. "Never speak of a child's faults," she continued. "Never reprove a child when excited. . . . Strive to inspire love, not dread." By these means, the virtuous mother could mold an unspoiled,

respectful, neat, and clean child. According to the *Family Visitant*, this was largely the call of a Baptist woman in her domestic life.[54]

Yet, the more-popular fiction published in the *Family Visitant* offered a synthesis of the Baptist gender message. This was especially true of the highly favored serial novel *Grace Truman*. This work, written by Sallie R. Ford herself,

Sallie Rochester Ford. Frontispiece, *Grace Truman*, 1886.

became one of the most popular items in the entire journal. Begun in 1856, the serialized story was one of many such novels included in the monthly journal, but in 1857 letters began to pour into the Fords' editorial office requesting *Grace Truman* in book form. By the end of that year, publishers in Nashville, New York, and Chicago had printed copies for distribution. Its success encouraged further printings in 1858 and 1859. On the thirtieth anniversary of its appearance as a serial, the American Baptist Publication Society published another edition in 1886, and again another in 1903. The novel also inspired another book by a competitor that replied to the propositions in Ford's book.[55]

The full title of the novel, *Grace Truman, or Love and Principle*, expresses the dual nature of the Baptist woman's life, which Sallie Ford tried to communicate through the work. The title character, a young Kentucky Baptist woman, marries a Presbyterian from a respectable family. Her marriage takes her to live at the home of her in-laws, which is a day's ride from her own family. The conflict driving the story rests upon Grace's reluctance to participate in the communion ceremony of her new family's Presbyterian church. Grace struggles to remain faithful to her Baptist principles, which include only communing with the baptized—more specifically, the immersed. Yet, her denial of Presbyterian communion begins to tear her new family apart and even appears to lead her husband down the path of degeneracy. In short, Grace struggles throughout the story with how to be a good wife, with all its demurring subjection, and still abide by the true doctrines and principles she embraces as a Baptist. Though her husband initially supports her determination not to commune, old Mr. Holmes, her father-in-law, drives them out of his house. Mr. Holmes rants that the immersive baptism Grace defends is a "low, indecent practice." The novel contains several theological debates in the Holmes' parlor. By the end of one debate, as Grace's logical arguments begin persuading others in Old Mr. Holmes's household and neighborhood, the patriarch feels his authority fading, along with the popularity of his dogmatism. "It's a vulgar, foolish thing," he shouts at his son, "this going down into muddy ponds and dirty creeks to be dipped under, head and ears, when a little water, sprinkled on the forehead, in a genteel manner, would do just as well. No daughter of mine should be caught doing it."[56] By the end of the novel, Grace convinces almost every major character, and a few minor ones, that Baptist practice is correct. They all become Baptists and organize a new church in the fictional town of Weston. Old Mr. Holmes, though, soon goes to his grave bitter, unrepentant, and Presbyterian.

In an afterword to the 1886 edition of the novel, Sallie Ford notes that the work was semi-autobiographical and reflects her own personal and public struggle as she converted from Presbyterianism to the Baptist movement. Many of the characters in the novel, she reveals, are based on real people she knew or are composites of actual figures from her past. She also recounts how she wrote the novel to argue against the practice of "open communion," which had been a point of Baptist controversy in the 1850s. In open communion, a church extended the privilege of communion to all the saints, regardless of whether or how they were baptized. To Ford, it appeared to be a doctrinal concession borne of a desire for respectability. A true Baptist woman like Grace Truman, she argued, would endure the ignominy of scandal and would even sacrifice family ties in favor of orthodoxy in fundamental beliefs and practices.[57]

The personal and pointedly doctrinal nature of Ford's *Grace Truman* is noteworthy in itself, but even more striking is the title character, whom Ford presents as a role model for her Baptist readers. In her struggles, Grace reveals the two facets of Baptist expectations of women. In many respects, she represents the height of true womanhood. Her manner is "gentle, yet unreserved." She is "attractive to those who could appreciate the 'poetry of form and motion.'" Her "well-formed features" are "kept in control by her habitual self-respect." She blushes when spoken about and demurs smilingly when Old Mr. Holmes first begins to proclaim, "We must make her a Presbyterian." When confronted by opposition, she prays for divine assistance. When she and her husband take up their own residence, Grace takes seriously the domestic duties in her "mystic round of housekeeping." In her own realm she creates a "cottage-home, plain and unpretending." Ford's narrator notes that homes like Grace's are "our city of refuge from the cares of the world, our holiest of sanctuaries. Domestic happiness! there is no earthly joy beyond it." A minor character who commands as much moral force as Grace is Mrs. Miller, the wife of the Baptist minister. Those who know her describe her as "a most excellent woman . . . loved and respected by all." One of her small, but significant, contributions to the story is to mark the life of a minister's wife. She notes that "there is but one class of people living that has a harder time than Baptist preachers, and that is their wives." Lest she be thought proud, Mrs. Miller adds, "If we women can't preach, we can stay at home and take care of things while our husbands go forth to sow the seed of truth and righteousness."[58]

In addition to representing an ideal of domestic strength in the novel, Grace Truman's actions also reveal the other side of Baptist gender expectations: that

when in the proverbial coliseum with the lions, female saints should become warriors. The story contains several scenes where the characters present and debate the issue of open communion and the definition of baptism. In the first intellectual contest, Grace confronts both her father-in-law and the local Presbyterian minister in a parlor debate. Though she holds her own, Grace gives in to some of her opponents' arguments. She decides that she will commune with the family on Sunday, but at the last moment she reneges. "Love had yielded to principle," the narrator explains.[59] There follows a second, more thrilling debate, wherein Grace faces Old Mr. Holmes and two Presbyterian ministers. In this dispute, she matches her opponents blow for blow intellectually, often revealing their arguments to be logically ill-founded or biblically indefensible. All the on-looking family members agree that Grace wins the debate, and they begin to consider the veracity of her Baptist claims. Despite her victory, Grace and her husband move out of the family home, and she grows weary of argument. Her cause is taken up by Edwin Lewis, her husband's cousin and a lawyer, whom she persuades during an earlier debate. Not feeling up to the task of replacing Grace in future debates, Edwin consults with her beforehand. The lawyer admires her rare wisdom and "the manner of her defence, her clear, convincing arguments," which have staved off rebuttals of her opponents. Another character, Grace's young Presbyterian sister-in-law Fannie, gains a sense of intellectual liberation from watching Grace in the debates. In a confrontation with her brother, Fannie asks rhetorically, "Haven't I a right to my own views about things; and isn't it as necessary for me to be right on all subjects as it is for older heads?" In the later debates, Grace avoids the bitter confrontations, believing them to be unproductive, especially given the hostility of her father-in-law. Reverend Gordon, one of the Presbyterian ministers who debates Edwin Lewis instead, privately reflects later that he is glad he did not have to face Grace who "would have been able to detect his weak points." In the end, it is Grace's humble piety in the home, as well as her shrewd and forceful logic in debate, that convinces most of the other characters—even the Reverend Gordon—that the Baptists are right.[60]

As Sallie Ford did in her popular fiction, by the mid-nineteenth century, the Baptists encouraged a conception of women that embraced the cult of True Womanhood, but also afforded them status as soldiers of the faith. Women were to embrace piety and submission, but were free and encouraged to defend the faith in personal interactions and through social reform movements. When Baptists began elevating the status of pastors in the 1840s, laity, both men

and women, were expected to honor that position and focus their criticism outwardly. But the deep-rooted independent spirit of the Baptist impulse offered a countervailing pull on the behavior of its members. Thus, women like Hannah Graves in the 1820s and Mary Bristow in the 1850s could feel free to voice their opinions to and about their preachers. In the same spirit, the Nelson Association could encourage the Baptists in central Kentucky that "religion is an individual matter, and everyone shall give an account for himself," and "the opinions of great and good men should be respected, but they should not be received for the teaching of the Spirit."[61] The actions of Baptist women from the late 1700s to 1860 show that through controversies and cultural accommodation, they embraced their faith, not as the product of someone else's devising, but as a meaningful and valid belief system that they could propagate and defend. And they upheld their church as an institution that captured both the independent nature of biblical Christianity and the democratic inclusivism of the American ideal. In tangible ways, then, Baptist women in early Kentucky participated in the preservation of the Baptist impulse, even as it weathered times of stress, and their presence and participation signify its resilience as a form of popular religion in America.

6

"Determined to Persist": African Americans and the Pursuit of Baptist Identity

I n 1857, seventy-four black members of the Baptist church at Paris, including both free and slave, applied to separate from the white membership and form their own church. In response, the church assigned a committee of white members to research the propriety of such a separation; eventually they concluded that an amicable schism would be acceptable, "with proper limitations." These restrictions were fivefold. First, the new black church had to adopt the old church's declaration of faith and practice. Second, though the new church members could elect their own officers and conduct their own business, they had to follow any advice given by the white-controlled church. Third, they could not represent themselves at the yearly associational gathering. Instead, they had to elect a white delegate to bear their letter and act as their representative. Fourth, they had to give a strict account of their business actions to the white-controlled church. Finally, if the separating members failed "to comply with these obligations, or maintain properly the worship of God,

or any other emergency shall make it necessary," the white-controlled church could rescind the act of separation. The African church members agreed to the restrictions and called Elisha W. Green as their pastor. Green already pastored the African church at Maysville, over forty miles away. Green's church in Maysville had proven popular and was the third largest in its association in 1856. By 1860, it was the largest. Given their petition and then their willingness to accommodate the white-controlled church's stipulations, the separating black members of the Paris church clearly desired to worship in their own environment and in their own way. They began holding Sunday worship services in an old horse stable behind their old church building. During inclement weather, the congregation sat under umbrellas to worship, because the rain leaked through the stable's roof. Pastor Green later recalled that given the restrictions and indignities faced by his congregation, anyone could see that "the colored church was a slave to the white Baptist Church." Still, the membership doubled in the first four years of the new church's existence.[1]

This was the paradox of black Baptists in Kentucky in the early to mid-nineteenth century: most white Baptists considered them second-class citizens of Zion, yet hundreds of thousands of slaves and free blacks joined the Baptist movement across the nation. In some respects, their status resembled that of white women. In many churches, they constituted the majority of members, yet they were barred from official positions of leadership. By other measures, African-American men enjoyed a few perquisites largely unavailable to white women. Black men could receive ordination to the ministry, whereas women of any race could not. In Baptist culture, of course, the lines between ordained preacher and lay exhorter were understood, but practically negligible. Yet Baptists saw divisive racial lines clearly. Thus it is a natural question why so many would embrace and commit themselves to a religious movement that only seemed to sacralize their subordination. The answers are complex and varied, but each helps to reveal the character of the larger Baptist movement, its democratic appeal, and the nature of what blacks experienced as participants. Historian Jon Butler asserts that "the attachment of American blacks to Christianity in antebellum society" is a myth that exaggerates the truth.[2] Still, the many who did attach themselves to the Baptist movement did so with fervor and with the goal of working out their own salvation.[3]

In the novel *Grace Truman,* a slave named Dolly approaches Grace, her mistress, wondering if Grace's Baptist beliefs have changed now that she is betrothed to a Presbyterian. "Massa John don't believe in baptizin' folks like we

do," Dolly begins, "but I think we's right, don't you?" Though a white woman authored the antebellum novel, Dolly's inquiry genuinely reflects the ownership black Baptists took of their faith, especially by the 1850s. Statistics on specific adherence rates by race prove difficult to determine. Since some slave owners would not allow their slaves to join the church, adherence was probably higher than the membership rates would suggest. Unlike membership rates for women, which consistently ran high throughout the period, black membership were low prior to 1800. In the central Bluegrass region of Kentucky, where one in every four households owned at least one slave, black Baptist church membership vacillated below 10 percent. Only during the waves of revivalism in 1800 and 1801 did Baptist churches see a great influx of African-American converts into the baptismal waters. After the revivals, black membership increased disproportionately to white membership. Ellen Eslinger's research on revivalism and black Baptists strongly suggests a connection between these revival conversions and the simultaneous development of African-American community.[4]

Since the vast majority of churches did not distinguish their membership by race in their annual reports to their associations, charting the rise of African-American participation using these reports is challenging. However, by the 1840s and 1850s, those churches that reported membership by race often revealed a high percentage of African-American membership. Some churches even had more black than white members. In the Bethel Association in 1845, for example, four of the thirty churches that distinguished members by race reported black majorities. By 1860, those same thirty churches included ten with black majorities, ranging from 52 percent to 74 percent of total membership.[5] In the Long Run Association in 1860, eight churches reported numbers of white and black members; two had black majorities.[6]

Despite Baptist complicity in the institution of slavery, blacks both slave and free joined with the Baptist churches in large numbers and desired to participate in leadership roles. Nathan Hatch contends that before 1800, Baptists and Methodists "earned the right to be heard," by embracing slaves as brothers and sisters and opposing slavery. Yet even after that opposition ceased, Baptists continued to welcome blacks and offered them membership status—though often it came with qualified benefits. Limitations on black members in the early nineteenth century affected those men who sought to preach. Eslinger observes that once blacks began expanding their presence in the Baptist churches, they also wanted to express themselves through general

participation and in positions of leadership. Since each Baptist church licensed and ordained its own ministers, when a black member (or white member) expressed a call to that position, the church members alone determined whether they would grant permission. If a man preached without prior approval, he could be cited for discipline. If a church denied approval and the man preached anyway, the harsh voice of the church would call him to order. When the issue of blackness or slavery entered the equation, the matter became more complicated. In May 1802, when the issue of slave preaching came before the Providence church of Clark County, the church decided that the laws of Kentucky required the slave to have his owner's consent before a church could license him. They added that slaves who thought they had "impressions of preaching or exhorting" could come before a committee for examination, "with the consent of their owner." All prospective preachers underwent an examination, but the Providence church exhibited a two-fold double standard based on race. First, a white candidate would obviously not need anyone's, much less an owner's, consent to apply for a license. Second, a white candidate would appear for examination before the whole church. A black applicant would come before a committee elected from the church for the purpose of questioning him. While this process still bore the hallmarks of a *representative* democracy, the committee blocked the candidate from the church as a whole. Baptists largely rejected the idea of committees doing the church's work until the antebellum period. Even then, committees were controversial due to their seemingly undemocratic and centralizing influence.[7]

African-American Baptists in Kentucky who desired to preach also faced common limitations based on the culture of slaveholding. Whereas the patriarchal cultural ethic helped keep women out of the pulpit, the slave culture restricted the ability of blacks to preach to white audiences. In the midst of a revival, the Providence church heard Brother Ambrose's application to preach in January 1811. In the previous three months, forty-three converts had joined the church, and in the following three months another forty-one joined. Many of these new converts were slaves. Ambrose had to wait until April to learn the church's verdict on his call. They voted that he could only "meet with his own color to sing, pray, and exhort." His license not only restricted his audience, but also his actions. Preaching, though similar to exhorting, remained out of bounds.[8]

The limits placed upon another slave preacher, Daniel, who attended the Stamping Ground church with his owner, reveal how the realities of the racial

hierarchy and Baptist cultural ideals meshed together. Daniel approached the church in February 1818, desiring to "exercise a public gift." The members agreed that he could do this "in his own way." Daniel's approval from the church, however, did not come without qualification. Like many candidates, he had to stay in the "bounds of the church," but unlike white candidates, he could only exercise his gift "at such places and times of the day as will enable the white male members to hear him." Daniel had control of his message, but would retain such control only as long as it stayed within white-approved limitations. Clearly a demand existed within that church and its neighborhood for Daniel's preaching. Slaves constituted a large portion of the membership at Stamping Ground and had been a significant part of the church for quite a while. Six months after Daniel's "gift" gained approval, the church agreed that he could use the meeting house for preaching on the first and third Sundays of the month. The church at this time generally only met one weekend a month, so the meeting house was available. That he had access to the meeting house two Sundays a month suggests a large demand and a fervency of the black faith that would compel multiple services in a month.[9]

Yet Daniel still faced restrictions in his access to the meeting house. If a white preacher in the neighborhood needed the meeting house, Daniel had to submit and surrender the pulpit. In November 1818, Daniel asked to add meetings during the week outside the meeting house. With the harvest season at an end, he and his congregants had more time for meetings. In response, the church extended his freedoms while still restricting him and his largely black congregation. The church declared he could "exhort among the people of his own colour at any time," but only when no white preacher was in his neighborhood. Also, the "anytime" allowance came with considerable qualification since he was allowed no night meetings whatsoever. The day meetings, likewise, had to break up at least one hour before sundown. The church's restriction cohered with civil regulations regarding slave mobility. The 1798 Kentucky slave codes limited the time slaves could spend away from their residences and mandated that extended absences required travel papers. Town ordinances typically supplemented these restrictions by imposing a curfew and appointing patrols to punish offenders.[10] Access always came with restriction, just as Baptist ideals often clashed with cultural demands.

The worst restriction a church could place on a prospective preacher was not to allow him to "exercise his gift" at all. As was the case with white members, black members sometimes ignored this prohibition. In 1798,

black Brother Abraham applied to the Mayslick church to take up preaching, and they refused. In December, the church members were notified that Abraham opposed their judgment "concerning his gift for preaching." They appointed a group of members to "labor with him," that is, to converse and settle differences for the sake of peace in the church. But Brother Abraham was firm in his opposition. In June 1799, a Brother Morris reported to the church that Abraham had "attempted to preach in public in direct opposition to the unanimous judgment of the church." When Abraham came to answer for his contempt, he stood before them defiantly unrepentant. The church clerk noted that Abraham appeared "determined to persist" and preferred "exclusion to submission to the church's judgment." The church excluded him "without a dissenting voice."[11] Baptist church membership had its privileges, but for African Americans like Abraham, commitment to a call took precedence over the church's judgment. In the case of slave preacher Madison Campbell, even his master's demands could not keep him from his calling. Campbell's master, a non-practicing Methodist, believed that only educated men should preach and told Campbell to stop preaching after he was licensed in 1852. Campbell replied that he "was called of God and sent to preach" and as he could read the Bible, he felt it his "duty to try." He said that he had always honored his master, but then Campbell emphatically announced to him, "I cannot promise you that I will not preach anymore." In the end, the master's wife, a Baptist, feared a divine curse would fall upon them if Madison were sold because of his commitment to preaching. Thus he continued his ministry in the neighborhood of Richmond, Kentucky, and eventually baptized over 2,000 black converts.[12]

The level of participation African-American Baptists enjoyed in the church's official meetings for business and worship is difficult to quantify, but records and primary accounts indicate that white church members viewed any activity at any time through the prism of race. As was the case for whites, the first voice a black member had in the church was when they delivered their conversion experience. Here, too, black members related their stories and church members evaluated them; and if the pattern of conviction, sorrow, and repentance were missing, the candidates were rejected. Preacher John Taylor's vast experience in early Kentucky reveals the ambivalent response of white Baptists toward African Americans in the church, in their conversion experiences and otherwise. Taylor, like many of his peers in the Bluegrass, owned slaves, some of whom he inherited and others he purchased. Through their labor, Taylor's fortune increased significantly.[13]

One of the most extensive and revelatory accounts on slaves in Taylor's memoirs relates the conversion of his long-time slave Letty. The story illuminates several aspects of race-colored Kentucky Baptist life. Taylor had inherited Letty in 1783 from his uncle when she was a child, and in 1800 she converted and joined the Bullittsburg church, located south of Cincinnati. According to Taylor, he recorded the account of her conversion and her relation of it so that his readers would not think him "partial to those of higher rank." In noting her early aversion to religion, Taylor comments casually that he found it difficult to bring her to family worship. "She could not be ruled (except by harsh means)." But sometime after her brother Asa's conversion, Letty began contemplating her own soul. During this period of introspection, she witnessed a Mr. Carrol in the "highest gale" of drunken revelry while his wife was giving birth. Attempting to record Letty's "phraseology," Taylor noted that she said, "[I] thought he was the wickedest man I ever saw. . . . But after reflecting on myself a while, I really thought I was worse." According to her conversion relation, she went to her newly converted brother, hoping he might validate that her conversion was near. But he denied seeing any evidence of divine conviction. In fact, he thought "all the work she talked of to be of the Devil." She turned to her overseer, whom Taylor described as a "very good, religious, old man." According to Letty, though, he treated her with "scorned contempt." She considered going to John Taylor and his wife, but she believed they would doubt her sincerity given her previous hostility to religion. At the edge of desperation, like many others who related such narratives, Letty ran to the Ohio River bank, intending to drown herself. Down by the riverside, though, she "confessed the justice of God in her eternal damnation," and then the burden lifted. As she told the church, her soul was secure because "Jesus Christ had made an angry God my friend." Commenting on the event over twenty years later, John Taylor stated that Letty had "given good evidence" that her conversion was genuine. More strikingly, he asserted that his readers "may see verified in this instance what the voice said to Peter that 'God is no respecter of persons.' And it is probable more slaves will go to Heaven than masters."[14] Obviously, the account of Letty's conversion comes to the reader filtered through Taylor's perspective, but the pattern matched that expected of and related by white and black converts alike; thus, the church received her into membership. The conversion experience served as an equalizer, hence Taylor's biblical observation that God was "no respecter of persons."[15] To African-American men and women both, the requirement of speaking before the membership and congregation actually offered them a chance to

"preach" the greatness and goodness of God, and it also offered them a way to influence—no matter how slightly—the rituals of the Baptist movement.

Baptism also served as a rite whereby African Americans experienced and contributed to an equalizing process in the faith. The Baptists saw baptism as a watery grave in which the convert symbolized her death to sin and resurrection to new life. In this context of watery graves, Letty's desire to drown herself in the Ohio River—the river in which she was likely baptized—takes on a greater significance. For Taylor, conversion and baptism were equalizers comparable to death in their ability to level humanity. Taylor extolled such idealistic equality and extended it in church life in general. After a ceremony wherein Taylor baptized twelve blacks and one white together, he reflected that "perfect equality" between master and servant only existed in the church and in death. A slave, he wrote, may have a "master in the shop or on the farm but not so in the church of Christ." Despite such high-sounding rhetoric, typical Baptist church practice, which restricted preaching rights and enforced segregated seating, did not rise to the same level. Taylor even seems to contradict his own statements later in his memoirs. In discussing the Buck Run church, he states that the church had two things in its favor: very few rich men among the membership, and very few blacks. "Very often by rich men and Negroes," Taylor reasoned, "the cause of religion suffers much, for while one is above, the other is below its native, godlike simplicity." To Taylor, the ideal faith equalized everyone, but homogeneity of race and class in a church seemed to be a formula for success and stability.[16]

After a church heard an African-American convert's conversion narrative, it might never hear from him again in official gatherings. Church records cite few instances of black members making a motion upon which the church would vote. Blacks did participate, however, in a church's discipline trials, both as accusers and the accused, but rarely ever brought charges against whites. African-American members, both men and women, were excluded from the church for social sins more than any other category of offense. Predominant male transgressions included drunkenness, theft, lying, and running away. White men shared in the sin of drunkenness with their black Baptist brothers, but faced exclusion for the other sins seldom or never. Thus, the primary slave resistance activities of theft, lying, and running away came under harsh rebuke from Baptist churches. While both white and black men committed adultery, the church excluded black men for the offense disproportionately.[17]

Church records reveal disjunctures by race among women as well. Whereas almost half of all white female exclusions were for crimes against the church, such as leaving to join another denomination, three-quarters of the excluding sins committed by black women were for social or sexual misdeeds. Social sins of black women, constituting over half of the total of all sins, included lying, theft, and running away. Here, too, violations of the slave code carried the stiffest religious penalty. Black women were also more likely to face exclusion for adultery and bearing illegitimate children. Little evidence exists to show how white Baptists confronted the dilemma of Christian purity and the sexual realities of slave life other than to show that they valued the former. Church records do show members attempting to punish sexual abuse of slaves, and they reveal blacks seeking assistance or redress. In July 1812, for instance, Judy, a slave woman belonging to Thomas Smith, informed the church at Mount Pleasant that her husband had left her and married another woman. Judy wished to know whether Christian ethical standards gave her liberty to marry another man. The church members agreed that she did have that freedom.[18]

African-American Baptists clearly saw the benefit of church discipline for obtaining justice, but that justice only ameliorated their slave experience, since their ability to complain against whites was limited or non-existent. When black Baptists separated from the white churches into their own fellowships, they took the discipline practice with them and showed little reluctance to exclude each other for transgressions. Their identity as Baptists had meaning for them and even during the conflicts over Alexander Campbell's theological innovations, black Baptists protected their churches. In 1842, at the Stamping Ground church, black Baptists discovered that Tom, a fellow slave, had gone over to the Reformers, and they excluded him.[19]

Churches rarely recorded the process of how church members debated any one particular issue; thus, if black members contributed to the discussion, such records offer little of substance on the content of their contribution. Preacher Wilson Thompson's recollection of his life includes an account of a black member speaking to a matter of great significance for the Mouth of Licking church. According to Thompson, the testimony of Brother Sumas, a mulatto member, resolved a church quarrel. The conflict in Thompson's church began in the first decade of the nineteenth century when one female member "trespassed against another." After the offended woman tried to follow the customary steps of resolving offenses and then brought the matter to the church, the transgressor's husband defended her and contradicted the testimony of another

witness. The church deadlocked for months on the case and factions began to form. In the midst of this turmoil, Brother Sumas addressed the church. Thompson notes that the church esteemed Sumas as "a sound, orderly brother, who, on account of being a mulatto, had never spoken on church business and had uniformly occupied a back seat." Trembling, Sumas pointed out his low status. "I know I am so very ignorant," Sumas began, "that I tremble at the very thought of saying a word." Yet Sumas claimed that he saw the issue plainly: that both the church and the two women were at fault for introducing and prolonging disorder in the fellowship. He then paused. The moderator assured Sumas that he had the floor and "told him to speak his mind freely; it was his privilege." Sumas concluded his explanation. Despite his repeated claims of ignorance, the church agreed with him and threw out the divisive matter entirely.[20] Such episodes suggest that while black members may have had the right to speak before the church, they did so rarely, gingerly, and obeisantly. It could also have been that African-American church members calculated that their voice would be unwelcome or unheeded in a predominantly white church. The right to speak would not matter much if action never followed.

As was the case with many aspects of western Baptist identity, the questions of slavery and African-American Baptist rights had to be resolved in the migration. The white response to the black embrace of Baptist identity varied, and Kentucky proved to be fertile ground for contestation and revision. Just as the Baptist movement migrated and spread into Kentucky in the late 1700s, so did slavery. Preachers who moved from Virginia and North Carolina brought their slaves with them, and so too did their church members. In this way, Baptists not only helped transplant religious institutions in the "wilderness," but social ones as well. Slave-holding ministers also resembled some of their congregants because of their slave ownership. Methodist itinerants, peripatetic and less financially stable, held fewer slaves. They also belonged to a movement more prone to condemn than accept slavery. The more-educated Presbyterian ministers tended to eschew slavery much more than Baptists. The most well-known western Presbyterian minister, David Rice, led the anti-slavery cause in Kentucky's constitutional debates in the 1790s. The three Baptist ministers who served as constitutional convention delegates in the 1790s also voted against slavery.[21]

In the late eighteenth century, churches and associations, in patchwork fashion throughout the state, debated their stances on the institution and how they should relate to it. In some cases, as happened in the Salem Association,

Baptists found safe ground in avoiding the topic. In 1788, the Rolling Fork church queried that association, "Is it lawful in the sight of God for a member of Christ's church to keep his fellow creature in perpetual slavery?" The delegates collectively refused to answer the question, deeming it "improper to enter into so important and critical a matter at present." The churches of this association again tried to stifle the issue in 1792 when the Lick Creek church sought associational assistance to resolve an intra-church dispute. Some of the Lick Creek church members opposed slavery and others did not. Once more the association decided, "We ought not to make any decision . . . . It is a subject which ought to be handled with the greatest caution." The association sent a committee of ten men to confer with the members of Lick Creek and seek a harmonious settlement, but the church split over the issue in 1795. Other churches within the association pressured their sister churches to take a firm stand on the issue, but the associational delegates repeatedly side-stepped the meddlesome questions. In 1793, the Severn's Valley church wanted the association to state "whether it was not the duty of us freemen" to present emancipationist memorials to the legislature so as to help end slavery. The delegates replied that "every individual in the Commonwealth [had] this privilege," but "it was improper for the association to present a memorial of any kind." In 1795, the Mill Creek church members wanted the association's stance on the question of whether slave owners should teach their slaves "to read the word of God" as well as provide for their physical needs. But the delegates dodged the issue deftly, citing it as among "domestic concerns" in which it was improper for the association to interpose. Without an answer, the Mill Creek church withdrew from the larger body in 1796, as did the Rolling Fork church which had broached the subject eight years earlier. The Salem Association was the first such group of churches to experience this much early disharmony, but other associations would wrestle with the issue of slavery in a generally less raucous fashion.[22]

The most radical and organized effort Baptists undertook in Kentucky against slavery proved both unpopular and fleeting. When hopes for state-wide emancipation sank in the revision-oriented 1798 state constitutional convention, a few individuals such as preachers David Barrow and Carter Tarrent held out hope for Baptists to forsake slavery on their own as a group. In 1805, however, Tarrent's efforts at emancipationist preaching came under associational attack. The Elkhorn Association's resolution that year modeled the position that future Baptists, and eventually Southern Baptists, would take

on slavery and race relations. They categorized slavery as a political issue and judged it "improper for ministers, churches, or associations to meddle with emancipation from slavery and any other political subject." In the same year, to prevent any more meddling by David Barrow, the North District Association appointed a committee of five preachers to put him on trial for preaching opposition to slavery. In 1806, the association charged Barrow with "preaching the doctrines of emancipation to the hurt and injury of the brotherhood," and then expelled him. The church of Mount Sterling, which Barrow pastored, also ejected him from fellowship.[23]

Put out from the larger Baptist community, the friends of emancipation gathered in 1807 in central Woodford County to organize their own association, called the "Licking-Locust Association, Friends of Humanity." The first meeting of the new emancipationist association included nine churches, represented by seven preachers and nineteen laymen. The total membership of these churches in September 1807 amounted to 190 people. Despite their bright hopes, the emancipationist association foundered. Their peak likely came in 1812 when they claimed twelve churches with about 300 members total. Such a low rate of membership meant that, at their height, the organized emancipationists represented less than 2 percent of all Kentucky Baptists in 1812. The association declined after 1812, dissolving in 1819 shortly after David Barrow's death.[24]

While Baptists battled on the associational level about slaves and slavery in the early 1800s, local churches also had to wrestle democratically with race-related practice and principle. The Stamping Ground church dealt with one of the most basic of questions in this regard in February 1798. One member inquired "whether bound slaves is [sic] fit members in the church or not." Rather than answer the question immediately, the members deferred it for later debate. By April, they had reached the conclusion that "any orderly Christian though in a state of slavery has a right to the privileges of a gospel church." The two-month interval between question and answer suggests the church took time to consider the issue carefully, since this three-year old church usually took a month to answer any query. The discourse on the matter also highlights how the Baptist principle of decentralization and democratic priorities often led churches and associations to "reinvent the wheel." They asked the question in 1798, but their association had asked and answered the same twelve years before—nine years before the Stamping Ground church existed.[25]

The conflict over slavery in the 1805 Elkhorn Association meeting reverberated beyond its borders and put such democratic processes to the test. Its effect

on the Mayslick church challenged their democratic ideals and their Baptist vision of congregational integrity and purity. Sitting as it did on the northern road into the Bluegrass, the Mayslick church body included a mixture of "old world" sentiments on the frontier. New Jerseyites founded the church in 1789, and later members came from New York and Pennsylvania, as well as Virginia, Maryland, and Delaware. The church had black members early on, but the issue of slavery never proved a major complication until three months before their association arranged for David Barrow (not a member of the Mayslick church) to face charges for preaching emancipation. In July 1805, John Davis made a motion in the church's business session that the "black Brethren & sisters at our Communion seasons be invited to sit on the same seats with their white Brethren." To this, the church agreed. At the same meeting, Thomas Longley moved that the church "consider whether unmerited, Involuntary, Hereditary slavery is supported by the word of god or not." To this, the church had no easy answer. Two months later, they met and answered that a large majority thought slavery was not biblically defensible. That same month, the Licking-Locust church drew censure and was excluded from the Bracken Association. Their exclusion, along with three other churches, sent shockwaves through the association. In November, the Mayslick church allowed some members of the excluded Licking-Locust church to take honorary seats at their monthly business meeting. This action offended the orderly Baptist sensibilities of Mayslick leader William Allen, who complained that his church should deny fellowship to excluded Baptists. After considering Allen's protest, the members disagreed and decided they had acted in an "orderly" manner. Following a discussion, Allen declared that he would not be reconciled to the majority. His obstinance paid off, because the next month, the members reconsidered and concluded they were mistaken. The anti-slavery majority apparently had allowed their views on slavery to color their decision to fellowship with the excluded.[26]

The confluence of democratic action, Baptist ideals of integrity, and quandaries over slavery continued to affect the Mayslick church in the months following, but in a different manner and with a more divisive result. By March 1806, fifteen members left the church because they believed slavery was a sin. The two men who forced the church to clarify its opinion, Thomas Longley and John Davis, were among this group. At least a third of this group hailed from the state of New Jersey, where the presence of slavery was less substantial than in Kentucky. That is not to say that the Jerseymen remained untouched by the lure of slavery. Among these Mayslick defectors were Isaac Drake and

his wife, Elizabeth. Isaac's son Daniel believed that of all the immigrants from New Jersey, his father "was the only one who did not become a slave holder." Even Daniel's uncle Cornelius, whom he respected dearly and who was one of the founders of the Mayslick church, purchased a slave and "argued from the Bible that it was right." Despite their previous statements on slavery, the church excluded the fifteen emancipationists for leaving the church. At least two of the excluded became leaders in the anti-slavery Licking-Locust Association. A few emancipationists stayed with the church, but over the next several years, the church either grew more comfortable with slavery or avoided the issue. Only occasionally did a few firebrands revive the topic. In 1808, the church excluded their emancipationist pastor, Jacob Grigg, after he lashed out at the Bracken Association. saying that its "ministers and messengers had made it the antechamber of Hell" by their acquiescence to slavery. Even as late as 1812, Brother Isaac, a black member of Mayslick, joined the emancipators and faced exclusion.[27]

By the 1810s, with the die-hard emancipationists largely separated out from the majority in the churches, Kentucky Baptists settled into an awkward compliance with the system of slavery. Churches continued to ask questions of themselves and others about proper policy for dealing with slaves in their meetings, rituals, and discipline, but the movement had set its course with slavery and would not be moved. As late as 1810, the Bear Grass church submitted a query to the Long Run Association, asking if it was "right to receive negroes, that are the property and slaves of other men, into churches, as members in full fellowship, or not?" The association agreed that slaves could enjoy full membership status, but only "by the consent of their owners." That same year, the South District Association devoted the annual message to its churches to the various Christian duties that render society happy. The letter promised to address the duties of the slave, as well as those of the husband, wife, parent, child, master, and servant. Nevertheless, almost half of the letter dealt with the subjection that was expected from servants. Servants, they wrote, should not lie or pilfer, but always show "good fidelity." The association stated that "the Christian religion imposes no necessity of a change in our condition, in respect to our standing in civil society." Servanthood, in their description, was one of the "adverse dealings of providence." That said, they quickly claimed they were not "discussing the question of slavery"; to do that would interfere with a political question. With their schisms over slavery behind them, these Kentucky Baptists wanted the message made clear—that Christians who do

their duty and churches that avoid such "political" issues do not "have the most remote tendency to disturb the public tranquility, or weaken the hands of government."[28]

As the nineteenth century progressed, as Kentucky Baptists became more settled in their complicity with the culture of slavery, and as more and more blacks joined Baptist churches, the separate status of African Americans became more apparent in various aspects of Baptist life. The annual association meetings, previously opportunities for social bonding, became venues for reinforcing a sort of separate-but-equal principle. The 1845 Bethel Association meeting, for example, drew a great number of black Baptists. The association's geography played a role in this. Its territory straddled the border between Kentucky and Tennessee, incorporating towns such as Russellville and Hopkinsville in Kentucky and Clarksville in Tennessee. This region included the counties of heaviest slave population in Kentucky outside the Bluegrass. The 1844 membership statistics submitted by the affiliating churches show that slaves represented a significant portion of the Baptist population. Of the thirty churches which submitted data by race, twenty-three of them had nine or more black members. The level of black membership ranged from 10 percent to 58 percent among these churches, with the great majority of them having a black membership of over 30 percent. Thus, when the association met in 1845, attendance was racially mixed. But in the times of preaching on Sunday, separation was the watchword. There were two different "houses of worship." In the morning, two preachers addressed the whites in one building while two others met with the blacks in a separate facility. Likewise, in the afternoon during the three o'clock preaching sessions, two preachers ministered to the whites, and Brother Kelly, "a colored man," spoke to the black Baptists. Even in the evening meetings, the segregation continued during preaching. What the black attendees may have thought of this arrangement remains unknown; however, the segregation of attendants by race in the association meeting, one of the most broad-based and inclusive forums, did not affect the continued flow of black converts into the churches of Bethel Association.[29]

The increased influx of African Americans into local Baptist churches coincided with the movement's pursuit of refinement—refinement not just of structure, but of conduct. Many churches lacked the financial resources to improve and dignify their houses of worship until the late 1830s and 1840s. This refinement of structure clearly signaled a pursuit of respectability, especially in the urban churches. But the members of some churches seemed to desire

a more dignified worship style within their as-yet-unrefined meeting houses. The growing numbers of black members did not seem to share this vision of sober worship, a fact which troubled the white members.[30]

As early as the 1810s, the practice of some Kentucky Baptist churches reveals that after a period of accepting revivalistic "excesses," they desired more order in their worship and rejected black ecstasy. The white members of the Stamping Ground church, in the heart of the Bluegrass, began a conflict with black members over conduct in worship just as the church started to concern itself with a finer look for their church building. Prior to 1819, this church had taken its name from the nearby stream called McConnell's Run. Then, in 1819, members chose to relocate to the growing town of Stamping Ground and reestablished themselves with a name that would identify them with the town. They erected a new church building at their new location, which preacher William Hickman labeled a "fine brick meeting house." That same year, as the church body renewed its identity and entered new and respectable quarters, the members appointed James Suggett, the church's one-time preacher, to meet with "the black people" on Sunday and inform them "that unless they keep better order in times of preaching, this church [was] determined to have the law put in force against them." Such a harsh threat signaled a different kind of disorder than the law of church discipline could fix.[31]

Studies of slave religion describe a common call-and-response style of black worship which highlighted the link between the preacher and the congregation. Historian Charles Joyner's analysis of such experiences portrays them as raucous affairs wherein a crescendo of murmurs and shouts, claps and stamps, united the soul and body, speaker and audience, in "religious transcendence." The white Baptists at Stamping Ground who desired more order during their times of preaching sought to censure such activity. Apparently their proscriptions worked for a while. Yet two years later, the white members resolved to use a different tactic to achieve order. In 1821, they appointed Martin Nimrod, a free black man, and Tony, a slave, to "use their influence in keeping the black people in order at all times of preaching in the meeting house." To make the point clear, they also appointed one of the church's trustees "to inform the blacks" of their orderly obligation. The issue lay dormant for over a decade, during which time the church continued to grow but was distracted by the controversies of Campbell's Reformation. By 1840, the black members of the church began holding a separate meeting after the monthly Sunday evening worship gathering. Theirs was not a separate and distinct church, nor was it

an "arm" of the church. Following the racially mixed meeting every fourth Sunday, the black members held their own church-like meeting, wherein they conducted discipline and approved those wishing to "exercise their gift" in exhortation. The white members still expected order, and appointed nine slaves to attend to "disorder" and to report any "difficulties that may occur among the black brethren."[32]

The experiences of the black and white Baptists at Stamping Ground reveal that both groups embraced the Baptist faith as their own and practiced it on their own terms. Conflict and concern grew out of the white pursuit of order and respectability amid the growing, enthusiastic black presence in the church. This tension continued until division seemed appropriate, but in the slave system of Kentucky, white churches maintained a "watch care" relationship with black churches that sought to break off from them. By 1855, the black church members of Stamping Ground had acquired their own "comfortable" meeting house and desired to separate. The white church members disagreed amongst themselves about the separation issue. Even the committee of members appointed to examine the issue in depth could not agree, but they asserted it was "a fact that cannot be contradicted that there is a growing disinclination upon our colored members to attend our meetings." Much is written in historical scholarship about how Baptists compromised their democratic and egalitarian values in denying black members full participatory rights, and the members of Stamping Ground admitted to as much. With a large constituency of black members desiring their own identity, limited as it would legally remain, the white members acknowledged their own racial double-standard. They remarked, "It is known to all that the coloured part of our church can not enter a complaint nor bear testimony against the white portion of the church." They confessed that the conflict between their Baptist theological values and their race-based practice compelled them to accept separation. "There seemed then to be such a glaring inconsistency," they argued, "in holding members in church fellowship who are denied this privilege of church membership that the objection brought against such an organization [a separate black church] do not weigh equal to the arguments in favor of it." Far from accepting the imminent separation of the church jubilantly, the white members viewed the reluctance of the blacks to attend the white meetings with "feelings of mystification and solicitude."[33]

In assessing why African-American Baptists sought to establish semi-independent churches, historians rightly tend to emphasize black agency. Ira

Berlin, for example, depicts black Baptists as desirous of independence after merely sipping at the fount of Baptist egalitarianism. Moreover, they accepted white limitations of their independence, "Confident they could outwit and outlast the white ministers and laymen who supervised their affairs." Church records strongly suggest that, in many cases, white Baptists in Kentucky desired separation as well, since the enthusiastic worship of black Baptists did not fit with the respectable image that white Baptists were trying to project. In the cities first, then in the towns, as the drive for refinement spread, black Baptists found themselves less welcome in white churches. Though Lexington had a black congregation as early as 1786, the first black church that was legitimated by other Baptists as properly constituted began in the early 1820s. Louisville Baptists quickly followed in 1829 with a small separate congregation of black members who were aligned with the white church of that growing city. In the 1840s and 1850s, the era Baptists tended to see as "the age of improvement," growing towns like Frankfort, Shelbyville, Danville, and Versailles saw the black members of the Baptist church granted separation. Over a dozen more such separations occurred in the 1850s in towns such as Maysville, Richmond, Nicholasville, and Paris.[34] Fortunately, their desires for independence and the ease with which Baptist churches could be created offered blacks new opportunities to express their own Baptist identities.

When black members established separate churches under the "watch care," or authority, of the predominantly white church, they did not turn their back on the larger Baptist movement and its priorities in the "age of improvement." If anything, they embraced them and then out-performed their white counterparts. The black churches at Louisville and Lexington, the vanguard of separating congregations, stand out in this regard. For example, white churches began supporting ministerial education and professionalization widely in the late 1830s. The acceptance of preachers as the managers of a refined denomination led the Baptist Association to opine in their 1850 circular letter that "those in the ministry should be the leaders in the age of improvement." But the urban black church members had already agreed and had actually been pursuing that course already. In 1842, the African church of Louisville became the first church in Kentucky to pay the money necessary to constitute their pastor as a life member of the Western Baptist Publishing and Sunday School Society. Even some white Baptists viewed black preachers as leaders of the movement. In Lexington, African-American pastor London Ferrill received accolades not only from his congregation of over 1,000, but from whites as

well. Baptist newspaper editor W. C. Buck heard one citizen of Lexington re-mark that Ferrill's leadership and influence did "more to suppress vice than all the police of the city." To Buck, this recognition exceeded all the college degrees and "vain honors" sought by white preachers. The church programs established in the urban African churches rivaled their white counterparts as well. The Louisville African church, which had 400 members in 1842, oper-ated a Sabbath school with 100 students. In addition, its Temperance Society, "pledged to total abstinence," numbered over 400 members.[35]

Some African-American Baptists even seem to have embraced the quest for refinement in their church buildings. Between 1857 and 1858, the United Baptist Church, Colored, of Richmond experienced significant internal con-troversy over the issue of improvement. The church had a pastor, John S. Irvine, but also had a licentiate preacher, Madison Campbell, among the member-ship. The church met in a small log cabin measuring eighteen by eighteen feet, but the members began to desire a new, brick building. To some members, Campbell seemed to have a greater influence in the church and seemed better suited to raise funds to pay for the expensive construction. This trust in the licentiate Campbell damaged his relationship with Irvine, the pastor. Tension between two or more preachers in any church was not unheard of, and the Richmond church split over whether Irvine should remain their pastor or if Campbell would better suit a church seeking to improve itself. In 1858, the church voted to call Campbell as pastor and to ask for Irvine's resignation. The Irvine minority, however, challenged the election. To quell the troubles, the church enlisted a committee of white Baptists to help. This committee proc-tored a secret ballot election and Campbell won. Thus, the church proceeded to pursue their refinement unabated.[36]

Still, as much as the practices of the African churches mirrored those of the white majority, the white Baptists kept a visible distance between the races. Despite any "solicitude" expressed when black Baptists separated from whites, the issue of race colored the Baptist sense of brotherhood. One of the clearest expressions of this differentiation appeared in S. H. Ford's *Christian Repository* in 1859. Though typically the pages of the monthly journal offered short biographies, historical essays, serial fiction, and theological treatises, in January 1859, Ford offered a brief essay on "Types of the Human Race." He ad-opted commonly mentioned categories of race—Caucasian, Mongolian, and Ethiopian—then discussed them according to their level of "advancement." At the apex of civilization, according to Ford, was the Caucasian race, wherein

"The Four Representatives of Mankind." *Christian Repository*, Louisville, Kentucky, January 1859.

"the moral feelings and intellectual powers . . . have been developed in the highest degree of perfection which human nature has ever exhibited." The Mongolians ranked somewhat lower since their "energies have been developed in an inferior degree." In contrast, the Ethiopian branch of the human race "has ever remained in a rude and comparatively barbarous state." In Africa, "They have retained their character unchanged, after centuries of intercourse with the most enlightened nations."[37]

Baptist newspaperman W. C. Buck had expressed a similar perspective in 1849 in *The Slavery Question*. Buck wrote the treatise during a heated debate that consumed the state of Kentucky after voters approved a revision of the 1799 constitution. Buck argued that the Bible justified slavery, though as practiced in the United States, the institution was "a perversion of slavery," since it made "no provision for the improvement and moral training of the slave" and disregarded "the marriage relation." This perverted brand of slavery had ill effects on the white population as well, given its "evil influences upon the moral and social interests" of whites. Buck believed the deficient nature of the institution called for "appropriate remedies," but only when the slaves had become "sufficiently enlightened for self-government." Though the system perniciously affected whites, Buck claimed slavery was ultimately good for the slaves. He argued that compared to "the condition of the native Africans," America's slave population had been "vastly improved by being brought as slaves to this country."[38]

The rhetoric and actions of Kentucky Baptists in the antebellum "age of improvement" thus reveal a complex amalgam of their ideals about polity and the realities of racism. After 1840, more than any time in their history, white Baptists accepted the prescriptions of the dominant culture. They desired educated ministers, stately meeting houses, refined and subdued worship, and subservient black members. Their fluid Baptist ecclesiastical structure easily allowed for separate black churches, but cultural assumptions and expectations compelled only semi-separate bodies of black believers. Rhetoric like Buck's indicated the belief that Kentucky's slaves were "rapidly approaching that state of intellectual improvement and moral refinement which will fit them for self-government and national independence." Yet in his own association, Buck and his fellow Baptists refused to recognize African-American preacher Henry Adams as a delegate, despite the fact that Adams ministered to the largest congregation in Louisville.[39]

Members from the Louisville African church attended the Long Run Association for one of the first times in 1843 along with the recognized delegates

from their white "mother" church. The highlight of the association's Saturday-morning business session occurred when the members from the Louisville African church requested that "their pastor be received as a messenger to the Association, in addition to the messengers chosen from the First [white] church." Many of the convened delegates did not wish to discuss the issue, and a motion was made to vote without debate. That motion narrowly failed, 30 to 35. After debating the African church's request, the association denied that Adams could represent his church independently. Adams then requested to speak, which the messengers unanimously granted. In his unrecorded remarks, Henry Adams asked if the association even "considered the Colored church a member of their body." The association members agreed that Adams's church was a part of the association, but they cited a proposition that the African church had accepted the previous year, their inaugural year, that the white church would represent them before the larger body. As happened with other black churches, the African-American leaders had sacrificed representation for quasi-independence. Adams's frustration was with the undemocratic result of this bargain, since his church was the most successful in the region. His was one of twenty-six churches in the association, but it was the largest in membership—almost twice as large as its mother church. Its membership alone accounted for almost 18 percent of the total associational membership. Even so, the church had no voting privileges in the association. This undemocratic pattern was common. The Bracken Association refused the messengers from the large African churches in Maysville and Mayslick—the two largest churches in its area. Together those churches accounted for 22 percent of the association's membership. Likewise, the 275-member African church of Tate's Creek was represented to its association by the 150-member white-controlled mother church.[40]

However much such restrictions at association meetings chafed black preachers like Henry Adams, the indignity—significant as it was—lasted only one weekend a year. Meanwhile, throughout the year, the presence and activity of black preachers worked to spread the Baptist impulse among ever-increasing circles of influence. The ordained and recognized black preachers, along with lay exhorters, dramatically affected the growth of the movement and shaped the foundation of post-Civil War black Baptist life. Some of these preachers who became leaders of the black Baptists came in contact with Christianity as a subversive influence. Elisha Green, for example, who was born a slave in Bourbon County around 1818, attended covert Sabbath schools as a boy. Reflecting on his youth after the days of slavery had passed, Green recalled

how some of the older slaves on his plantation would organize such schools, being careful to change the time and place to evade the slave patrollers, who might have mistaken the meetings for sessions to plot escape. Though Green first encountered faith practices covertly, he converted as a teenager while plowing in the fields of his owner, the Baptist preacher Walter Warder. Several years later, Green noted that while he was a member of the church in Mayslick, he began to feel a call to preach. In 1845, the church approved his license and gave him relatively great latitude to preach "in the public before the colored population of this city or any others before whom in the providence of God he may be cast." Green gained a name for himself in Flemingsburg after the Methodists allowed him to use their meeting house. He gained quite a following there until, as he recalled, the Methodists "saw that the influence of the Baptists, through my instrumentality, was becoming strong." By 1860, Green pastored two churches, the larger being the African church in Mayslick. With a membership of 264 in 1860, Green pastored over 11 percent of the members of the Bracken Association.[41] Along with Green, other significant black preachers worked within the established ecclesiastical norms of Baptist life and helped bring thousands of black Kentuckians into the Baptist fold.[42]

When African-American Baptists in Kentucky began requesting and forming their separate institutions, they were participating in and expressing the Baptist impulse. The relative ease with which they established a new church came out of the democratic, locally driven ethic. All that was necessary to create a semi-independent black congregation was a desire on the part of the blacks and a vote from the local white church. This accomplished, the black Baptists in most respects governed themselves like members of any other Baptist church. Their converts entered the church through the same "watery grave" of baptism that whites came through. Even as the larger movement tended to embrace the priorities of the culture of slavery and defended slavery as a positive good, black converts continued to affiliate themselves with the Baptist churches. Then, as the white Baptists desired to refine their churches in structure and practice, and grew uncomfortable with the black adherents' enthusiasm—which had been part of the Baptist's "primitive" past—black Baptists found even more opportunities in their own decidedly Baptist congregations. Their rapidly growing churches also became the seedbed for other black churches. Henry Adams's African church in Louisville, for example, had grown to 744 members in 1844, when some members separated to form a new black church, the Second Colored Church, Louisville. By 1860, the original

church had almost 1,000 members while the filial church claimed 690.[43] The opportunities in the Baptist church which grew out of the movement's theology and polity appealed to many blacks, both slave and free. Their unabashed commitment to their churches was clearest after emancipation, when the black Baptist churches continued to grow and then voluntarily aligned in their own associations beginning in 1867. After an ill-fated attempt in 1865, Kentucky's black Baptists also formed a successful state-wide convention in 1869 to promote unity of effort among their churches and associations.[44] Clearly, the experiences of Kentucky's black Baptists in the nineteenth century reveal their ability to create their own Baptist identity in a developing African-American community.

7

Refining and Radiating the Impulse

"Infant baptism is a doomed institution," wrote the 1859 Tate's Creek Association in their circular letter, quoting the writings of recently deceased Baptist newspaperman John Lighthorse Waller. The letter continued, "The evangelical current is sweeping it into the ocean of things that were." This kind of doctrinal pugnaciousness matched Waller's temper. His career as pastor, newspaper editor, debater, and publisher had brought his name and views into the homes and churches of antebellum western Baptists, and his bellicosity made him famous as a Baptist champion in the post-Campbell era. One of his contemporaries noted, "Waller loves controversy; it is his vital air, without it his energies remain dormant, he languishes and must be unhappy." The art of polemic and apologetic were Waller's stock-in-trade. That the delegates at the 1859 Tate's Creek Association, representing over 2,000 Baptists in the heart of the Bluegrass region, would quote him directly and so dramatically shows not only their approval of Waller's opinions, but the shared optimism pervading the Baptist movement on the cusp of the Civil War. They truly believed that their pedobaptist rivals were destined for the ash heap of religious history. Their confidence was not entirely unfounded. By 1860, the Baptists

in Kentucky numerically dominated other religious groups. Counting official membership only, one out of every twelve Kentuckians was Baptist. Given the hesitance of Baptists to accept children, a more accurate calculation would preclude that portion of the population. Of Kentuckians age ten and over, roughly one in every eight was a member of a Baptist church. The actual representation of Baptist adherents in the state was undoubtedly much higher, since many more men and women affiliated themselves with a church in doctrine but not

John L. Waller. Frontispiece, *Christian Repository*, Louisville, Kentucky, 1856.

as official members. Nationwide, there were three Methodists for every two Baptists. In Kentucky, however, as in six other states, the Methodist juggernaut had failed to outpace the Baptists. Though they could not know it, the Baptists' hopes for continued growth would be fulfilled.[1]

Before the Baptists entered this new stage of growth, the movement gradually completed the transformative process they had begun in the struggles and revisions between 1825 and 1845. Among the important elements aiding this process was the formation of the Southern Baptist Convention (SBC) in 1845 over the issues of slavery and missionary activity. From 1814 onward, foreign and domestic missionary organizations served as the foremost recognizably Baptist efforts on the national level. In the late 1830s, state conventions like Kentucky's funded missionaries on the state level, and large associations did likewise on a regional level. Mission societies unaffiliated with conventions and associations also enjoyed the support of some Baptist individuals. These local organizations served particularly destitute regions where individual churches could not effectively preach the gospel. However, the nationally focused Baptist mission organizations had to deal with the growing sectional tensions between the North and South. Tensions flared as controversy erupted in the early 1840s over the issue of slavery. Georgia and Alabama Baptists, testing the allegedly neutral position of the national mission societies, forced the slavery question in 1844. Those southern states tested whether a slave owner could be appointed as a missionary. Southerners asserted that the slavery issue had never been a point of orthodoxy for those doing mission work. If the mission boards became dogmatic, they would violate their own constitutions. In response to these test cases, the domestic mission society declined to act and the foreign mission society sided with northern anti-slavery interests. Thus, in 1845, delegates representing offended southerners formed the Southern Baptist Convention: an organization that would allow slave owners to become missionaries.[2]

The attitude of Kentucky's borderland Baptists during the crisis and after the schism ranged widely from fervent to practically dismissive, with caution abounding in the middle. W. C. Buck, who succeeded John L. Waller as editor of the largest Baptist newspaper in the West, began his tenure in 1841 by addressing the crisis. Like many other Kentuckians, Buck saw himself as a westerner. Regarding the union of the denomination, Buck wrote, "'United we stand—divided we fall,' and the West, we trust, will interpose and prevent a serious division in our ranks, apparently so earnestly desired by the fierce ultraists, North and South."[3] A year later, in the context of denominational

strife, Buck addressed the looming national crisis in religious terms, suggesting that sectionalism itself was a punishment from "the Moral Governor of the Universe to rebuke us for our sins." The majority of Christians, cried Buck in his jeremiad, had been "so entirely identified with the great political parties" that they forgot that "God was the ruler of nations." The Bethel Association in southwest Kentucky echoed Buck's fears in 1844. Their concerns coincided with the most passionate days of the Baptist crisis and the virulently partisan national election of 1844. Complaining of the spiritual debility and languor that characterized "our American Zion," they blamed a lack of dependence on God and a preponderance of partisan spirit. Getting right with God, they suggested, would allow Christians to pursue political matters as "religious, conscientious men," armed with "a calm, serene patriotism" that would be "the more effectual because of its moderation and firmness, its conscientiousness and sanctity."[4]

While acknowledging this same spirit of partisanship had led to a "year of unexampled spiritual declension," the Long Run Association took a more aggressive stand regarding the Southern Baptist Convention than other associations had. The churches of Long Run were located near Louisville, and, in 1845, noting that the association occupied "a more extended border line upon the free States than any other Association of Baptists," they asserted, "Here the struggle upon the slavery question has to be met." Rather than seek a moderating position based upon their distinct identity as westerners, the Long Run delegates claimed that the mission boards had been "subversive of the rights of the churches in the slaveholding States," and had "elevated the pride of the Anti-Missionary Baptists." Thus, the association advised their fellows to "make common cause upon the subject of missions with our brethren of the South." And the new SBC was a conspicuously southern enterprise. At its 1845 constituting convention, 93 percent of those present came from Georgia, South Carolina, or Virginia. With the support of such likeminded associations and churches, the new southern mission boards served as focal points for creating a greater sense of denominational identity. They also provided the needed cohesiveness to encourage creation of other denominationally oriented, southern institutions.[5]

Though a sense of national denominational identity existed before the 1845 sectional split, the concerns expressed about Baptist disunion are ironic, since no real union existed in the first place. Mission boards and publishing houses allowed for common cause, but Baptists cherished congregational localism.

In 1846, one year after the sectional separation, the West Union Association, composed of churches in far-west Kentucky and northwestern Tennessee, made this point apparent in their circular letter. The association exhorted their members to continue in the "true faith," which they characterized as being true to the Bible and defending their congregational and democratic form of church government. To be sure, this association supported missionary boards without hesitation. In fact, they recommended preacher Henry H. Richardson to serve with the Home Mission Society. Still, they forcefully resisted the idea of a denomination whose "written formulas have a binding force, which extends to the remotest churches." In such a system, they earnestly exclaimed, any "errors, when they obtain place, must become denominational!!!" On the other hand, the Baptists, they said, manifested the "practical working of this simple scriptural machinery," wherein "errors may exist in one, two, or more churches," but not across the denomination. Without an actual link or connection binding the churches beyond the local association, most Baptists continued their work much as they had before the sectional division.[6]

Though no real institutional unity existed among antebellum Baptists on par with that of the Methodists or Presbyterians, by the mid-1840s the collective Kentucky Baptist self-image had begun to evolve from sectarian to denominational. The very success of the Baptist movement in the pluralistic early republic invited a new denominational mindset. This evolution coincided with, indeed, was a key component of, a religious quest for refinement. Concerned about this evident transformation, the churches of the Concord Association voiced their worry about how success would affect Baptist purity and piety. Baptist churches, they claimed, had granted membership to applicants without proper examination, and had been too relaxed in discipline. Such churches could not claim to be the kind of pure church that would "be as a city set upon a hill." Foundational to this concern was the new image of Baptists in the nation. The association wrote in their letter to the churches that Baptists were once "a poor and despised people in this country, and it was not supposed that any man would be a Baptist, if he could help it." But times were different, and "things have greatly changed," they continued. "The Baptists have become a popular denomination of Christians." Baptists wanted and celebrated their numerical dominance in the state, but even in the midst of their prosperity, they expressed anxiety over the possible loss of their distinctiveness and purity.[7]

The newly refined Baptist image hinged upon an educated pastorate. The drive for ministerial education in Kentucky, which had been an important

result of the conflict with Alexander Campbell, continued after that turmoil had ceased. Likewise, a competitive drive remained a part of associational advisory admonishments. In 1849, the Bethel Association heard one of the first reports from their committee on education. The committee appealed to their fellow Baptists' patriotism first. They argued in democratic terms that "the welfare and prosperity of a free nation require a large amount of virtue and intelligence in the mass of the people," though "knowledge, if unsanctified, is power for evil." They warned, however, that Baptists should not rely on other religious groups to provide such sanctified education. Rather, the very "prosperity of the Baptists as a denomination, demands that they should . . . anticipate the moral and intellectual wants of the community." To make the danger of inaction as clear as possible to their fellow Baptists in southwest Kentucky, they declared, "If we do not meet the demand, other denominations will." Without effort and success in the endeavor, "We shall eventually find ourselves dispossessed of the land."[8] The North Bend Association's 1854 circular letter articulated the same message in more tempered tones and offered a connection to the not-to-distant frontier past. They desired an educated ministry, but believed that men "with warm hearts and strong minds" though without the means to "acquire a thorough preparation for the field" should still be sent to work. In militaristic language they concluded, "Well-disciplined regulars may form the nucleus of an army, while much of its efficiency and power, may be given by active and ardent volunteers." They conceived that, like Christian soldiers, educated Baptist ministers would combat the errors propounded by the dark powers of papacy and pedobaptism.[9]

Along with educating the clergy, another aspect of creating denominational gentility dealt with sobering up the Baptist image. As with most Americans, alcohol intake among Baptists in the early 1800s was considered no vice. In fact, for most Kentuckians, it was part of common hospitality. In the 1830s, when the temperance movement began to gain a following in Kentucky, it unsurprisingly encountered resistance in the state where much of the nation's grain for alcohol took root. Zachariah Worley, a Baptist preacher and the son of a distiller, noted the occasion that drove him to temperance. At an association meeting, the older preachers and many others in the neighborhood celebrated the close of the first day with decanters of brandy and whiskey, as was their custom. Worley and several other young preachers resolved to condemn drinking alcohol in every sermon they delivered over the next year. Despite their best efforts, alcohol consumption was simply woven into the

economic and social fabric of life.[10] Still, Baptists, for all their tippling, drew the line at drunkenness and the accompanying loss of self-control. Though evidently not a problem for women, Baptist men succumbed to drunkenness in epidemic proportions. Upwards of 25 percent of male exclusions followed convictions of drunkenness.[11] The plague of intemperance infected ministers and laity alike. J. H. Spencer's two-volume history of early Kentucky Baptists is suffused with accounts of inebriated pastors, many of whom were excluded by their own congregations. The few clergymen who dared and desired to introduce temperance reform into their churches met deep resistance. Orson Holland Morrow, for example, formed a temperance society in the Sulpher Spring church in 1833. News of the resultant congregational disharmony drew crowds from the region to watch the heated church debates over the propriety of Morrow's decision. In the end, a slim majority of members voted to divide the church amicably and allow the minority to form their own church.[12]

By the 1850s, while some controversy still occurred, Baptists appeared more willing to merge the quest for piety with total abstinence from alcohol. Part of this change of heart resulted after the ultra-primitivist minority separated themselves from the more mainstream Baptist majority in the 1840s. To the Primitivists, reform societies like temperance organizations seemed to sap the moral energies from the church. Further, according to some Baptists, organizations like the Sons of Temperance, which utilized secret passwords, initiation rites, and symbolism, resembled dangerous secret societies. Such organizations threatened to secretively conjoin the powers of church and state, which might strip the liberties of the church or usurp a man's primary allegiance to the church. For some Baptists, these secretive groups ran contrary to the public nature of their faith. The movement thrived in part due to its very public initiatory baptismal ceremonies and symbolic communion rituals, which openly reinforced the sense of solidarity.[13]

After the Primitivist schism, and as temperance became a more prominent part of political life in Kentucky, most Baptists embraced the temperance movement. Some churches allowed their meeting houses to be used for temperance assemblies, even allowing the Sons of Temperance to use the facilities. Other churches, though, began to exclude members who joined the secretive Sons of Temperance, prompting several associations to condemn such disfellowshipping. Many associations took the next step and encouraged their churches to support their local temperance efforts and to oppose the traffic and production of alcohol. Most of the associations that condemned intemperance did so with

more than simple piety in mind. Rather, they seemed much more interested in the institutions of respectable society. The Campbell County Association, in its lengthy attack on intemperance, noted the ill effects of alcohol on the drunkard's physiology, its corrupting influence on democratic elections, and its direct impact on crime, poverty, and insanity. Wine and grog, they wrote, ripped open the "domestic circle" where "lies the wife and mother, weltering in her blood, and the husband . . . stands over her with the death weapon in his hand"; thus, Baptists should use the state's legal institutions to follow New England's prohibitionist example. Otherwise, the future of "noble, chivalrous, glorious old Kentuck, looks dark and gloomy."[14]

The advent of Sabbath schools among Kentucky Baptists also reflects the evolution of the Baptist self-image in the West. Generally speaking, the Sabbath school movement was an early nineteenth-century, evangelical, and reformist effort to promote uplift and activity among children who would otherwise find themselves idle and prone to mischief on Sundays. Historians in the mid-twentieth century were quick to label benevolence efforts like Sabbath schools as attempts by bourgeois evangelicals to exert control over the working class. In the case of Sabbath schools, the effort was primarily aimed at working class children. Historian Lois W. Banner's study of benevolence, however, revealed a larger element of Christian, moral republicanism in the voluntary benevolence organizations than had previously been recognized. According to Banner, historical reality is not always "mean, hidden, and sordid," and historical actors did not always act "from fear and from considerations of status and gain."[15]

Baptists in Kentucky were generally cool to the very idea of Sabbath schools before the 1840s. As an innovation, Sabbath schools threatened the primitivist core of Baptist sentiments and had little scriptural foundation. Since most churches lacked the resources to establish their own schools, they held them in cooperation with one another. But to some, that cooperation threatened the commitment to democratic localism. Before their defection in the 1840s, the opinion of the ultra-localist, Primitivist minority on the evils of Sabbath schools stifled early efforts. After all, they reasoned, if God wanted children saved from sin, he would accomplish it without the aid of extra-biblical, human efforts. Besides, by rejecting infant baptism, the Baptists lacked the same emphasis on children found in many other religious groups.[16]

While western Baptists initially approached Sabbath schools hesitantly, their attitudes to the effort quickly warmed. So swift was the change that, by 1849,

one group of Baptists could claim that "the utility and importance of Sabbath schools" as an issue was "settled and no longer debatable." Nevertheless, most Baptist churches did not manifest this certitude in their practice. One denominational historian has estimated that, in 1845, there were less than 500 Sabbath schools in the entire South. Figures from Kentucky support these low statistical estimations. For example, only three of the twenty-three churches in the Russell's Creek Baptist Association had Sabbath schools in 1834. Likewise, just four of the South District Association's seventeen churches operated schools in 1845. As late as 1892, only about half of all churches in the entire South operated schools.[17]

Perhaps unsurprisingly, churches in towns and cities with a large support base and a more concentrated field of mission initiated Sabbath school programs earlier. In 1842, the twenty-three churches of the Long Run Association operated only six schools: four in Louisville, and one each in New Castle and Shelbyville. Thomas Smith taught in the Sabbath school at Georgetown and his diary reveals both the pious idealism of his fellow teachers and the realities of the work. On one September Sunday, with 150 children in attendance, Smith remarked, "With their bright faces, cleanly attired, and learning eyes they form a scene beautiful and enchanting to the eyes of the Christian." Not long after, the gilded veneer wore away, and he noted on one occasion that his young students were "inattentive, disposed to laugh at anything I told them." In another instance, Smith asked a young girl, "Would you not rather have the favor of God, than anything else?" She replied no, and stated matter-of-factly that "she would rather have a new dress." Even with his eyes open to the challenges of teaching, Smith felt "each day more and more convinced of the tremendous importance of Sabbath schools. If it be a fact that the eternal destiny of my scholars is in some measure confided to my hands, with what humility of heart and deep concern should we enter upon . . . our several duties!"[18]

Beyond the destinies of their students, Sabbath schools worked to affect the fortunes of the Baptist denomination—a fact not lost on the Kentucky faithful. While no organized scheme effected the proliferation of schools, town churches in and around the central Bluegrass region led the way. Later, by the mid-1850s, Baptists in the east and west extremes of the state began making earnest appeals for Sabbath schools. The eastern Greenup Association, for example, issued a fourfold argument in its 1858 circular letter for the utility of Sabbath schools. First, they wrote, since churches met only once a month, idle youth needed to be taken "out of the way of

Satan." Second, schools would work to develop latent lay talent, "bringing the mind into activity . . . and the powers of speech into use." Third, both the teachers and the students alike would develop more religious constancy and gain important Bible knowledge. Finally, in an example of the emergent modified Calvinism, the association argued that God could use the schools for the "conversion of sinners." The same year, the western Daviess County Association used similar arguments as they approved a committee's report on Sabbath schools, particularly the best kinds of publications to use for instruction. They recommended materials written by Baptists, even mentioning the specific works produced by southern conservative Baptists like A. C. Dayton. To justify their rejection of northern, ecumenical American Sunday School Union literature, these westerners claimed that "to unite with other denominations" would work to suppress "the very truths the holding of which constitutes us as Baptists." The result would be "not only suicidal to us as a denomination, but treasonable to the King of Zion."[19] By meeting the schools every Sunday, churches which met only once a month for worship would become accustomed to weekly services. By training up children and even their families in organized and frequent Baptist instruction, Sabbath schools, it was believed, would "work a complete revolution in the churches."[20] The scattered voices and actions that signaled the acceleration of the Sabbath school movement among Baptists in Kentucky point also to the increasing convergence of piety, institutional refinement, and denominational identity that began in the 1830s. The Baptist commitment to local islands of democracy only kept these developments from occurring more rapidly and smoothly.

Of all the issues creating denominational turbulence among Baptists in antebellum Kentucky, none fomented more tumult than the emergence of Landmarkism. According to historian James E. Tull, Kentucky Baptist newspaperman John L. Waller inadvertently prompted the "actual beginning of the Landmark controversy" when he published his thoughts on the validity of immersions performed by pedobaptists.[21] Waller's 1848 essay responded to a letter from Richard B. Burleson, one of his readers in Alabama, asking for the editor's views on the topic. Burleson feared his Muscle Shoals Association might divide on the issue without an amicable solution. Waller summarized the problem: "If the administrator be necessary to the validity of baptism *now,* he was *always* necessary. . . . Every administrator from now to the Apostles must be proved to be a proper administrator, or else

all baptisms coming from him will be null and void."[22] To Waller, such sure knowledge of a proper succession of baptisms to the ancient past was "utterly out of the question."[23] Just as significantly, the Kentucky editor asserted "that honest, upright and intelligent brethren may entertain different opinions" on the matter. Practically speaking, and more relevant to his Alabama reader's query, Waller maintained this was a question which "should be left to the decision of the individual church," and that "Associations certainly have nothing whatever to do with it."[24]

Two months after the publication of Waller's essay, a letter to the editor appeared in the *Tennessee Baptist*, J. R. Graves's paper rivaling Kentucky's *Baptist Banner and Western Pioneer* for the attention of the western Baptist mind. Writing with great "sorrow and disappointment" under the pseudonym "Fidus," the author disagreed with his "warm friend" John L. Waller, asserting that Baptists had never accepted the validity of pedobaptist immersions. With certitude, Fidus claimed that Waller's convictions clashed with "the fifty thousand Baptists of Tennessee and North Alabama." Indeed, Fidus averred, Baptists "have invariably, so far as their annals inform us, re-immersed those whom they have received from Rome, or any one of her numerous daughters."[25] In a brief column near this letter, editor Graves echoed Fidus's conviction, further claiming that the "churches in the South West are unanimous in sentiment and feeling on this question."[26]

Throughout the summer of 1848, a heated exchange of correspondence, both personal and theological, was printed in the pages of the *Tennessee Baptist*, between R. B. Burleson, Fidus, and another anonymous writer, known only as "Veritas." Then, in August, Waller offered a fifteen page reply to Fidus and Graves in the *Western Baptist Review*. He wrote that after reading the months of increasingly hostile letters prompted by his essay, he was "perfectly unruffled and as cool as if seated upon an iceberg," and he described Fidus as a writer with a "sound heart, but a very weak head." He pitied Fidus's "bad state of mind," the gall in his heart, his "bad English, and worse logic," and that he seemed "to be afflicted too with an over portion of wind." Countering the assertion made by both Fidus and Graves that the Kentuckian was challenging the accepted wisdom of Baptists across the Southwest, Waller claimed he stood with historical Baptists, who would "rather be right than in a majority." To the contention that Baptists had always re-immersed those received from pedobaptists, Waller parried that Fidus had no proof for his argument, and thus all he said on the subject

was "mere empty sound."[27] More to the point, Waller wrote, Fidus espoused an "anti-Baptist notion of *official grace*—that to a privileged order in the Church is confined the right—the *jus divinum* to administer the ordinances," which further must flow from "regular succession of ecclesiastical officers, from the Apostles to the Baptist ministers of our generation!"[28] At the heart of this controversy were issues pertinent to the core of the Baptist impulse: the nature of the church, the duties of the minister, the importance and nature of baptism. The questions the arguments portended would color the future of the movement in America: how close would the Baptists be with non-Baptists and just how old *was* the Baptist impulse?

Despite their disagreements in 1848, Waller and Graves shared an antipathy to pedobaptism in American life. In an 1849 essay that Graves would later reprint, Waller crowed that infant baptism was on the decline in America. Based on his reading of eastern newspaper articles, he claimed that the Methodists, Episcopalians, and Presbyterians were baptizing fewer and fewer infants as the practice fell into disuse for a variety of reasons. For Waller, the reasons were clear enough: "Infant baptism does not seem to flourish in a free and evangelical atmosphere," but rather in those "countries where Church and State are united and among Papists and those parties of religionists the least removed from Papists."[29] The next year, Waller would echo his own sentiments, condemning the "evils and the corrupting influence of infant baptism." Its character, to Waller, was a "loathsome, monstrous thing." "Its native goblin hideousness" was in other continents, but "the American is an Anti-Pedobaptist atmosphere."[30] To the south, J. R. Graves waged his own campaign against the pedobaptists, depicting himself as a modern-day Jesus or Paul, an agitator defending the truth. Even so, he wrote, "Let the battle still rage, and the war cry still go up—and ten years hence, far greater conquests will have been gained."[31] After the pedobaptist press responded to Graves's hostility, he thundered: "The tremendous conflict has begun, the battle cry resounds upon every side."[32] Both of these two western Baptist editors seemed eager to wage the ultimate religious battle with the pedobaptists.

In this climate of doctrinal contention between friend and foe alike, Graves called for a mass meeting of Baptists at Cotton Grove, Tennessee, which James E. Tull would call the "*official* commencement of the Landmark movement."[33] After an address to the assembled crowd on the topics of Christian unity, the proper mode of baptism, and the error of the pedobaptists, Graves issued and later printed a set of questions:

1st. Can Baptists, consistently with their principles or the Scriptures, recognize those societies not organized according to the pattern of the Jerusalem church, but possessing different *governments*, different *officers*, a different class of *members*, different *ordinances, doctrines,* and *practices*, as churches of Christ?

2nd. Ought they to be called gospel churches, or churches in a religious sense?

3rd. Can we consistently recognize the ministers of such irregular and unscriptural bodies as gospel ministers?

4th. Is it not virtually recognizing them as official ministers to invite them into our pulpits, or *by any other act that would or could be* construed as such recognition?

5th. Can we consistently address as *brethren* those professing Christianity who not only have not the doctrine of Christ and walk not according to his commandments but are arrayed in direct and bitter opposition to them?

A few weeks later, the same questions were posed to the Big Hatchie Association in Tennessee. As had happened at Cotton Grove, the questions were answered in such a way as to cast doubt on the salvation of all non-Baptists and on the legitimacy of their churches and ministers. Other associations across the South and Southwest would follow suit, becoming a grassroots movement.[34] In the pluralistic religious marketplace of mid-nineteenth-century America, the Landmark movement offered Baptists an opportunity to transcend mere rectitude by comparison, that is, which religious group was "*most* right." Rather, Landmarkism encouraged Baptists to claim essential and absolute rightness.

In 1854, James Madison Pendleton would help provide a label for Graves's movement with a small, but controversial, tract. Pastor of the Baptist church in Bowling Green, Kentucky, sixty miles north of Nashville, Pendleton began contributing notices to *The Tennessee Baptist* in 1850. He and Graves affiliated more closely in 1852 when they preached together during a protracted, four-week meeting in Bowling Green. Though Pendleton would later deny Graves's influence, Graves took credit for convincing Pendleton of the Cotton Grove truths during this meeting. Then, in 1854, the Kentuckian contributed a series

of essays to Graves's paper which the newspaperman soon compiled and published as *An Old Landmark Re-set*. The title alluded to a biblical admonition found in Proverbs 22:28: "Remove not the ancient landmark, which thy fathers have set."[35] The original title for Pendleton's treatise better reflects his subject: "Ought Baptists to Recognize Pedobaptist Preachers as Gospel Ministers?" This title seems to correlate well to the fourth Cotton Grove question, but Pendleton's brief tract highlighted how they all interconnected. He argued that if the only true baptism was immersion of believers and baptism was the only door into a true church, then pedobaptist churches were not true churches of Christ at all, but mere societies. It followed, according to Pendleton, that ministers of such societies, lacking true scriptural authority to preach, should not be invited to preach in Baptist pulpits. Pendleton allowed that pedobaptists could be called on to pray, but preaching was a different matter. Baptists, he said, should not commune with pedobaptists at all, lest such affiliation suggest connivance. If these stances should lead to the unpopularity of Baptists in America, Pendleton asked, "What Baptist is afraid of odium? If our people are not yet familiarized with it they ought to be." Lastly, regarding affiliation with Alexander Campbell's Reformers, who also rejected infant baptism and insisted upon immersion, Pendleton merely stated, "I take it for granted that ministerial and religious intercourse between Baptists and Campbellites would be utterly unjustifiable." Fundamental differences on other theological matters disallowed communion.[36]

Despite his assertion that the ideas in *An Old Landmark* were indeed old, Pendleton rapidly encountered resistance within the Kentucky Baptist fold against his treatise. John L. Waller asserted, "The views of Bro. P are not the views of the Baptists, past or present. These views are something new under the sun."[37] Graves vociferously responded to Waller's contention, reiterating, "It is an old landmark, which a modern and false charity and an unscriptural liberality have well-nigh removed, that is sought to be replaced." Quoting numerous sources on early Baptist history, Graves connected the current controversy with his earlier battle with Waller in 1848 over re-immersing those received from pedobaptist churches. For the Tennessee editor, all such issues were resolved by the fact that Baptist churches were the only true churches of Christ.[38]

Pendleton's tract faced criticism from other sources as well, including W. W. Everts, the new pastor of the genteel Walnut Street Baptist Church in Louisville. An ecumenical abolitionist, Everts had just moved to Kentucky

from New York in 1853, and had quickly established his influence in Louisville's Baptist community by investing in Kentucky's two major Baptist periodicals, the *Western Recorder* and the *Christian Repository*.[39] In his review of Pendleton's tract, Everts condemned how this "new dogma" would create a new and "ill-timed" controversy which would distract western Baptists from missionary work and "disaffect them towards the great evangelical unions of our country."[40] According to the review, the controversial tract's argument suffered from two fallacies. First, Pendleton "confounds the essence with the form of the church," which Everts likened to denying the essential "tree-ness" of a sickly, deformed, leafless tree. To Everts, an "imperfectly organized," error-ridden, "irregular and unscriptural" church was nevertheless still a church. Indeed, such a church would be preferable to Everts than a scripturally organized church without "faith, charity, and good works."[41] The second fallacy was that Pendleton "assumed that preaching is exclusively an official act. . . . All may preach what they know of the gospel to all who will hear." Everts asserted that the "commission to preach the gospel was given to the church, and not to an order of men merely." On the issue of communion, the reviewer argued that "a free pulpit does not require a free communion table." In the end, Everts said Pendleton's views seemed less an old landmark than a "new stake, which can be set down and maintained only in sectarian arrogance."[42] Not to be put down, Pendleton offered a twenty-eight page reply to Everts to vindicate his earlier essay. Pendleton denied the existence of such a thing as an ill-timed controversy, noting that "Romanists thought it very unnecessary in the days of Luther." Pendleton's reply and Everts's own subsequent rejoinder largely offered elaboration on previous debate points. Neither writer signaled that they found the other persuasive.[43]

If Baptist churches were the only essentially true churches of Christ and true baptism depended upon a proper succession of immersion baptisms, it flowed logically that the Baptist impulse had ancient roots, extending back to the days of Jesus. Thus, as J. R. Graves and his Landmarkist allies researched the Christian past, they perceived links which logically had to exist and they constructed their arguments on the work of earlier Baptist writers. Though seventeenth-century English Baptists were loath to trace their origins beyond their separation from the Church of England, a few Baptist apologists perceived varying degrees of ancient heritage. For example, Baptist lay preacher Henry Danvers, in his 1674 work entitled *A Treatise of Baptism*, attempted to trace believers' baptism through the ages. He provides numerous examples of

baptism after conversion, but makes no attempt to connect them "genealogically." Likewise, writing in early Georgian England, Thomas Crosby traced opposition to infant baptism as a principle back to the first century, but he made little effort to locate Baptist beginnings much earlier than the Anabaptists of Europe. In England, at best, John Wycliffe and the Lollards had provided an evangelical seedbed in the fourteenth century fertile for anti-pedobaptist ideas.[44] Decades after Crosby, Robert Robinson continued the hunt for Baptist roots. While asserting that "uninterrupted succession is a specious lure, a snare set by sophistry . . . necessary only to such churches as regulate their faith and practice by tradition," Robinson surveyed early and medieval European Christian groups, finding anti-pedobaptist principles as well as dissent for the sake of conscience. These he connected with Baptist principles in the 1780s.[45]

The effort to trace Baptist continuity in genealogical fashion flowered in the early nineteenth century. As pedobaptist attacks increased against the growing Baptist movement, the inclination grew stronger to articulate and defend Baptist origins. Though several American Baptist preachers gave arguments for succession of belief, arguably the most influential writing to early Landmarkers was that of G. H. Orchard, an English Baptist minister and historian.[46] Leaning heavily on secondary sources such as Danvers and Robinson, Orchard offered *A Concise History of Foreign Baptists* in 1838, which proposed a "connected history" to link Baptists with the New Testament apostles. In 1855, arguing that "if the world is ever favored with a faithful history of Christian Churches, it will receive it from Baptists," J. R. Graves reprinted Orchard's work, adding a preface wherein he described the book as "the most valuable chronological history of the Churches of Christ, now extant."[47]

Prominent Kentucky Baptist authors agreed with and built upon Orchard's model even prior to Graves's reprint. Even as John L. Waller and Graves vehemently contended with each other on issues such as baptism's "proper administrator," they agreed on church successionism. In 1852, Waller used the pages of the *Christian Repository* to explain his views at length, concluding "that the churches of the first ages of Christianity, were Baptist churches. We might trace the existence of these churches, step by step, through every successive age from that time to the present."[48] In the same year and in similar fashion, publisher S. H. Ford preached a sermon to the West Union Baptist Association in far western Kentucky on the "Past and Future of the Baptist Churches." At best a sketch, and largely dependent on the thought of eighteenth-century Lutheran historian J. L. Mosheim, Ford's sermon rhetorically asked where the origins of

the denomination lay. Touching on the Lollards, the Waldenses, the Arnoldists, the Paulicians, the Donatists, and the Novations, Ford found signs of Baptist principles, but not the origins. These, he claimed, lay "in the Apostolic age, amid Judea's hills."[49] Ford would later expand his sketch to a full-fledged book, first serialized in the *Christian Repository* in 1857 and then published as *The Origin of the Baptists* in 1860 at J. R. Graves's publishing house.[50]

Because of the fluid and democratic nature of the Baptist impulse, Landmarkist ideas spread to Kentucky's Baptist churches in irregular fashion. Churches had to decide for themselves whether they would embrace the ideas of Graves, Pendleton, and others. The 1858 gathering of the Sulphur Fork Association reveals how Baptists could grapple with new ideas and remain true to their ethic. Among many resolutions passed at that meeting, the association resolved each member church should decide and report the following year on "a question that has never been decided among us, as Baptists, whether it is consistent and scriptural to receive immersed Reformers and Pedobaptists into our fellowship on their baptism." Though each church could respond how it wished, the association resolved that "consistency and uniform action in practice" were preferred. Delegates from several churches asked that a committee be appointed to give advice on this topic. The following year the committee delivered their report, and using many of the Landmarkist arguments, concluded that churches should consider "members from alien denominations just as if they came from no denomination at all."[51]

The rise of Baptist successionism and Landmarkism among Kentucky Baptists was slowed by the sectional conflict between the North and South. Publishers W. C. Buck and John L. Waller probably best represent the border-state Baptist position on the burgeoning conflict. Early on, as Kentucky's legendary Senator Henry Clay pushed his omnibus bill through Congress, Buck editorialized how extremists in North and South forced division upon the nation. Buck claimed the duty he owed to his readers was "to harmonize public sentiment in regard" to the national questions.[52] The next year, Waller warned that sectional separation would not only drag the country down but "the altar fires of our religion would be extinguished in blood, and the cause of Christianity and civilization would suffer throughout the world."[53]

The advent of war did leave Kentucky's churches in a stagnant condition. Widespread social disruption occurred, as thirty to forty thousand Kentucky boys and men joined the Confederate forces and more than twice that number fought for the Union. Raids and guerilla warfare plagued the state and

characterized the conflict in the borderland region. In early September 1861, as Union and Confederate troops occupied key river towns such as Columbus, Paducah, and Louisville, the Long Run Association held its annual meeting. As was their custom, delegates and members from Louisville's seven Baptist churches and from almost two dozen other churches gathered to hear preaching, to socialize, and to conduct business. But J. H. Spencer observed that "there was more war-excitement than spirituality," since many churches split into factions and many were left pastorless. As a preacher, Spencer found it difficult to propound his faith to hearers "in such constant fear of losing their lives or their property." Amid the harsh realities of war, the preacher was at a loss "to get their attention to the gospel." Another chronicle of the period described Baptist churches as "monuments of desolation."[54]

Though the gloom of war restored the "dark and bloody ground" image to Kentucky, the Baptist impulse which pioneers such as William Hickman had brought so many years before survived and thrived. Eighty-five years after preachers like Hickman planted Baptist seeds in western soil, the churches of his faith had become much more organized and refined. Preachers like him now faced greater expectation to be educated and had much more opportunity to be so. They, likewise, had much greater chance to be salaried. The African-American presence and leadership in Baptist life had expanded beyond what could have been imagined. Indeed, some of the largest Baptist churches in the state by mid-century were African-American churches. In the Baptist churches, as in society at large, women played significant cultural roles as genteel warriors of the faith. Theological innovators like Alexander Campbell had tested the resilience of the Baptist impulse in Kentucky, while controversialists like J. R. Graves tried the extent to which that impulse could be intensified before becoming distorted.

Even with dark days on the horizon, Kentucky Baptists celebrated what the future held for their truths. Gathering in 1859 just south of the Ohio River in Owen County, the Baptists of the Ten Mile Association met in north-central Kentucky, but positioned themselves in an eternal schema. "When we look back, not a century ago, the place where we have assembled . . . was one wide wilderness," they wrote in their annual letter. To the Baptists in their rural association, numbering near 1,700, they exclaimed, "The prowling monsters of the forrest [sic] have fled before the march of civilization . . . amid ascending hosannas to God." But it was not just in Kentucky, they asserted, where God's grace would yield "an approaching reign of righteousness." Rather, a "glorious

display of gospel light and liberty" flew across America, "melting the icy hearts of the frozen North, taming the burning passion of the South, and illuminating the dark wilderness of the West."[55] Despite their many differences, Kentucky's Baptists saw their goal as spreading that illuminating light of God, embodied specifically in the Baptist impulse. They committed to disciplined communities of believers "born of the spirit" and immersed into the fellowship; to ministers not from a "limited privileged class"; and to independent churches, "little republic[s] executing the laws of [their] Supreme Lawgiver."[56] Though they could not know that among all the prominent Christian faiths thriving in the Second Great Awakening theirs would be the only one continuing to thrive a hundred years later, they optimistically believed this impulse would transform America and the world.[57]

Appendix: Maps

Kentucky Baptist Associations, associational boundaries, circa 1830.

Pikeville

Greenup

Nez

Ashland

GREENUP

West Liberty
Prestonsburg

Hindman
Hazard
Whitesburg

Maysville

Brooksville

Mt Olivet

BRACKEN

Mount Sterling
Frenchburg
Campton
Stanton

BOONE'S
CREEK
Irvine
Sandgap
Beattyville
Booneville

Harlan

NORTH
CONCORD

Covington
CAMPBELL
COUNTY
Alexandria
UNION

Williamstown
CRITTENDEN
Cynthiana

Paris
ELKHORN
Georgetown
Versailles Winchester
Lexington
Nicholasville

Richmond

TATES
CREEK

Mt Vernon
IRVINE

LAUREL
RIVER

SOUTH
UNION
Whitley City

NORTH
BEND

TEN
MILE

Oventon
CONCORD

FRANKLIN
Frankfort

BAPTIST
Harrodsburg
Stanford
SOUTH
DISTRICT
Lebanon

SOUTH
KENTUCKY
Liberty
CUMBERLAND
RIVER
Somerset

SOUTH
CONCORD

Monticello

Bedford
SULPHER
FORK
Newcastle

Shelbyville
LONG RUN
Louisville

Sherpherdsville

Bardstown

Elizabethtown

Campbellsville
RUSSELL'S
CREEK
Columbia
Glasgow

FREEDOM
Albany

MIDDLE
DISTRICT

SALEM
Hodgenville

LYNN

LIBERTY

BARREN
RIVER
Tompkinsville

Hardinsburg

GOSHEN

Morgantown
Bowling
Green
BAYS
FORK
Green

Franklin

Owensboro

DAVIESS
COUNTY

GASPER
RIVER
Lewisburg

CLEAR
FORK
Russellville
BETHEL

Henderson

LITTLE
BETHEL
Madisonville

Greenville

Hopkinsville

Marion

LITTLE
RIVER

WEST
UNION
Murray

Paducah

MOUNT
OLIVET
Mayfield

Kentucky Baptist Associations, associational boundaries, circa 1860.

Notes

Introduction

1. Minutes of the Baptist (Baptist) Association, 1850, Southern Baptist Historical Library and Archives, Nashville, TN (SBHLA). While most Baptist associations took their names from nearby geographic landmarks, particularly rivers, the members of the Baptist Association chose just the name "Baptist" purposefully at their founding in 1826. They wanted to express their disdain for the Elkhorn Association's efforts to assert what appeared to them to be excessive associational influence. The name choice was unique in Kentucky and led to confusion among the members and other associations. They finally changed their name to the Anderson Baptist Association in 1956. Frank M. Masters, *A History of Baptists in Kentucky* (Louisville: Kentucky Baptist Historical Society, 1953), 243–45.

2. William M. Newman and Peter L. Halvorson, *Atlas of American Religion: The Denominational Era, 1776–1990* (Walnut Creek, CA: AltaMira Press, 2000), 18, 39; H. Leon McBeth, *The Baptist Heritage: Four Centuries of Baptist Witness* (Nashville: Broadman Press, 1987), 200–87 (title hereafter cited *Heritage*); Mark A. Noll, *A History of Christianity in the United States and Canada* (Grand Rapids, MI: William B. Eerdmans, 1992), 91–113; Harry S. Stout, *The Divine Dramatist: George Whitefield and the Rise of Modern Evangelicalism* (Grand Rapids, MI: William B. Eerdmans, 1991); William G. McLoughlin, *New England Dissent, 1630–1833: The Baptists and the Separation of Church and State,* 2 vols. (Cambridge: Harvard University Press, 1971); Clarence C. Goen, *Revivalism and Separatism in New England, 1740–1800* (New Haven, CT: Yale University Press, 1962); William L. Lumpkin, *Baptist Foundations in the South: Tracing through the Separates the Influence of the Great Awakening, 1754–1787* (Nashville: Broadman Press, 1961); Rhys Isaac, *The Transformation of Virginia, 1740–1790* (New York: W. W. Norton, 1982).

3. Of the scores of studies covering this time period, the seminal works include: Gordon S. Wood, *The Radicalism of the American Revolution* (New York: Vintage Books, 1991); Charles Grier Sellers, *The Market Revolution:*

Jacksonian America, 1815–1846 (New York: Oxford University Press, 1991); Steven A. Watts, *The Republic Reborn: War and the Making of Liberal America, 1790–1820* (Baltimore: Johns Hopkins University Press, 1987); Alan Taylor, *William Cooper's Town: Power and Persuasion on the Frontier of the Early American Republic* (New York: A. A. Knopf, 1995); and Sean Wilentz, *Chants Democratic: New York City and the Rise of the American Working Class, 1788–1850* (New York: Oxford University Press, 1984).

4. Significant studies for the early to mid-nineteenth century include: on the social impact of the emergent class stratifications, Wilentz, *Chants Democratic;* Stuart M. Blumin, *The Emergence of the Middle Class: Social Experience in the American City, 1760–1900* (New York: Cambridge University Press, 1989); Mary P. Ryan, *Cradle of the Middle Class: The Family in Oneida County, New York, 1790–1865* (New York: Cambridge University Press, 1981); on the impact of technological developments, Carol Sheriff, *The Artificial River: The Erie Canal and the Paradox of Progress, 1817–1862* (New York: Hill and Wang, 1996); George Rogers Taylor, *The Transportation Revolution, 1815–1860* (New York: Harper Torchbooks, 1951); on social ills and the reform movements responding to them, Ronald G. Walters, *American Reformers, 1815–1860* (New York: Hill and Wang, 1978); Robert H. Abzug, *Cosmos Crumbling: American Reform and the Religious Imagination* (New York: Oxford University Press, 1994); W. J. Rorabaugh, *The Alcoholic Republic: An American Tradition* (New York: Oxford University Press, 1979); and on the sectionalism leading to war, William W. Freehling, *The Road to Disunion*, vol. 1 (New York: Oxford University Press, 1990); and David M. Potter, *The Impending Crisis, 1848–1861* (New York: Harper & Row, 1976).

5. Walter B. Shurden, "The Southern Baptist Synthesis: Is It Cracking?" *Baptist History and Heritage* (April 1981): 2–11.

6. Masters, *A History of Baptists,* 10–53; John B. Boles, *Religion in Antebellum Kentucky* (Lexington: University Press of Kentucky, 1976), 2–8; Leo Taylor Crismon and George Raleigh Jewell, *Kentucky Baptist Atlas* (Middletown, KY: Kentucky Baptist Historical Society, 1964), 1–4.

7. Robert G. Gardner, *Baptists of Early America: A Statistical History, 1639–1790* (Atlanta: Georgia Baptist Historical Society, 1983), 120–23; Masters, *A History of Baptists,* 157, 197, 222; Boles, *Religion in Antebellum Kentucky,* 28–29.

8. Masters, *A History of Baptists,* 257.

9. Masters, *A History of Baptists,* 276, 295, 329; Mark A. Noll, *America's God: From Jonathan Edwards to Abraham Lincoln* (New York: Oxford University Press, 2002), 244; Gardner, *Baptists of Early America,* 21, 35, 57, 77, 117, 121; Newman and Halvorson, *Atlas of American Religion,* 39. The growth of Methodism in Kentucky lagged behind, but grew on par with the Baptists. Comparison of the Baptist population to the Methodists: 1800, 5,119/1,742; 1810, 16,555/7,057; 1830, 39,957/28,189; 1860, 94,759/56,815. Masters, *A History of Baptists,* 157, 160, 222, 329. For further comparisons of Baptists and the Methodists, see Roger Finke and Rodney Stark, *The Churching of America, 1776–1990: Winners and Losers in Our Religious Economy* (New Brunswick, N.J.: Rutgers University Press, 1992), 282–288. The distinction between membership and adherence rates is significant. Each church had a number of regular attendants who never joined the membership due to the harsh demands of entry and continued membership. Yet these "hangers-on" in the congregation still adhered to Baptist doctrines and sentiments. This study accepts the statistical procedures of Finke and Stark for calculating the adherence rate of early religious groups; this work is found in *The Churching of America,* 24–28, and "Turning Pews into People: Estimating Nineteenth-Century Church Membership," *Journal for the Scientific Study of Religion* 25 (1986): 180–192. That said, the ratios presented here are based upon Robert Gardner's estimation of actual membership. Thus, the ratios are conservative estimates.

10. Seminal works on Puritanism include: Perry Miller, *Errand into the Wilderness* (New York: Harper & Row, 1956); Edmund S. Morgan, *Visible Saints: The History of a Puritan Idea* (New York: New York University Press, 1963); and Edmund S. Morgan, *The Puritan Family: Religion & Domestic Relations in Seventeenth-Century New England* (New York: Harper & Row, 1966). Revivalism has long been an object of scholarly fascination. Significant early works on revivals include: William Warren Sweet, *Revivalism in America: Its Origin, Growth, and Decline* (New York: Abingdon Press, 1944); Whitney R. Cross, *The Burned-Over District: The Social and Intellectual History of Enthusiastic Religion in Western New York, 1800–1850* (New York: Octagon Books, 1950); Charles A. Johnson, *The Frontier Camp Meeting: Religion's Harvest Time* (Dallas: Southern Methodist University Press, 1955); Bernard A. Weisberger, *They Gathered at the River: The Story of the Great Revivalists and Their Impact upon Religion in America* (Boston: Little, Brown and Company, 1958). More recent scholarship on revivals has included: John B. Boles, *The Great Revival, 1787–1805: The Origins of the Southern*

Evangelical Mind (Lexington: University Press of Kentucky, 1972); Dickson D. Bruce, *And They All Sang Hallelujah: Plain-Folk Camp-Meeting Religion, 1800–1845* (Knoxville: University of Tennessee Press, 1974); Paul K. Conkin, *Cane Ridge: America's Pentecost* (Madison, WI: University of Wisconsin Press, 1990); Leigh Eric Schmidt, *Holy Fairs: Scottish Communions and American Revivals in the Early Modern Period* (Princeton, NJ: Princeton University Press, 1989); Kenneth O. Brown, *Holy Ground: A Study of the American Camp Meeting* (New York: Garland, 1992); George M. Thomas, *Revivalism and Cultural Change: Christianity, Nation Building, and the Market in the Nineteenth-Century United States* (Chicago: University of Chicago Press, 1989); Ellen Eslinger, *Citizens of Zion: The Social Origins of Camp Meeting Revivalism* (Knoxville: University of Tennessee Press, 1999).

11. Some of the best works covering these marginal early movements are: Richard L. Bushman, *Joseph Smith and the Beginnings of Mormonism* (Urbana: University of Illinois Press, 1984); Marvin S. Hill, *Quest for Refuge: The Mormon Flight from American Pluralism* (Salt Lake City: Signature Books, 1989); Lawrence Foster, *Women, Family, and Utopia: Communal Experiments of the Shakers, the Oneida Community, and the Mormons* (Syracuse: Syracuse University Press, 1991); Jan Shipps, *Mormonism: The Story of a New Religious Tradition* (Urbana and Chicago: University of Illinois Press, 1985); Jay P. Dolan, *The American Catholic Experience: A History from Colonial Times to the Present* (Garden City, NY: Doubleday, 1985); Jay P. Dolan, *Catholic Revivalism: The American Experience, 1830–1900* (Notre Dame: University of Notre Dame Press, 1978); and Paul E. Johnson and Sean Wilentz, *The Kingdom of Matthias: A Story of Sex and Salvation in 19th-Century America* (New York: Oxford University Press, 1994).

12. The phrase is quoted from Joel A. Carpenter, who himself adapted it from Timothy L. Smith. Joel A. Carpenter, *Revive Us Again: The Reawakening of American Fundamentalism* (New York: Oxford University Press, 1997), 4; Timothy L. Smith, "The Evangelical Kaleidoscope and the Call to Christian Unity," *Christian Scholar's Review* 15 (1986): 125–140.

13. Nathan O. Hatch, *The Democratization of American Christianity* (New Haven, CT: Yale University Press, 1989), 39; Jon Butler, *Awash in a Sea of Faith: Christianizing the American People* (Cambridge: Harvard University Press, 1990), 272, 287.

14. Christine Leigh Heyrman, *Southern Cross: The Beginnings of the Bible Belt* (New York: Knopf, 1997); Philip N. Mulder, *A Controversial Spirit: Evangelical Awakenings in the South* (New York: Oxford University Press, 2002).

15. James R. Rohrer, *Keepers of the Covenant: Frontier Missions and the Decline of Congregationalism, 1774–1818* (New York: Oxford University Press, 1995); Jonathan D. Sassi, *A Republic of Righteousness: The Public Christianity of Post-Revolutionary New England Clergy* (New York: Oxford University Press, 2001); Douglas A. Sweeney, *Nathaniel Taylor, New Haven Theology, and the Legacy of Jonathan Edwards* (New York: Oxford University Press, 2003).

16. Hatch, *Democratization,* 220–224; Nathan Hatch, "The Puzzle of American Methodism," *Church History* 63 (June 1994): 175–189. Also opening the door to further study of Methodism was Russell E. Richey, *Early American Methodism* (Bloomington: Indiana University Press, 1991). This wealth of recent scholarship on Methodism includes: A. Gregory Schneider, *The Way of the Cross Leads Home: The Domestication of American Methodism* (Bloomington: Indiana University Press, 1993); David Hempton, *The Religion of the People: Methodism and Popular Religion, c. 1750–1900* (London: Routledge, 1996); Cynthia Lynn Lyerly, *Methodism and the Southern Mind, 1770–1810* (New York: Oxford University Press, 1998); Christopher H. Owen, *The Sacred Flame of Love: Methodism and Society in Nineteenth-century Georgia* (Athens: University of Georgia Press, 1998); William R. Sutton, *Journeymen for Jesus: Evangelical Artisans Confront Capitalism in Jacksonian Baltimore* (University Park: Pennsylvania State University Press, 1998); John H. Wigger, *Taking Heaven by Storm: Methodism and the Rise of Popular Christianity in America* (New York: Oxford University Press, 1998); Dee E. Andrews, *The Methodists and Revolutionary America, 1760–1800: The Shaping of an Evangelical Culture* (Princeton, NJ: Princeton University Press, 2000); Philip F. Hardt, *The Soul of Methodism: The Class Meeting in Early New York City Methodism* (Lanham, MD: University Press of America, 2000); and Nathan O. Hatch and John H. Wigger, eds. *Methodism and the Shaping of American Culture* (Nashville: Kingswood Books, 2001).

17. Wigger, *Taking Heaven by Storm,* 6; Newman and Halvorson, *Atlas of American Religion,* 39.

18. Noll, *America's God,* 149.

19. Hatch, *Democratization,* 101; Paul K. Conkin, *The Uneasy Center: Reformed Christianity in Antebellum America* (Chapel Hill: University of North Carolina Press, 1995), 59.

20. McBeth, *Heritage,* 205–206, 229–235; William H. Brackney, ed., *Baptist Life and Thought: 1600–1980* (Valley Forge, PA: Judson Press, 1983), 95–105; W. Glenn Jonas, Jr., ed., *The Baptist River: Essays on Many Tributaries of a Diverse Tradition* (Macon, GA: Mercer University Press, 2008). Jewel L. Spangler has challenged the widely held consensus and argued that the differences between Regular and Separate Baptists are "overemphasized." She asserts that the "groups at times acknowledged that there was little difference between them, and both groups sought union at various times." This study finds and accepts well-documented evidence of substantial differences, but seeks to peer beyond these differences to capture those elements that allowed for the eventual (but contentious) synthesis of the Regulars and Separates. Jewel L. Spangler, "Becoming Baptists: Conversion in Colonial and Early National Virginia," *Journal of Southern History* 67 (May 2001): 248, n. 10. Spangler also asserts, based on her in-depth study of two Virginia churches, that the Baptist movement grew in the South primarily because of "its promise to provide social order through a heightened self-discipline and its ability to elicit intimate interpersonal contact and intense emotional release." Spangler, "Becoming Baptists," 246. While these factors are hard to deny, they apply just as well if not better to the Methodist movement. This study will analyze common characteristics such as these, but will also search for distinctions.

21. William G. McLoughlin, *Isaac Backus and the American Pietistic Tradition* (Boston: Little, Brown, 1967); Guy Thomas Halbrooks, "Francis Wayland: Contributor to Baptist Concepts of Church Order" (Ph.D. diss., Emory University, 1971); James A. Rogers, *Richard Furman: Life and Legacy* (1985; reprint, Macon, GA: Mercer University Press, 2001); A. James Fuller, *Chaplain to the Confederacy: Basil Manly and Baptist Life in the Old South, 1798–1868* (Baton Rouge: Louisiana State University Press, 2000); and Anthony L. Chute, *A Piety Above the Common Standard* (Macon, GA: Mercer University Press, 2004).

22. Susan Juster, *Disorderly Women: Sexual Politics and Evangelicalism in Revolutionary New England* (Ithaca, NY: Cornell University Press, 1994); Janet Moore Lindman, "A World of Baptists: Gender, Race, and Religious Community in Pennsylvania and Virginia, 1689–1825," (Ph.D. diss., University of Minnesota, 1994); and Gregory A. Wills, *Democratic Religion: Freedom, Authority, and Church Discipline in the Baptist South, 1785–1900* (New York: Oxford University Press, 1997). Lindman's focus on the faith of the Baptists as

"body-centered" was later published as *Bodies of Belief: Baptist Community in Early America* (Philadelphia: University of Pennsylvania Press, 2008).

1. From One World to Another

1. John Taylor, *Baptists on the American Frontier: A History of Ten Baptist Churches of which the Author has been Alternately a Member*, ed. Chester Raymond Young, 3rd ed. (Macon, GA: Mercer University Press, 1995), 9–14, 94–99, 116–117 (this title hereafter cited *History of Ten Baptist Churches*); John Taylor, *Thoughts on Missions; Biographies of Baptist Preachers*, (Frankfort, KY: s.n., 1820), 35–36; John Taylor, "The Rev. John Taylor's Experience," *Kentucky Missionary and Theological Magazine* 1 (May 1812): 33. Taylor's *History of Ten Baptist Churches* was originally published in 1823. His account, written for many reasons, including to establish his own bona fides in the missionary crisis of the 1820s, is one of the few which captures Baptist life on the frontier. Young's edition is a harmony of three eighteenth century editions. Dumas Malone, ed., *Dictionary of American Biography* (New York: Charles Scribner's Sons, 1964), 330–331.

2. Taylor, *History of Ten Baptist Churches*, 95–96.

3. Ibid., 96–99.

4. Ibid., 99–102.

5. Ibid., 102–103.

6. Ibid., 103–104. The hymn Taylor recalled was Isaac Watts's "I'm Not Ashamed to Own My Lord."

7. Ibid., 14, 19, 76, 116–117.

8. On the cultural and literary significance of "wilderness" and "Canaan" as archetypal images in early American thought, see David R. Williams, *Wilderness Lost: The Religious Origins of the American Mind* (Selinsgrove, PA: Susquehanna University Press, 1987).

9. A remarkable similarity is evident in the "morphology of conversion" of Baptist narratives, but more notable are the similarities between Baptist and earlier Puritan narratives, as well as those of Methodists. Jonathan Edwards offered a classic account of Puritan conversion, wherein sinners awaken to their sin-sick condition, pursue sinlessness, suffer distress at the futility of the pursuit of perfection, combat their own corruption and envy of the saints, and then accept absolute dependence on God's grace. Jonathan Edwards, "A Faithful Narrative of the Surprising Work of God (1737)," in *A Jonathan Edwards Reader*, ed. John E. Smith, Harry S. Stout,

and Kenneth P. Minkema (New Haven, CT: Yale University Press, 1995), 57–87. Edmund S. Morgan's oft-cited study of Puritan life observes a five-fold pattern in line with Edwards's explanation. Morgan saw patterns of "knowledge, conviction, faith, combat, and true, imperfect assurance." Morgan, *Visible Saints*, 66–72. Other insightful works on Puritan conversion include Patricia Caldwell, *The Puritan Conversion Narrative: The Beginnings of American Expression* (Cambridge: Cambridge University Press, 1983); Norman Pettit, *The Heart Prepared: Grace and Conversion in Puritan Spiritual Life* (New Haven, CT: Yale University Press, 1966); and Owen C. Watkins, *The Puritan Experience: Studies in Spiritual Autobiography* (New York: Schocken Books, 1972). Harry S. Stout suggests that colonial preachers went over the sequence of salvation in their sermons and that the congregations internalized that sequence, giving themselves a "vocabulary for self-examination." Harry S. Stout, *The New England Soul: Preaching and Religious Culture in Colonial New England* (New York: Oxford University Press, 1986), 38. Despite the Methodists' famed Arminianism, Dee E. Andrews's research depicts a strikingly similar pattern in their conversion narratives. She argues for a kind of Methodist exceptionalism by claiming that Congregationalists, Presbyterians, and "many Baptists came to their religious experiences after years of familiarity with Scripture and Reformed theology." That said, her many examples of Methodist conversion reveal the same pattern described by Morgan. Andrews, *Methodists and Revolutionary America*, 73–91. Jon Alexander has found a similar, though less detailed, pattern in personal religious accounts in America from the early seventeenth century into the modern era. This fourfold pattern involved, first, a shattering of complacency; second, a struggle between two worlds; third, a miraculous moment; and fourth, a new consciousness. Jon Alexander, *American Personal Religious Accounts, 1600–1980: Toward an Inner History of America's Faiths* (New York: Edwin Mueller Press, 1983), 11–28.

10. James Pendleton, *Reminiscences of a Long Life* (Louisville: Baptist Book Concern, 1891), 25; *James Ross, Life and Times of Elder Reuben Ross* (Philadelphia: Grant, Faires, and Rodgers, 1882), 63–69; Taylor, *History of Ten Baptist Churches*, 186–188.

11. Taylor, *History of Ten Baptist Churches*, 94; Thomas Smith, Jr., Diary, 14 September 1845, Special Collections, James P. Boyce Centennial Library, Southern Baptist Theological Seminary, Louisville, Kentucky (this collection hereafter cited SBTS J. H. Spencer, *A History of Kentucky Baptists* (1886;

reprint, Lafayette, TN: Church History Research and Archives, 1976), 1:221, 233, 288–89, 2:282–83 (this title hereafter cited *History*).

12. Wilson Thompson, *The Autobiography of Elder Wilson Thompson: His Life, Travels, and Ministerial Labors* (Greenfield, IN: D. H. Goble, 1867; reprint, Conley, GA: Old School Hymnal Co., 1978), 37 (this title hereafter cited *Elder Wilson Thompson*); Spencer, *History*, 1:222.

13. On Methodism and dreams, see Mechal Sobel, *Teach Me Dreams: The Search for Self in the Revolutionary Era* (Princeton, NJ: Princeton University Press, 2000), 30–31, 50–54, 79–81; Andrews, *Methodists and Revolutionary America*, 85–88; and Wigger, *Taking Heaven by Storm*, 53–55, 106–108, 111–116, 129–130, 189.

14. Thompson, *Elder Wilson Thompson*, 6–9.

15. Ibid., 9–10.

16. Ibid., 11–13. On one occasion, Thompson witnessed several youths accepted into church membership whom he saw as "wicked children." He was "utterly astonished" to hear his father agree that the youths had "passed from law to gospel" beautifully (meaning having surely converted). Thompson was at a loss, lamenting, "I could not understand their system. This something they called law and gospel was with them the great matter. . . . I could not understand what they meant by the phrase, 'passing from law to gospel.'" Thompson went to several church meetings hoping to hear from the sermon what the phrase meant, but to little avail. Later, he heard a group of his young Christian cousins singing,

> *The glorious day is drawing nigh,*
> *When Zion's light shall come;*
> *She shall arise and shine on high,*
> *Bright as the morning sun.*

In the midst of his miserable soul-searching, he noted, "They were at peace in their minds. . . . but I felt I was a condemned rebel." He began to understand that under the law, he was rightfully doomed. At a high point in his long conversion process, when he was feeling a new love for Christians, he recalled some "words of the poet, Keble":

> *Keep me, O keep me, king of kings,*
> *Beneath Thine own almighty wings.*

These lines helped Thompson understand the dependence necessary for conversion. For those with limited literacy, the oral world and not catechisms or extensive theological study guided them toward resolving their conversion. Thompson, *Elder Wilson Thompson,* 18–33. Thompson misattributes the verse; Anglican priest and poet John Keble (1792–1866) was a child when Thompson underwent his conversion experience. The hymn he recalled was "All Praise to Thee, My God, This Night" written in 1709 by Thomas Ken. John R. Griffin, *John Keble: Saint of Anglicanism* (Macon, GA: Mercer University Press, 1987); "An Evening Hymn," Hymnary.org, accessed April 11, 2014, http://www.hymnary.org/text/all_praise_to_thee_my_god_this_night.

17. McBeth, *Heritage,* 74, 171–72. The influence of Calvinism in the early nineteenth century was pervasive, with roots stretching back to the colonial era. Harry S. Stout argues that the "providential" underpinning of American's view of their history and corporate identity has its roots in the covenant theology of early colonial Puritans. The unity of New England's resistance in the revolution and the "leap from monarchy to republicanism," Stout contends, "was not that great a leap," because of their valuation of the purity of God's churches. Stout, *The New England Soul,* 7, 310. Stout elsewhere asserts that the libertarian, Calvinist rhetoric of George Whitefield galvanized and united the colonies in the decades before the revolution. Stout, *The Divine Dramatist,* 249–87. By Paul K. Conkin's estimation, nine out of ten American church members in 1800 were part of the Reformed tradition, though he broadens the definition considerably. Conkin, *The Uneasy Center,* 295.

18. William Conrad, *The Journal of Elder William Conrad, Pioneer Preacher,* ed. Lloyd W. Franks (Lexington, KY: RF Publishing, 1976), 26; Taylor, *History of Ten Baptist Churches,* 234–35.

19. Charles Woodmason, *The Carolina Backcountry on the Eve of the Revolution: The Journal and Other Writings of Charles Woodmason, Anglican Itinerant,* ed. Richard J. Hooker (Chapel Hill: University of North Carolina Press, 1953), 102; Taylor, *History of Ten Baptist Churches,* 188–89, 229; Smith, Diary, 4 October 1845, SBTS; Thompson, *Elder Wilson Thompson,* 16; P. Donan, *Memoir of Jacob Creath, Jr.* (Cincinnati: R. W. Carroll and Co., 1872), 53. In his analysis of the conversion relation, Philip N. Mulder describes the ceremony, and much of Baptist life, as a Calvinist "doctrinal litmus test." However, there was a subtle richness in the occasion wherein prospective Baptists had to

relate their experience truthfully and confidently. The hearers then evaluated whether or not it matched with their own experiences as well as their biblical understandings. Mulder, *A Controversial Spirit*, 44–45. Significantly, Congregationalists in the early republic did practice such a doctrinal litmus test before allowing converts to join the church. James R. Rohrer argues that this practice helped to hinder Congregationalist growth. Rohrer, *Keepers of the Covenant*, 145–46.

20. William Hickman, *A Short Account of My Life and Travels* (1828; reprint, Louisville: Kentucky Baptist Historical Society, 1969), 13–14; Masters, *A History of Baptists*, 72.

21. Taylor, *History of Ten Baptist Churches*, 238. On the varieties of religious experiences of slave children, see Wilma King, *Stolen Childhood: Slave Youth in Nineteenth-Century America* (Bloomington: Indiana University Press, 1995), 80–90. Susan Juster argues that salvation was a gendered experience. Men tended to resolve moral dilemmas through "agency" while women did so through "communion." They expressed these principles in their conversion narratives, though in reverse; men sought help and advice from others and women found exultation through loneliness. Juster, *Disorderly Women*, 197–208.

22. Smith, Diary, 28 September 1845, 1 October 1845, SBTS.

23. William Warder, Diary, as quoted in Spencer, *History*, 2:378.

24. Minutes of the Sulpher Fork Baptist Association, 1837, SBHLA (first quotes); Minutes of the Bethel Baptist Association, 1837, SBHLA (latter quotes).

25. Woodmason, *Carolina Backcountry*, 103; McBeth, *Heritage*, 47–48, 80, 105–6, 141–42; Keith Harper and C. Martin Jacumin, *Esteemed Reproach: The Lives of Reverend James Ireland and Reverend Joseph Craig* (Macon, GA: Mercer University Press, 2005), 120. See also Isaac, *Transformation of Virginia*, 161–322.

26. In Philip N. Mulder's analysis of Baptist immersion, he states, "The ritual marked a defining moment of salvation . . . in which an individual was no longer condemned." He bases this on the Baptist opposition to pedobaptism, wherein "there was no clear moment of choice." While decisionism was important to Baptists, they knew salvation occurred prior to the conversion relation and the baptismal rite. Baptism was not a "defining moment of salvation," but the definitive, outward imprimatur given by the church after the

salvation had been deemed genuine and acceptable for entry to the church. Mulder, *A Controversial Spirit*, 45.

27. New Testament passages informing Baptist understandings of baptism include; Matthew 3:1–6, 13–16; Mark 1:9, 10:38; Luke 12:50; John 4:2; Acts 1:5. For expressions of Baptist beliefs on baptism and other rites, see William L. Lumpkin, *Baptist Confessions of Faith* (Valley Forge, PA: Judson Press, 1959) and Timothy and Denise George, eds., *Baptist Confessions, Covenants, and Catechisms* (Nashville: Broadman & Holman, 1996).

28. Passages in the book of Acts include: 2:41; 9:18; 16:15, 33; 19:5.

29. Pauline passages include: Romans 6:3–4, Colossians 2:12, and Galatians 3:27.

30. Passages include: I Corinthians 12:13 and Ephesians 4:5.

31. Minutes of the West Union Baptist Association, 1843, SBHLA; Smith, Diary, 7 and 14 September 1845, SBTS.

32. Smith, Diary, 26 and 27 September 1845, 5 October 1845, SBTS.

33. Thompson, *Elder Wilson Thompson*, 38–39.

34. Hickman, *A Short Account*, 14 (first quote); Daniel Drake, *Pioneer Life in Kentucky: 1785–1800*, ed. Emmet Field Horine (New York: Henry Schuman, 1948), 193 (second quote); J. S. Higgins, letter to the editor, *Baptist Banner*, 8 August 1837, 2.

35. Taylor, *History of Ten Baptist Churches*, 222; Higgins, 2–3; Masters, *A History of Baptists*, 28–29; Thompson, *Elder Wilson Thompson*, 38.

36. McBeth, *Heritage*, 47–48; Taylor, *History of Ten Baptist Churches*, 192

37. Alfred Taylor, letter to the editor, *Baptist Banner*, 10 May 1838, 2; Editorial, *Baptist Banner*, 30 January 1838, 2.

38. Taylor, *History of Ten Baptist Churches*, 257–59.

39. Ibid., 291–93.

40. Smith, Diary, 14 September 1845, SBTS; Taylor, *History of Ten Baptist Churches*, 291–94, 222.

41. Related passages include: Matthew 26:19–29, Mark 14:17–25, Luke 22:15–20, John 13:1–2, and I Corinthians 10:15–21 and 11:23–34.

42. McBeth, *Heritage*, 82–83.

43. Spencer, *History*, vol. 2:315.

44. William Warren Sweet, *Religion on the American Frontier*, vol. 1, *The Baptists* (New York: Henry Holt and Co., 1931), 259 (this title hereafter cited *Baptists*); Church Book, Sardis Baptist Church, Boone County, 27 October 1831, Special Collections and Archives, Margaret I. King Library, University

of Kentucky, Louisville (this archive is hereafter cited as UK); Minutes of the South District Baptist Association, 1828, SBHLA.

45. Church Book, Mount Pleasant Baptist Church, Jessamine County, August 1801, November 1840, UK; Church Book, Bethel Baptist Church, Wayne County, August 1811, August 1823, October 1824, UK; Church Book, Mayslick Baptist Church, Mason County, May 1797, UK; Church Book, Providence Baptist Church, Clark County, November and December 1791, December 1792, UK.

46. Sweet, *Baptists*, 48; Taylor, *History of Ten Baptist Churches*, 247; Wigger, *Taking Heaven by Storm*, 88.

47. Eric Foner, *The Story of American Freedom* (New York: W. W. Norton, 1998), 47–85; Watts, *The Republic Reborn*, xvii–xxi, 7–16; Wood, *The Radicalism of the American Revolution*, 229–369 passim; Hatch, *Democratization*, 3–16.

48. On developing bonds of labor in the early republic, see Wilentz, *Chants Democratic*; Stephen Innes, ed., *Work and Labor in Early America* (Chapel Hill: University of North Carolina Press, 1988).

49. For different perspectives on developing bonds within reform movements in the early republic, see Abzug, *Cosmos Crumbling*; Walters, American *Reformers*; and Bruce Dorsey, *Reforming Men and Women: Gender in the Antebellum City* (Ithaca, NY: Cornell University Press, 2002).

2. First among Equals

1. Basil Manly, Jr., *The Kentucky Baptist Pioneers: A Discourse for the Kentucky Baptist Centennial, May 25, 1876, at Louisville, Ky.* (Louisville, KY: Western Recorder, 1876), 26–31; Masters, *A History of Baptists*, 369–70. The ratios of Baptists to population are based on membership. Adherence rates would be several times the rate of membership.

2. Hatch, *Democratization*, 9–14, 44–46; Sweet, *Baptists*, 21–22, 36; Taylor, *History of Ten Baptist Churches*, 159; Wigger, *Taking Heaven by Storm*, 58–63, 71.

3. Sweet, *Baptists*, 36; Pendleton, *Reminiscences*, 49. For the use of nostalgia in evangelical religion, see Schweiger, *The Gospel Working Up*, 196.

4. Spencer, *History*, 1:88, 164, 201, 217, 313; 2:64, 258, 381; on Hiram Curry, see Drake, *Pioneer Life in Kentucky*, 34. After 1840, Georgetown College, a Baptist institution founded in 1829, emerged from a decade of administrative turbulence and began educating aspiring ministers in earnest, helping to mark a new era for Baptists' expectations for an educated clergy. Masters, *A History of Baptists*, 223–30.

5. Spencer, *History,* 1:220, 256, 285, 316, 351–52, 358, 373, 380, 399; 2:29, 71, 115, 153, 186, 232, 247, 260, 375, 470, 529; Conrad, *Elder William Conrad,* 25. This group represents a small percentage of those men preaching prior to 1840, but provides a picture of the diversity of professions that bi-vocational preachers undertook. Firm, quantitative data on both vocation and salary is difficult if not impossible to establish for early (pre-1840) preachers. For example, Beth Barton Schweiger, whose research focuses on Virginia, has written one of the best treatments of early Baptist and Methodist preachers, and yet her pre-1860 data for Baptist preachers accounts for only twenty percent of the total number. Schweiger, *The Gospel Working Up,* 197.

6. Spencer, *History,* 1:438.

7. Stout, *The New England Soul,* 162–63.

8. Wigger, *Taking Heaven by Storm,* 91–92; Mulder, *A Controversial Spirit,* 82–83.

9. Smith, Diary, 24 November 1845, SBTS; Conrad, *Elder William Conrad,* 26–29.

10. Thompson, *Elder Wilson Thompson,* 40–43. Thompson wrote this in the 1860s after Baptists had come to the view that some ministerial training was acceptable. Thus, his assertion that certain qualifications were "essential" shows the change that occurred in the antebellum period, discussed here in chapters four and seven. For context, see David B. Potts, *Baptist Colleges in the Development of American Society, 1812–1861* (New York: Garland Publishing, 1988).

11. Thompson, *Elder Wilson Thompson,* 43–44, 49–52. According to John Taylor, exhortations could be delivered by preachers or congregants, young or old. They typically involved relating conversion experiences or invitations to seek God's mercy. In his evaluation of preacher Lewis Craig's particularly moving exhortations, Taylor seems to use the term "exhortation" interchangeably with "preaching." Taylor, *History of Ten Baptist Churches,* 133, 136–37, 165–66, 199, 249, 268, 287. For the Methodist practice of exhortation, see Wigger, *Taking Heaven by Storm,* 29–30.

12. Thompson, *Elder Wilson Thompson,* 52–60.

13. Masters, *A History of Baptists,* 84; Thompson, *Elder Wilson Thompson,* 61–65.

14. Spencer, *History,* 1:180, 290–91. The church's clerk was the member designated to record church business and maintain records.

15. James P. Brooks, *The Biography of Elder Jacob Locke, of Barren County, Ky.* (Glasgow, KY: Times Print, 1881; reprint, South Central Kentucky

Historical and Genealogical Society, 1976), 17–19; Church Book, Mayslick Baptist Church, January 1793, UK; Church Book, Stamping Ground Baptist Church, Scott County, September 1798, UK.

16. Thompson, *Elder Wilson Thompson*, 69; Conrad, *Elder William Conrad*, 29–31.

17. Church Book, Mayslick Baptist Church, October-November 1803, April 1805, UK. Nathaniel Hickson's name was also recorded as Hixon.

18. William Carey Taylor, Sr., *Biography of Elder Alfred Taylor* (Louisville, KY: Caperton and Cates, 1878; revised and privately reprinted by Wendell Holmes Rone, Sr., 1983), 4.

19. Pendleton, *Reminiscences*, 34–36.

20. Spencer, *History*, 1:139–41, 201–2.

21. Taylor, *History of Ten Baptist Churches*, 302–305; Spencer, *History*, 1:297–99, 316–19; John H. Spencer, "Autobiography of Dr. John Henderson Spencer," SBTS, 83 (this title hereafter cited "Autobiography").

22. Pendleton, *Reminiscences*, 36–38.

23. "R.," letter to the editor, *Baptist Banner and Western Pioneer*, 30 September 1841, 2; "Remarks," *Baptist Banner and Western Pioneer*, 30 September 1841, 2.

24. Walter Brownlow Posey, *The Baptist Church in the Lower Mississippi Valley, 1776–1845* (Lexington: University of Kentucky Press, 1957), 22–23. Although uncommon, laymen could serve on ordination councils. The church at Bullittsburg queried their fellow Baptists at the 1807 meeting of the North Bend Association, "Whether a church when sent to may properly send laymembers as a help to judge of the gift and qualifications of a minister, who is set forward for ordination." The association answered the query in the affirmative. Minutes of the North Bend Baptist Association, 1803, SBHLA.

25. Pendleton, *Reminiscences*, 42; Taylor, *History of Ten Baptist Churches*, 341; Masters, *A History of Baptists*, 114. See Matthew 25 for Jesus's distinction between sheep and goats.

26. Taylor, *History of Ten Baptist Churches*, 264, 324–25.

27. Spencer, *History*, 1:312, 314–15; 2:28, 160–61; Hickman, *A Short Account*, 19.

28. Spencer, *History*, 1:296–301; Minutes of the North Bend Baptist Association, 1818, SBHLA; Taylor, *History of Ten Baptist Churches*, 307.

29. Spencer, *History*, 1:300–04, 326, 393; William Carey Taylor, Sr., *Elder Alfred Taylor*, ii, 2, 4; Spencer, "Autobiography," 81–84, 91–92, SBTS; Minutes of the Barren River Baptist Association, 1858, SBHLA.

30. Conrad, *Elder William Conrad*, 32–33; Pendleton, *Reminiscences,* 64–65.

31. Minutes of the Salem Baptist Association, 1820, SBHLA; Pendleton, *Reminiscences,* 37.

32. Taylor, *History of Ten Baptist Churches,* 236.

33. "Slanders on Preachers of the Gospel," *Baptist Banner,* 28 February 1837, 2. The elevation of ministers' status coincided with a broad-based quest for refinement, discussed in greater detail in chapter four.

34. Minutes of the Little River Baptist Association, 1846, SBHLA.

35. Minutes of the Salem Baptist Association, 1812, SBHLA.

36. Minutes of the Goshen Baptist Association, 1825, SBHLA; Minutes of the Baptist Association, 1831, SBHLA; Minutes of the Long Run Baptist Association, 1811, SBHLA; Minutes of the Licking Baptist Association, 1827, SBHLA.

37. Hickman, *A Short Account,* 16–17; Masters, *A History of Baptists,* 38.

38. Newman and Halvorson, *Atlas of American Religion,* 39; Finke and Stark, *The Churching of America,* 55; "Church Statistics," *Baptist Banner and Western Pioneer,* 23 September 1841, 2; Spencer, *History,* 1:675; Wigger, *Taking Heaven by Storm,* 60. For extensive analysis of Methodist itinerants, see Wigger, *Taking Heaven by Storm,* 48–79.

39. William R. Estep, *Renaissance and Reformation* (Grand Rapids, MI: William B. Eerdmans, 1986), 155; Posey, *The Baptist Church,* 23–25; Taylor, *History of Ten Baptist Churches,* 129–30, 196, 204, 217, 270, 272, 307; Minutes of the Elkhorn Baptist Association, 1785–1805, in Sweet, *Baptists,* 417–504.

40. Posey, *The Baptist Church,* 25; Taylor, *History of Ten Baptist Churches,* 129; Ross, *Elder Reuben Ross,* 142–44.

41. Taylor, *History of Ten Baptist Churches,* 139; Drake, *Pioneer Life in Kentucky,* 193. On William Wood, see Drake, *Pioneer Life in Kentucky,* 7–8, 29–30; Spencer, *History,* 1:68; and Masters, *A History of Baptists,* 36.

42. On John Gano, see Drake, *Pioneer Life in Kentucky,* 7–8, 10–11; William B. Sprague, *Annals of the American Pulpit,* vol. 6, *Baptist* (New York: Robert Carter and Brothers, 1865; reprint, New York: Arno Press, 1969), 62–63; Spencer, *History,* 1:126; Stephen Gano, ed., "Biographical Memoirs of the Late Rev. John Gano," in *The Life and Ministry of John Gano, 1727–1804,* by Terry Wolever (Springfield, MO: Particular Baptist Press, 1998), 97–99. In his memoirs, Gano actually paraphrases the passage as, "So we got all safe to land." On Hiram Curry, see Drake, *Pioneer Life in Kentucky,* 34.

43. Regarding ministerial education as a principle, the colonial Baptists varied in their opinions. Regulars appreciated education, while Separates retained a prejudice against it. Until the 1830s, Kentucky's Baptists remained relatively ambivalent on the matter, reflecting the blending of the Regular and Separate attitudes. However, with institutional maturity and the elevation of the ministerial role in the 1830s, Baptists struggled over the issue. For a more in-depth discussion of this transformation, see chapters four and seven. Randall Allen Corkern, "A Study of the Education, Morals, Salary, and Controversial Movements of the Frontier Baptist Preacher in Kentucky from its Settlement until 1830" (Ph.D. diss., Southern Baptist Theological Seminary, 1952), 72–84; Spencer, *History,* 1:164–65, 329, 386–87; 2:68–70; Thompson, *Elder Wilson Thompson,* 48. See Potts, *Baptist Colleges.*

44. Spencer, *History,* 1:316; 2:28–30, 369–71.

45. Taylor, *History of Ten Baptist Churches,* 166, 171.

46. Noll, *History of Christianity,* 91–103; Taylor, *History of Ten Baptist Churches,* 188, 214, 233, 247; Thompson, *Elder Wilson Thompson,* 38–39; Spencer, *History,* 1:339–41, 373; 2:65–66.

47. Taylor, *History of Ten Baptist Churches,* 201. On Baptists and the Great Revival of 1800–1803, see Eslinger, *Citizens of Zion,* 197–209, 228, 237.

48. S. H. Ford, "History of the Kentucky Baptists: Extravagances of the Great Revival—Rise of the Reformation," *Christian Repository* 6 (January 1857): 6–12.

49. McBeth, *Heritage,* 99–120; McLoughlin, *New England Dissent,* vol. 1, 3–91; Isaac, *Transformation of Virginia,* 161–63, 172–77, 200–3. The biblical reference is Matthew 5:10–11.

3. Divine Channels of Democracy

1. Spencer, "Autobiography," 29, 54, 60–63, SBTS.

2. Church Book, Sardis Baptist Church, 1–12, UK.

3. Minutes of the Little Bethel Baptist Association, 1836, SBHLA.

4. On gender disparities in church memberships, see Noll, *History of Christianity,* 180–81; Nancy F. Cott, *The Bonds of Womanhood: "Woman's Sphere" in New England, 1780–1835* (New Haven, CT: Yale University Press, 1977), 126–41; Ann Braude, "Women's History *Is* American Religious History," in *Retelling U. S. Religious History,* ed. Thomas A. Tweed (Berkeley: University of California Press, 1997), 88–92.

5. Minutes of the Barren River Baptist Association, 1858, SBHLA (first quote); Minutes of the Liberty Baptist Association, 1847, SBHLA (second quote).

6. "Methodism on the Wane," *Baptist Banner and Western Pioneer,* 11 August 1842, 4 (first quote); Minutes of the West Union Baptist Association, 1846, SBHLA (second quote).

7. Hatch, *Democratization,* 167–70 (quote on 167); Noll, *History of Christianity,* 33; Nathan O. Hatch, *The Sacred Cause of Liberty: Republican Thought and the Millennium in Revolutionary New England* (New Haven, CT: Yale University Press, 1977), 66–70, 84–86; Bernard Bailyn, *The Ideological Origins of the American Revolution* (Cambridge: Harvard University Press, 1967), 79.

8. Minutes of the Nolynn Baptist Association, 1833, SBHLA. For other early views of the church, see E. Brooks Holifield, *The Gentlemen Theologians: American Theology in Southern Culture, 1795–1860* (Durham, NC: Duke University Press, 1978), 155–85.

9. Bill J. Leonard, *Baptist Ways: A History* (Valley Forge, PA: Judson Press, 2003), 6–7; Robert G. Torbet, *A History of the Baptists,* 3rd ed., (Valley Forge, PA: Judson Press, 2000), 29–32. On Methodists, see Wigger, *Taking Heaven by Storm,* 25, 27, 34–35, 46, 164. Though Wigger makes an argument for the decentralized aspects of Methodism, he acknowledges the critical role coordinated and controlled effort played in the movement's formation. On Presbyterians, see William Warren Sweet, *Religion on the American Frontier,* vol. 2, *The Presbyterians* (New York: Harper & Brothers Publishers, 1936), 8–11, 24–25, 28–29, 32, 46.

10. Minutes of the Ten Mile Baptist Association, 1831, SBHLA (first quote); Church Book, Providence Baptist Church, October 1811, February 1812, UK (second quote); Records of Forks of Elkhorn Baptist Church, in Sweet, *Baptists,* 274–83; Minutes of the Elkhorn Baptist Association, 1800–1801, in Sweet, *Baptists,* 484–88.

11. Taylor, *History of Ten Baptist Churches,* 278–81. In the end, after getting over his worries, Taylor says he consulted with his "family," including his wife, teenage son, and seven slaves, who were all members of the church. With the exception of one slave woman, they decided to transfer their membership to the new church.

12. Taylor, *History of Ten Baptist Churches,* 281–83; Spencer, *History,* 1:454–55.

13. Gordon S. Wood, *The Creation of the American Republic, 1776–1787* (Chapel Hill: University of North Carolina Press, 1969), 12–13, 288–90, 600–1; Charles William Deweese, "The Origins, Development, and Use of Church Covenants in Baptist History" (Th.D. diss., Southern Baptist Theological Seminary, 1973), 8–31, 100–1 McLoughlin, *New England Dissent*, 2:753–54.

14. Deweese, "The Origins, Development, and Use of Church Covenants," 102. Specific church covenants or articles of faith referenced include those in Church Book, Beaver Creek, 5 November 1798, in Sweet, *Baptists*, 258–259; Church Book, Mayslick Baptist Church, 27 November 1789, UK; and Church Book, Sardis Baptist Church, 27 October 1831, UK. Other church covenants and articles used include: Church Book, Stamping Ground Baptist Church, Scott County, 1795, UK; Church Book, Paris Baptist Church, Bourbon County, 5 March 1818, UK; Church Book, Particular Baptist Church, Williamstown, KY, Grant County, November 1826, UK (this church book is hereafter cited as Williamstown); Church Constitution, Buck Run Baptist Church, Franklin County, 1788, as quoted in Taylor, *History of Ten Baptist Churches*, 347–348.

15. Church Book, Williamstown Baptist Church, UK (first quote); Buck Run in Taylor, *History of Ten Baptist Churches*, 347–48. Church books consulted for these articles of faith include those from Beaver Creek, Sardis, Stamping Ground, Paris, and Bethel. For the terms of the General Union, see Masters, *A History of Baptists*, 158–59. Bethel Baptist Church constituted their church in 1810 "on the principles of the union." Church Book, Bethel Baptist Church, July 1810, UK.

16. As doctrinal confessions tended to be systematic statements of theology, it is likely that the ordinances appeared close to the end, since they logically followed the articles that included God, salvation, conversion, and so forth. Lumpkin, *Baptist Confessions of Faith*, 117–23, 154–71. Church confessions referred to here include those from Beaver Creek, Sardis, Williamstown, Buck Run, as well as the terms of the General Union, in Masters, *A History of Baptists*, 159.

17. On use of confessions, see McBeth, *Heritage*, 68. On Buck Run, see Taylor, *History of Ten Baptist Churches*, 347–48. Confessions referred to here include those from Stamping Ground and Paris, as well as the terms of the General Union, in Masters, *A History of Baptists*, 159. The church at Stamping Ground adopted its name in 1819. Previously it had been called the church

at McConnell's Run. The name of longer usage is used in this work. Church Book, Stamping Ground Baptist Church, October 1799, June–July 1801, UK.

18. Timothy and Denise George, eds., *Baptist Confessions*, 9–10; Church Book, Mount Pleasant Baptist Church, August 1801, April 1802, June 1807, UK; Charles W. Deweese, *Baptist Church Covenants* (Nashville: Broadman Press, 1990), 42–43.

19. Hatch, *Democratization*, 9. Hatch analyzes Methodists, Disciples of Christ, Mormons, Baptists, and black religion, specifically listing the ways in which the first three could be considered less than democratic. But he does not mention Baptists and black religion in this regard. Baptist deviation from their own egalitarian ideals most often occurred in their discipline of church members. For studies of such discrimination in discipline, see Juster, *Disorderly Women*, 75–107; Heyrman, *Southern Cross*, 214–15, 249–52; Lindman, "A World of Baptists," 210–35; and Wills, *Democratic Religion*, 54–56, 65–66.

20. The representative sample of church books consulted regarding rules includes those of Beaver Creek, Sardis, Paris, Williamstown, Mount Pleasant, and Buck Run.

21. Quoted from Arthur M. Schlesinger, "What Then is the American, This New Man," *American Historical Review* 48 (1943), 238.

22. Church Book, Bethel Baptist Church, July 1810, February 1811, May 1811, March 1812, May 1812, July 1812, March 1815, May 1815, December 1816, October 1817, December 1817, July 1825, August 1827, UK; Minutes of the Cumberland River Baptist Association, 1815, 1822, SBHLA. On John Smith, see Spencer, *History*, 1:261. On Methodists and Presbyterians, see T. Scott Miyakawa, *Protestants and Pioneers: Individualism, and Conformity on the American Frontier* (Chicago: University of Chicago Press, 1964), 28–29, 48–49.

23. Church Book, Mount Pleasant Baptist Church, August 1801, January 1802, January 1803, December 1810, June 1843, UK; Spencer, *History*, 1:202–5; 2:22; Church Book, Mayslick Baptist Church, February 1814, April 1836, October 1843, October 1844, UK.

24. James M. Pendleton, *The Condition of the Baptist Cause in Kentucky in 1837: An Address delivered at the Jubilee of the General Association of Kentucky Baptists, in Walnut Street Baptist Church, Louisville, October 20, 1887* ([Louisville?]: s. n., 1887), 16–17 (this title hereafter cited *Condition of the Baptist Cause*). Apparently, the "joke" Pendleton's father told him was an

old Baptist barb. Another along the same lines was the apocryphal gibe of the unpaid minister who told his congregation, "You love the gospel—but you love your money better." David Benedict, *A General History of the Baptist Denomination in America, and Other Parts of the World,* (Boston: Lincoln & Edmands, 1813; reprint, Freeport, NY: Books for Libraries Press, 1971), 2:458.

25. Taylor, *History of Ten Baptist Churches,* 146; Taylor, *Thoughts on Missions,* 10–12, 20; McBeth, *Heritage,* 344. The full title of the mission organization was the General Missionary Convention of the Baptist Denomination in the United States for Foreign Missions, though it was popularly referred to as the General Convention or the Triennial Convention.

26. Taylor, *History of Ten Baptist Churches,* 186; Church Book, Mayslick Baptist Church, March 1801, UK; Ross, *Elder Reuben Ross,* 293–94; Church Book, Stamping Ground Baptist Church, February 1806, UK; Church Book, Mount Pleasant Baptist Church, March 1811, UK; Minutes of the Goshen Baptist Association, 1825, SBHLA. Given their commitment to congregational autonomy, Baptists had no set amount for a minister's renumeration. In addition, early nineteenth century church records might cite a salary figure and pay much less. Thus it is difficult to establish how typical Taylor's compensation was. The experiences of the Paris Baptist Church give some idea of the futility of finding a norm even in the antebellum period. Between 1837 and 1858, the church contracted with at least ten ministers for their preaching services. This was one of the few churches that had preaching four times per month, but some preachers were only contracted for two Sundays per month. Adjusting for this, the annual salaries promised to the preachers for full-time service were $500, $500, $214, $400, $400, $1000, $300, $350, $300, $600, $500. Thus, the church agreed to pay its pastor as much in 1858 as it had twenty years before, with significant variation in between. Church Book, Paris Baptist Church, February 1837, October 1838, November 1845, January 1849, February 1851, January 1852, May 1853, March 1854, August 1855, February 1857, February 1858, UK.

27. Taylor, *History of Ten Baptist Churches,* 186; Pendleton, *Condition of the Baptist Cause,* 16–17. Pendleton's rant should be compared with Basil Manly's praise in 1876; see *The Kentucky Baptist Pioneers,* 26–31. For the connections between republicanism, revolution, and religion, see George M. Marsden, *Religion and American Culture* (San Diego: Harcourt Brace Jovanovich, 1990), 39–42.

28. W. E. Vine, *Expository Dictionary of Bible Words* (London: Marshall, Morgan & Scott, 1981), 272–73, 348. Relevant biblical passages include Acts 6:17 and I Timothy 3:8–13.

29. Church Book, Paris Baptist Church, March, May, and October 1818, UK; Church Book, Mayslick Baptist Church, August 1795, September 1798, May 1802, January 1803, UK; Church Book, Forks of Elkhorn Baptist Church, April–November 1804, in Sweet, *Baptists,* 305–11. The rite of "laying on of hands" was a highly and frequently contested practice throughout Baptist history. Some churches incorporated the rite to symbolize their support for a pastor, deacon, or new convert. When, whether, and upon whom the rite should be used could be a point of fierce contention. In the crucible of Kentucky, where differing traditions collided, Baptists tended to compromise more readily on the rite rather than make it a divisive issue. McBeth, *Heritage,* 195; Benedict, *A General History,* 2:106–7.

30. Posey, *The Baptist Church,* 10; Minutes of the Baptist Association, 1831, SBHLA; Church Book, Mayslick Baptist Church, December–March 1802, UK.

31. Hatch, *Democratization,* 64–66.

32. By 1800, only three American publications existed for use as manuals in Baptist churches. Bob Compton, "Baptist Church Manuals in America: A Study in Baptist Polity and Practice" (Th.D. diss., Southern Baptist Theological Seminary, 1967), 7–8; Posey, *The Baptist Church,* 11–12. A witty, satirical piece in the *Christian Repository* reveals both that most Kentucky Baptist churches continued to meet only monthly in the 1850s, and that the fact was a concern for urbane leaders such as S. H. Ford. Presumably, Ford believed that frequent meetings would lead to greater denominational advancement. In Ford's piece, called "The Paydoontoe Letters," the fictional Able Paydoontoe of Delaware writes his cousin Osmar to inquire if there are any "Seventh Day Baptists" in the West. Osmar comically replies that few "Seven Day Baptists" reside in the Southwest; most are "Thirty Day Baptists." He explains that a few town and city churches meet every seven days, but perhaps "not one in ten or twenty" country churches do. Significantly, Osmar notes that while a few more churches meet bi-weekly, "The great body of our good substantial brethren in the country who compose the strength and exert the controlling influence of the denomination are *thirty* day Baptists, who have meeting one Saturday and Sabbath in each month." Given the satirical nature of the work, it is difficult to assess Ford's motivation in attributing significant denominational influence to the country churches. Schweiger and Wills have argued that shortly after the

Civil War, by the 1870s, denominational influence had shifted to the growing cities. "The Paydoontoe Letters," *Christian Repository* 7 (May 1858): 367–69; Schweiger, *Gospel Working Up*, 129–48; Wills, *Democratic Religion*, 127–28.

33. For the importance of "perfectionist theology," see Noll, *History of Christianity*, 172, 181–2, 235. The categories of formative and corrective discipline come from J. M. Pendleton, *Church Manual, Designed for the Use of Baptist Churches* (Philadelphia: Judson Press, 1867), 117–124. Pendleton's manual would have been influenced by his experience with early church tradition in Kentucky. Church Book, Mount Pleasant Baptist Church, August 1801, UK. For biblical context of Baptist ideas of discipline, see Matthew 18:15–17.

34. James Edward Humphrey, "Baptist Discipline in Kentucky, 1781–1860" (Th. D. diss., Southern Baptist Theological Seminary, 1959), 104–105; Miyakawa, *Protestants and Pioneers*, 37–39; Posey, *The Baptist Church*, 38–53. For further use of the categorization of infractions presented here, see Lindman, "A World of Baptists," 210–23.

35. This accounting is based upon a sample of Kentucky Baptist church records from the churchs' founding until 1860. These churches include Mount Pleasant, Mayslick, Providence, Paris, Mount Zion (Graves County), Williamstown, Bethel, and McCormack's (Lincoln County). The issue of women joining other denominations is taken up in chapter five.

36. Recent and pertinent studies of Baptist discipline include those of Lindman, Juster, and Wills. For more on this relationship of Baptists to slavery, see John B. Boles, *Masters & Slaves in the House of the Lord: Race and Religion in the American South, 1740–1870* (Lexington: University Press of Kentucky, 1988).

37. See Sweet, *Baptists;* Miyakawa, *Protestants and Pioneers;* and Juster, *Disorderly Women*. Susan Juster argues that Baptists in the early republic "targeted" women as the "chief source" of disorder in their inherently fragile democratic system. Likewise, as Baptists sought respectability, they adopted a "feminized model of sin" to purge women from the church. This study, like many others, finds that Baptists clearly had gender expectations that are reflected in discipline records. However, it is also true, as Gregory A. Wills remarks, that "it was the waywardness of the male majority that kept Baptist church discipline in business." Kentucky Baptist church records and other contemporary documents do not harmonize with Juster's thesis. Juster, *Disorderly Women*, 145–178; Wills, *Democratic Religion*, 54–57; Randy J. Sparks, *On Jordan's Stormy Banks: Evangelicalism in Mississippi, 1773–1876* (Athens: University of Georgia Press, 1994), 153–57.

38. Wills, *Democratic Religion*, 8.

39. Minutes of the Salem Baptist Association, 1815, (first quote), SBHLA; Minutes of the Ten Mile Baptist Association, 1831, (second quote), SBHLA.

40. Minutes of the Bracken Baptist Association, 1823, SBHLA. This holistic Baptist view of history is also evident in the 1819 circular letter of the Little River Association in western Kentucky. Part of that letter reads, "When necessity compelled the sons of America to assert their rights to liberty and independence, he [God] manifested himself the God of battle. . . . When the Lord of hosts sends forth a Gideon, a Cyrus or a Washington to deliver his people, they are his appointed means and cannot fail of success. Hence brethren the Lord has blessed us with peculiar blessings above all other nations."

41. Minutes of the Bracken Baptist Association, 1823, SBHLA.

42. Watts, *The Republic Reborn*, 5, 48–49, 64–65, 154–55.

43. Walter B. Shurden, *Associationalism among Baptists in America, 1704–1814* (New York: Arno Press, 1980), 1–5, 11, 15. Shurden's work, still cited as the definitive study of early Baptist associationalism, finds the beginnings of associations in England in the 1650s. Immigration of Baptists to the English colonies brought associations to America. In the early eighteenth century, the few Baptist churches in America founded near Philadelphia met quarterly. One of these four meetings, the one that always convened in Philadelphia, was called the "general meeting." Delegates there conducted business that might serve the common good of the churches. In 1707, the conferees of the general meeting organized the Philadelphia Association, the first in America. By 1775, there were ten associations in America. The similarities between the long-time associational practices of Baptists and those adopted by the Methodists in their conferences and quarterly meetings are intriguing, and require a more in-depth study. Shurden, *Associationalism*, 8–13.

44. Posey, *The Baptist Church*, 115–116. Though Baptists made much of the "designation" of attendants to the associations, they sometimes used the terms "delegate" and "messenger" interchangeably, the latter predominating. The purposeful use of "messenger" was to denote the lack of authority of a church's representative to make laws for that church through the association.

45. Minutes of the Elkhorn Baptist Association, 1795, in Sweet, *Baptists*, 468–9; Minutes of the Long Run Association, 1813, SBHLA; Taylor, *History of Ten Baptist Churches*, 253–54.

46. Posey, *The Baptist Church*, 115–19; Minutes of the Long Run Association, 1838, SBHLA.

47. Church Book, Stamping Ground Baptist Church, July 1822, UK; Church Book, Paris Baptist Church, July 1826, UK; Minutes of the Ten Mile Baptist Association, 1847, SBHLA; Minutes of the North Bend Baptist Association, 1846, SBHLA; Minutes of the Green River Baptist Association, 1851, SBHLA.

48. Shurden, *Associationalism*, 58–60. Associational divisions are addressed in chapter four.

49. For discussion of national consciousness among Baptists, see Shurden, *Associationalism*, 64. For representative examples of the state of correspondence between associations at mid-century, see Minutes of the Salem Baptist Association, 1857, SBHLA; Minutes of the Long Run Baptist Association, 1846, SBHLA; Minutes of the Bethel Baptist Association, 1845, SBHLA; Minutes of the Little River Baptist Association, 1852, SBHLA.

50. Shurden, *Associationalism*, 61–62. For the representative ratios of attendance and laity in this accounting, see the minutes of the following associations from SBHLA: Long Run, 1812; Franklin, 1815; Green River, 1824, 1830, 1851; Little River, 1825; Ten Mile, 1831, 1845, 1851; Russell's Creek, 1831, 1842; Salem, 1839; North Bend 1843; and Bethel, 1860.

51. Shurden, *Associationalism*, 64–68; Minutes of the Elkhorn Baptist Association, 1803, in Sweet, *Baptists*, 499.

52. Wills, *Democratic Religion*, 98–102.

53. Sellers, *The Market Revolution*, 159. In 1789, the influential Elkhorn Association advised that foot-washing was a "Christian duty," but it was "to be practiced at discretion." At the same meeting a question on hand-laying was withdrawn. Minutes of the Elkhorn Baptist Association, 1789, in Sweet, *Baptists*, 436. The 1788 Salem Association announced that the practice or non-practice of hand-laying would not be a "breach of fellowship." In the same way, that association in 1804 could not give advice on foot-washing, since there was such "a difference of opinion respecting the interpretation of [John 13:14]." "The History of the Salem Baptist Association," in Minutes of the Salem Baptist Association, 1826, 4–8, SBHLA.

54. For the typical pattern of coordinating quarterly meetings, see Minutes of the Goshen Baptist Association, 1824, SBHLA. On Haycraft, see Minutes of the Salem Baptist Association, 1823–1824, SBHLA; and Masters, *A History of Baptists*, 26.

55. McBeth, *Heritage*, 344.

4. Reforming the Impulse, 1825-1845

1. Minutes of the Long Run Baptist Association, 1831, 1832, SBHLA.

2. James E. Tull, *Shapers of Baptist Thought* (Valley Forge, PA: Judson Press, 1972), 103–106; Robert Richardson, *Memoirs of Alexander Campbell* (Philadelphia: J. B. Lippincott & Co., 1870), 2:71. On the sources of Campbell's theology, see David Edwin Harrell, Jr., *Quest for a Christian America: The Disciples of Christ and American Society to 1866* (Nashville: Disciples of Christ Historical Society), 27–28; George G. Beazley, Jr., "Who Are the Disciples?" in *The Christian Church (Disciples of Christ): An Interpretive Examination in the Cultural Context*, ed. George G. Beazley, Jr. (n.p.: Bethany Press, 1973), 24–26; Winfred E. Garrison, *The Sources of Alexander Campbell's Theology* (St. Louis: Christian Publishing Company, 1900), 107–114; Robert Frederick West, *Alexander Campbell and Natural Religion* (New Haven, CT: Yale University Press, 1948).

3. Alexander Campbell, *Memoirs of Elder Thomas Campbell* (Cincinnati: H. S. Bosworth, 1861), 125–26; Tull, *Shapers of Baptist Thought,* 106–9.

4. E. Brooks Holifield, "Theology as Entertainment: Oral Debate in American Religion," *Church History* 67 (September 1998): 501–2.

5. Richardson, *Memoirs of Alexander Campbell*, 2:82–83, (emphasis in the original).

6. Ibid., 2:80–83, 90–93.

7. Hatch, *Democratization,* 125, 141–146; Tull, *Shapers of Baptist Thought,* 106, 110–118; Nathan O. Hatch, "The Christian Movement and the Demand for a Theology of the People," *Journal of American History* 67 (December 1980): 557–58.

8. Noll, *History of Christianity,* 185–187; McBeth, *Heritage,* 344–46, 350; Masters, *A History of Baptists,* 189–92.

9. Taylor, *History of Ten Baptist Churches,* 51–55; Taylor, *Thoughts on Missions,* 9–10, 15–24; "Rev. John M. Peck's First Journey through Kentucky in 1817," *Christian Repository* 8 (April 1859): 257–67 (this title hereafter cited "Peck's First Journey").

10. Taylor, *History of Ten Baptist Churches,* 53–54; Larry Douglas Smith, "The Historiography of the Origins of Antimissionism Examined in the Light of Kentucky Baptist History" (Ph.D. diss., Southern Baptist Theological Seminary, 1982), 46, 177, 194.

11. Church Book, Providence Baptist Church, March–April 1817, UK; "Peck's First Journey," 260–261.

12. S. Morris Eames, *The Philosophy of Alexander Campbell* (Bethany, WV: Bethany College, 1966), 87–94.

13. Spencer, *History*, 1:271, 348–353; Z. T. Cody, *History of the May's Lick Baptist Church* (Maysville: G. W. Oldham, 1890), 25–26; Tull, *Shapers of Baptist Thought*, 118–24.

14. Cody, *May's Lick Baptist Church*, 24–25; Spencer, *History*, 1:199–203; Richardson, *Memoirs of Alexander Campbell*, 2:118; Thomas M. Vaughan, *Memoirs of Rev. Wm. Vaughan, D. D.* (Louisville: Caperton & Cates, 1878), 166–167; Church Book, Mayslick Baptist Church, January–July 1828, UK. For the dispersed nature of the 1827–1828 revival, see Spencer, *History*, 1:142, 203, 248, 334, 419, 424, 430, 437, 444, 468; 2:35, 208, 267, 382; and James DeForest Murch, *Christians Only: A History of the Restoration Movement* (Cincinnati: Standard Publishing, 1962), 104.

15. Church Book, Mayslick Baptist Church, July 1805–March 1806, January 1829, UK; Cody, *May's Lick Baptist Church*, 30–31; Richardson, *Memoirs of Alexander Campbell*, 2:330.

16. Cody, *May's Lick Baptist Church*, 31–35; Church Book, Mayslick Baptist Church, August 1830, February 1838, November 1838, October 1841, UK; Minutes of the Bracken Baptist Association, 1830, SBHLA.

17. Minutes of the Long Run Baptist Association, 1825, SBHLA; "Historical Memoranda," in Minutes of the Long Run Baptist Association, 1843, SBHLA; Minutes of the Bracken Baptist Association, 1828, SBHLA; Minutes of the Tate's Creek Baptist Association, 1831, SBHLA. For associations issuing statements in favor of creeds, see Minutes of the Franklin Baptist Association, 1826, SBHLA; Minutes of the Baptist Association, 1830, SBHLA.

18. McBeth, *Heritage*, 686–687; E. Y. Mullins, *Baptist Beliefs*, 6th ed., (Philadelphia: Judson Press, 1951), 6–7; H. Wheeler Robinson, *The Life and Faith of the Baptists*, 2nd ed., (London: Kingsgate Press, 1946), 78.

19. Clifton J. Allen, ed. *Encyclopedia of Southern Baptists* (Nashville: Broadman Press, 1958), s. v. "Church Covenant, Baptist," by Raymond A. Parker; Allen, ed. *Encyclopedia of Southern Baptists*, s. v. "Confessions of Faith, Baptist," by William L. Lumpkin; Masters, *A History of Baptists*, 41, 159, 218; Church Book, Williamstown Baptist Church, November 1826, UK; Taylor, *History of Ten Baptist Churches*, 93; Minutes of the Baptist Association, 1830, SBHLA; Minutes of the North District Baptist Association, 1831, SBHLA.

20. Minutes of the Franklin Baptist Association, 1826, SBHLA; Minutes of the Salem Baptist Association, 1819, SBHLA; Minutes of the Long Run Baptist Association, 1821, SBHLA. Gregory A. Wills finds a similar ideal in his study of Georgia Baptists, though he does not emphasize how Baptists limited confessions or creeds to fundamentals. Wills, *Democratic Religion*, 108–115.

21. Minutes of the Franklin Baptist Association, 1826, SBHLA; Minutes of the Long Run Baptist Association, 1821, SBHLA; Minutes of the Salem Baptist Association, 1819, SBHLA; Minutes of the Bracken Baptist Association, 1831, SBHLA; Minutes of the Green River Baptist Association, 1832, SBHLA; Minutes of the Goshen Baptist Association, 1830, SBHLA.

22. Masters, *A History of Baptists,* 222; Richardson, *Memoirs of Alexander Campbell*, 2:370–374, 382–397.

23. Hatch, *Democratization,* 179; Noll, *History of Christianity,* 185; Justo L. González, *The Story of Christianity* (San Francisco: Harper & Row, 1985), 2:179–82; Marsden, 24–28. According to Robert G. Gardner, by 1770 approximately one-sixth of all Baptists in America held Arminian views. Gardner, *Baptists of Early America*, 20–63.

24. Philip Schaff, *The Creeds of Christendom* (Grand Rapids, MI: Baker Books, 1996), 3:545ff; Wigger, *Taking Heaven by Storm,* 15–20.

25. McBeth, *Heritage,* 211–27; Masters, *A History of Baptists,* 158–159.

26. McBeth, *Heritage,* 181–83; Phil Roberts, "Andrew Fuller," in *Baptist Theologians,* eds. Timothy George and David S. Dockery (Nashville: Broadman Press, 1990), 121–125; Tull, *Shapers of Baptist Thought,* 98–99.

27. McBeth, *Heritage,* 181–83; Roberts, 124–33.

28. Vaughan, *Rev. Wm. Vaughan,* 92–93, 114; Ross, *Elder Reuben Ross,* 278–87; Minutes of the Bethel Baptist Association, 1825, 1826, 1836, SBHLA.

29. Minutes of the Tate's Creek Baptist Association, 1831, SBHLA; Editorial, *Baptist Banner,* 5 December 1835, 2; "Ultra Calvinism or Antinomianism," *Baptist Banner,* 5 March 1836, 3; Minutes of the Nolynn Baptist Association, 1820, 1834, SBHLA.

30. Masters, *A History of Baptists,* 190–91, 256–64; Pendleton, *Condition of the Baptist Cause,* 3–10; Doyle L. Young, "The Place of Andrew Fuller in the Developing Modern Mission Movement" (Ph.D. diss., Southwestern Baptist Theological Seminary, 1981), 259–67.

31. Wigger, *Taking Heaven by Storm,* 176; A. H. Redford, *The History of Methodism in Kentucky* (Nashville: Southern Methodist Publishing House, 1868–1870), 512, 553; Roy Hunter Short, *Methodism in Kentucky* (Rutland, VT:

Academy Books, 1979), 4; Francois Andre Michaux, *Travels to the West of the Allegheny Mountains*, in *Early Western Travels 1748–1846*, ed. Reuben Gold Thwaites (Cleveland: Arthur H. Clark, 1904), 3:249. Redford pins the number of Methodists in 1832 at approximately 27,000. Short finds 52,000 in 1845. For hostility between Methodists and Baptists, see "The Journal of Benjamin Lakin, 1794–1820," in *Religion on the American Frontier, 1783–1840*, vol. 4, *The Methodists*, ed. William Warren Sweet (Chicago: University of Chicago Press, 1946), 254–258; Edward Stevenson, *Biographical Sketch of the Rev. Valentine Cook* (Nashville: Southern Methodist Publishing House, 1858), 105; William Moody Pratt, Diary, University of Kentucky, 84. For the rivalry between Valentine Cook and Jeremiah Vardeman, see Stevenson, *Biographical Sketch*, 94–95. Stevenson's description of a "Mr. V." fits that of the very popular Vardeman.

32. Minutes of the Long Run Baptist Association, 1838, SBHLA; Posey, *The Baptist Church*, 59; Wigger, *Taking Heaven by Storm*, 97, 185–186; Spencer, *History*, 1:487. In 1832, the Kentucky Baptist Convention appointed a four-man committee to oversee protracted meetings. But the nature of these meetings is unclear. J. H. Spencer cites a revival on 1832 that occurred "before protracted meetings came in vogue." "Minutes of the Kentucky Baptist Convention, 1832," quoted in S. H. Ford, "History of the General Association of Kentucky," *Christian Repository* 8 (July 1859), 483; Spencer, *History*, 2:262.

33. Minutes of the Gaspar River Baptist Association, 1835, 1836, SBHLA. The seven innovating ministers included David Mansfield, William Tatum, J. B. Dunn, Alfred Taylor, Simeon Vaught, J. H. Felts, and G. B. Dunn. Alfred Taylor's biography, written by his son, has led subsequent denominational historians to conclude that Taylor, the youngest of the seven, took the lead in these protracted efforts in December 1837. The associational records, however, show the efforts beginning in October 1835 and also show Mansfield and Tatum holding elected positions of leadership in the associations. Taylor, *Thoughts on Missions; Biographies of Baptist Preachers*, 7. On the ministers who died in 1834–35, see Taylor, *Thoughts on Missions; Biographies of Baptist Preachers*, 7; Spencer, *History*, 1:332–36, 363; 2:313, 315, 369–71, 376–81.

34. W. R. McFerron, letter to the editor, *Baptist Banner and Western Pioneer*, 7 November 1837, 201; Thomas J. Fisher, letter to the editor, *Baptist Banner*, 7 November 1837, 201; "Revivals," *Baptist Banner*, 22 August 1837, 162; John Dale, letter to the editor, *Baptist Banner and Western Pioneer*, 9 April 1840, 2; "Revival in Burksville," *Baptist Banner and Western Pioneer*, 16 July

1840, 2. For Methodist emotionalism, see Wigger, *Taking Heaven by Storm*, 104–24.

35. McFerron, *Baptist Banner*, 7 November 1837, 201; Fisher, *Baptist Banner*, 7 November 1837, 201; Letter from Elizabethtown, *Baptist Banner*, 7 November 1837, 201; Rice Maxey, letter to the editor, *Baptist Banner and Western Pioneer*, 12 August 1841, 2; Josiah Leake, letter to the editor, *Baptist Banner and Western Pioneer*, 12 August 1841, 2.

36. Hatch, *Democratization*, 195–206; Richard L. Bushman, *The Refinement of America: Persons, Houses, Cities* (New York: Alfred A. Knopf, 1992), 313–352; Butler, *Awash in a Sea of Faith*, 270–272; Church Book, Mayslick Baptist Church, July 1847, UK; Church Book, Mount Zion Baptist Church, November 1844, UK; *Baptist Banner and Western Pioneer*, 7 July 1842, 7; Hickman, *A Short Account*, 17–19.

37. Minutes of the Goshen Baptist Association, 1825, SBHLA; Masters, *A History of Baptists*, 266–269.

38. "Circular letter to the Baptist Churches and Associations in the State of Kentucky," *Baptist Banner*, 21 November 1837, 1; Minutes of the Long Run Baptist Association, 1838, SBHLA. Among the associations favoring ministerial professionalization between 1837 and 1847 were South District (1838), Goshen (1839), Gaspar River (1840), Liberty (1840), Franklin (1841), Middle District (1842), Nolynn (1842), Freedom (1846), Little River (1846), and Cumberland River (1847).

39. Spencer, *History*, 1:200–203; Church Book, Mayslick Baptist Church, February 1814, February 1825, UK; Richardson, *Memoirs of Alexander Campbell*, 2:118; Masters, *A History of Baptists*, 223.

40. Potts, 32, 76, 155, 158, 208; Charles D. Johnson, *Higher Education of Southern Baptists: An Institutional History, 1826–1954* (Waco, TX: Baylor University Press, 1955), 91–93; Masters, *A History of Baptists*, 224–30.

41. Masters, *A History of Baptists*, 229–30; Johnson, *Higher Education of Southern Baptists*, 93; Potts, 101, 181, 204, 233–34.

42. Minutes of the Bethel Baptist Association, 1839, SBHLA; Minutes of the Franklin Baptist Association, 1841, SBHLA; Minutes of the Bracken Baptist Association, 1845, SBHLA; For other motivations for founding evangelical colleges, see Donald G. Mathews, *Religion in the Old South* (Chicago: University of Chicago Press, 1977), 88–97.

43. Minutes of the Middle District Association, 1842, SBHLA. Other associations offering similar advice, though less perspicuously, were Goshen

(1839), Long Run (1841, 1845), West Union (1843, 1860), Baptist (1850, 1853), North Bend (1854), Tate's Creek (1856), and Liberty (1858).

44. Smith, "Historiography," 13, 177, 193–198; Jeffrey Wayne Taylor, "Self-Definition in the Formation of the Primitive Baptist Movement as Expressed in their Three Major Periodicals, 1832–1948" (Ph.D. diss., Baylor University, 2000), 1–5, 18–21, 48, 64; Lumpkin, *Baptist Foundations in the South*, 147–49, 153. See also James Rhett Mathis, *The Making of the Primitive Baptists: A Cultural and Intellectual History of the Antimission Movement, 1800–1840* (New York: Routledge, 2004) and Michael Andrew Dain, "The Development of the Primitivist Impulse in American Baptist Life, 1707–1842" (Ph.D. diss., Southwestern Baptist Theological Seminary, 2001).

45. Minutes of the Russell's Creek Baptist Association, 1841, SBHLA; "Revivals," *Baptist Banner and Western Pioneer*, 16 July 1840, 2; Minutes of the Ten Mile Baptist Association, 1851, SBHLA; Minutes of the Daviess County Baptist Association, 1860, SBHLA.

46. Editorial, *Baptist Banner and Western Pioneer*, 3 September 1840, 2; Minutes of the Sulpher Fork Baptist Association, 1840, SBHLA; "HAPAX [a pseudonym]," letter to the editor, *Baptist Banner and Western Pioneer*, 30 May 1839, 2; Newman and Halvorson, *Atlas of American Religion*, 39; Editorial, *Baptist Banner and Western Pioneer*, 1 August 1839, 2. When the Sulpher Fork Association split in 1840, both parties recorded their own versions of the schism and both claimed to be the true representatives of the association. Both accounts are preserved at the SBHLA.

47. Vido, "Committees—Baptist Presbyterianism!" *Christian Repository* 5 (April 1856): 223; "Committees," *Christian Repository* 5 (May 1856): 301; Minutes of the Concord Baptist Association, 1857, SBHLA.

5. Sisters, Friends, and Proprietors

1. Untitled poem, Mary Bristow, Diary, 1857, Special Collections, James P. Boyce Centennial Library, SBTS, Louisville.

2. Ibid. This latter quotation likely refers to Isaiah 2:22: "Cease ye from man, whose breath is in his nostrils: for wherein is he to be accounted of?"

3. McBeth, *Heritage*, 197, 690–91; Carolyn DeArmond Blevins, "Women and the Baptist Experience," in *Religious Institutions and Women's Leadership: New Roles Inside the Mainstream*, ed. Catherine Wessinger (Columbia: University of South Carolina, 1996), 158. Catherine A. Brekus has deftly redis-covered the voices of female preachers in the Second Great Awakening. She

analyzes Free Will Baptists, a religious group concentrated in the northeast in the early nineteenth century. She argues that as Free Will Baptists became more "respectable," they shunned women in the ministry. In Kentucky, the first signs of a quest for refinement occured in the 1820s, reaching a peak after the 1830s, yet Baptists in the state (mostly Regular, or United, Baptists) gave no impression of their acceptance of female ministers or deacons prior to this. Catherine A. Brekus, *Strangers and Pilgrims: Female Preaching in America, 1740–1845* (Chapel Hill: University of North Carolina Press, 1998).

4. Braude, "Women's History," 87–107.

5. Blair A. Pogue, "'I Cannot Believe the Gospel That Is So Much Preached': Gender, Belief, and Discipline in Baptist Religious Culture," in *The Buzzel About Kentuck: Settling the Promised Land,* ed. Craig Thompson Friend (Lexington: University Press of Kentucky, 1999), 237–38, n. 11.

6. Minutes of the Goshen Baptist Association, 1860, SBHLA. Such a breakdown of membership was uncommon in antebellum membership reports to associations. The extent of female majority in these thirteen churches ranged from narrow (14 men to 15 women in Millerstown) to wide (34 men to 95 women in Cloverport). Of the sixteen churches that reported black membership, only one also reported them by gender.

7. Taylor, *History of Ten Baptist Churches,* 218; Church Book, Stamping Ground Baptist Church, July 1859, UK.

8. Morgan Edwards, *The Customs of Primitive Churches* (Philadelphia: Printed by Andrew Stewart, 1768), 102.

9. Leon McBeth, *Women in Baptist Life* (Nashville: Broadman Press, 1979), 30–38, 40–42.

10. Church Book, Providence Baptist Church, March 1788, UK.

11. "A Relation of My Experience," Mary Bristow, Diary, 1857, SBTS; Taylor, *History of Ten Baptist Churches,* 325. The final consequence of Mary Bristow's hearing her aunt's conversion experience was that Mary decided to join the Particular Baptist Church at Sardis rather than the church at Bryant's Station. It had been the members at Bryant's Station who had asked to hear her relation on that "miserable day." Nancy A. Hardesty's study of women and Finneyite revivalism likewise notes how conversion was "democratic. . . led to a questioning of traditional ways of thinking . . . [and] had the potential to eradicate racial and sexual prejudices." Nancy A. Hardesty, *Women Called to Witness: Evangelical Feminism in the Nineteenth Century* (Knoxville: University of Tennessee Press, 1999), 48–51.

12. Spencer, *History,* 1:236, 672; 2:442–444; Thompson, *Elder Wilson Thompson,* 40–41; Taylor, *History of Ten Baptist Churches,* 219, 359–360.

13. Taylor, *History of Ten Baptist Churches,* 225, nn. 200–2.

14. Ibid., 225–27.

15. Ibid., 235–36. A similar, though more gender-oriented, interpretation of Hannah Graves's activity is in Pogue, "I Cannot Believe the Gospel," 228–29.

16. Letter to aunt, Mary Bristow, 5 September 1844, SBTS.

17. Mary Bristow, Diary, June 1851, SBTS.

18. Barbara Welter, "The Cult of True Womanhood, 1820–1860," *American Quarterly* 18 (Summer 1966): 152–54. Just as Laurel Thatcher Ulrich observed in her study of Martha Ballard, Kentucky Baptist women did not see a disjuncture between their religious life and their "ordinary life." Their religion was "not a calling out from ordinary life but a validation of it." For Ballard, a Congregationalist, "Seeing her friends and neighbors gathered in orderly rows in the meeting house confirmed her place in the universe and in the town." One easily gets the sense from the available sources that Baptist women experienced something similar. "Laurel Thatcher Ulrich, *A Midwife's Tale: The Life of Martha Ballard, Based on Her Diary, 1785–1812* (New York: Vintage Books, 1990), 76, 108.

19. Spencer, *History,* 1:299–300. For similar, though less descriptive, accounts of such influence, see Spencer, *History,* 1:395; 2:591; Taylor, *History of Ten Baptist Churches,* 285–286, 293.

20. Taylor, *History of Ten Baptist Churches,* 357–358.

21. Taylor, *History of Ten Baptist Churches,* 168–69; Spencer, *History,* 1:328–29.

22. Spencer, *History,* 2:440–41.

23. On the concept of republican motherhood, see Linda Kerber, *Women of the Republic: Intellect and Ideology in Revolutionary America* (Chapel Hill: University of North Carolina Press, 1980). For a view of the "costs" of domesticity and an interpretation that perceives antagonistic gender interests, see Barbara Leslie Epstein, *The Politics of Domesticity: Women, Evangelism, and Temperance in Nineteenth-Century America* (Middletown: Wesleyan University Press, 1981). The records used for this study reveal not so much antagonism between Baptist men and women as pursuits of truth in doctrine and religious practice that only sometimes came into gender-based conflict.

24. E. P. Rogers, "Woman's Proper Sphere," *Baptist Banner and Western Pioneer,* 10 October 1849, 4.

25. Drake, *Pioneer Life in Kentucky*, 29, 193, 197–198.

26. Thompson, *Elder Wilson Thompson*, 9, 54–55.

27. Church Book, Particular Baptist Church at Williamstown, December 1831, July 1832, UK. For a similar case in Elizabethtown in 1826, see Pogue, "I Cannot Believe the Gospel," 234–35.

28. In the case of Brother Wiley, the church appointed a committee to investigate the matter further. In both cases, however, the church did not record the eventual outcomes. It might be safe to assume that Daniel repented of any charge, since he was licensed to preach fifteen years later in February 1818. Church Book, Stamping Ground Baptist Church, August 1801, August 1803, February 1818, UK; Church Book, Mayslick Baptist Church, February 1825, UK.

29. Church Book, Stamping Ground Baptist Church, UK. See also the church book of the Sardis church for representative examples of this popular commitment. The Buck Run church placed this commitment in the context of its disciplinary activities. As members watched over each other's conduct, they also strove "for the benefit of the weak of the flock; to raise up the hands that hang down and strengthen the feeble knees." Covenant of Buck Run Church, as quoted in Taylor, *History of Ten Baptist Churches*, 345.

30. Church Book, Mount Pleasant Baptist Church, March 1821, UK; Church Book, Mayslick Baptist Church, December 1820, February 1821, UK.

31. Church Book, Stamping Ground Baptist Church, June 1847, December 1847, UK.

32. Harrell, 203–205; Alexander Campbell, "Woman and Her Mission: An Address Delivered before the Henry Female Seminary, New Castle, Ky., May 30, 1856," in *The Writings of Alexander Campbell*, ed. W. A. Morris (Austin: Eugene Von Boeckmann, 1896), 454–58.

33. Harrell, 72–76; Minutes of the Sulpher Fork Association, 1840, SBHLA.

34. Cott, *Bonds of Womanhood*, 133, 142; Mary P. Ryan, "A Woman's Awakening: Evangelical Religion and the Families of Utica, New York, 1800–1840," *American Quarterly* 30 (1978): 602–23.

35. Pendleton, *Church Manual*, 130–43.

36. "A Combat Written in '45," Mary Bristow, Diary, SBTS.

37. Pogue, "I Cannot Believe the Gospel," 226. The five churches whose records were used for the analysis of exclusions were Mount Pleasant, Mayslick, Paris, Williamstown, and Providence. These records comport with other studies of church discipline, including Melissa Haynes's unpublished study

of over a dozen churches in North Carolina. She found that women were five times as likely as men to be indicted for defection. Melissa G. Haynes, "Piety, Purity, and Baptist Femininity: Gender and Religious Discipline in Wilkes County, North Carolina, 1777 to 1890" (M.A. Thesis, Appalachian State University, 2001), 59.

38. Pogue, "I Cannot Believe the Gospel," 226.

39. Church Book, Providence Baptist Church, August 1830, UK.

40. Minutes of the Bracken Baptist Association, 1829, 1830, 1831, SBHLA; Church Book, Mayslick Baptist Church, June–August 1830, UK; Cody, *May's Lick Baptist Church*, 31–33.

41. Church Book, Paris Baptist Church, January 1833; Masters, *A History of Baptists*, 119.

42. Perhaps the most extensively described associational split in Kentucky is recorded in the minutes of the 1840 Sulpher Fork Association, wherein an anti-mission minority, representing 275 members, broke with the larger group, representing 1,012 members. Both factions wrote their own description of the acrimonious split and both versions are available at the Southern Baptist Historical Library and Archives. Minutes of the Sulpher Fork Association, 1840, SBHLA.

43. Church Book, Mount Pleasant Baptist Church, June–December 1833, UK; Church Book, Williamstown Baptist Church, January–May 1842, UK.

44. Minutes of the South District Baptist Association, 1826, 1830, 1832, SBHLA; Masters, *A History of Baptists*, 170. "United Baptists" was a label for those who agreed with the terms of union fashioned in 1801 to bond the Regulars and the Separates.

45. Minutes of the Russell's Creek Baptist Association, 1834, SBHLA. While it is apparent from available records that women played integral roles in the battles for Baptist identity, whether pro-Reformation or not, what is not as clear is why they chose the sides they did. Alexander Campbell's movement upheld an even more conservative view of women's roles than did Baptists. The biographer of Campbell's wife Selina notes that "fewer Disciples women joined reform movements than did female members of other Protestant groups." She also provides little reason for Selina Campbell's joining the movement other than her family's Baptist background. Loretta M. Long, *The Life of Selina Campbell: A Fellow Soldier in the Cause of Restoration* (Tuscaloosa: University of Alabama Press, 2001), 22–43. Other scholarly treatments of Campbell's movement agree that Disciples women had more

opportunities after the Civil War and Campbell's death in 1866. Antebellum female Disciples, however, were just as much a part of and subject to the separate-spheres mentality as Baptist women, if not more so. Fred Arthur Bailey, "The Status of Women in the Disciples of Christ Movement, 1865–1900" (Ph.D. diss., University of Tennessee, 1979), 1–34; John R. Lup, Jr., "A History of the Nineteenth Century Women's Issue in the Restoration Movement" (M.A. Thesis, Cincinnati Bible Seminary, 1993), 30–98; Long, 21, 82.

46. Church Book, Mayslick Baptist Church, February 1853, UK; Church Book, Paris Baptist Church, December 1856, April 1857, March 1860, UK.

47. Biblical passages for the Ruth archetype include Ruth 1:16 and 4:17–22, and Matthew 1:5. Passages for Jael include Judges 4:17–24. To a more extensive degree, Laurel Thatcher Ulrich uses the archetypal images of Bathsheba, Eve, and Jael to discuss the roles of colonial women in New England. Laurel Thatcher Ulrich, *Good Wives: Image and Reality in the Lives of Women in Northern New England, 1650–1750* (New York: Vintage Books, 1980).

48. John L. Waller, "A Good Wife," *Baptist Banner*, 19 September 1835, 1.

49. John L. Waller, "Directions for Ladies," *Baptist Banner*, 3 October 1835, 4.

50. Susan Hill Lindley, *"You Have Stept out of Your Place": A History of Women and Religion in America* (Louisville: Westminster John Knox Press, 1996), 109; Hardesty, *Woman Called to Witness*, 103–104; John L. Waller, "Insurrection of the Ladies!!!" *Baptist Banner and Western Pioneer*, 4 June 1840. The newspaper was at an early peak in 1840, with over 5,000 subscribers. In 1839, the paper absorbed *The Baptist* from Tennessee and the *Western Pioneer* of Illinois giving it a wide circulation and a key position of cultural influence in the West.

51. George Raleigh Jewell, "The Ford's Christian Repository," *Encyclopedia of Southern Baptists,* ed. Clifton Judson Allen (Nashville: Broadman Press, 1958), 1:457; Spencer, History, 1:702–3; 2:191–92.

52. "Receipts," *Christian Repository* 7 (February–November 1858). The receipt lists were printed on the inside of the journal's back cover.

53. Editorial, *Christian Repository* 5 (January 1856): 67. Leonard I. Sweet has analyzed the larger significance of ministers' wives in the nineteenth century, describing how they assumed the roles of companion, sacrificer, assistant, and partner. Ford's comment suggests that these wives' roles did not end as adjuncts of their husbands, but also extended to encompass propagators of the faith generally. Leonard I. Sweet, *The Minister's Wife: Her*

Role in Nineteenth-Century American Evangelicalism (Philadelphia: Temple University Press, 1983), 3–11.

54. Mrs. A. O. Smith, "Woman," *Christian Repository* 6 (January 1857): 59–60; "Duties of a Christian Mother," *Christian Repository* 5 (June 1856): 384.

55. *Christian Repository* 6 (March 1857): 194. *Grace Truman* received at least eight different printings between 1857 and 1903. The novel written in response to Ford's book was *Constance Wright, or The Heroine of Truth* by W. S. May. Richard Traylor, "Sallie Rochester Ford: Fiction, Faith, and Femininity," *Baptist History and Heritage* 40 (Summer/Fall 2005): 91–99.

56. Sallie Rochester Ford, *Grace Truman, or Love and Principle* (1886; reprint, Philadelphia: American Baptist Publication Society, 1903), 179–80.

57. Sallie Ford, "How I Came to Write *Grace Truman*," Appendix to *Grace Truman*, i–ix.

58. Ford, *Grace Truman*, 34–35, 48, 245–46, 259.

59. Ibid., 70–112.

60. Ibid., 138–58, 166, 170, 364.

61. Minutes of the Nelson Baptist Association, 1859, SBHLA.

6. Determined to Persist

1. Church Book, Paris Baptist Church, May–October 1857, UK; Elisha W. Green, *Life of the Rev. Elisha W. Green* (Maysville, KY: Republican Printing Office, 1888), 12–13; Minutes of the Bracken Baptist Association, 1856, 1860, SBHLA. After the separation of many black members from the Paris Church, the original church entered into a period of decline. The church's associational letter from August 1857, before the split, lists the membership at 93 white and 117 black. One year later, membership was listed at 92 white and 33 black. By 1860, the church had 78 white and 31 black members. The new African Baptist church, on the other hand, began to grow rapidly. Beginning with 74 members, by 1860 it had 138 members. Other African churches in the region matched Paris's success. In 1856, the African church at Maysville had 204 members and the African church at Mayslick had 212 members. In 1860, Maysville had 264. Because of this growth, by 1860 the two largest churches in the Bracken Association were African churches.

2. Butler, *Awash in a Sea of Faith*, 247–248.

3. William Courtland Johnson claims that "mainstream historians have too often overlooked evidence" that challenges the "assumption that slaves exposed to Christianity embraced enthusiastically the religion of their

oppressors." He asserts that "ill-prepared" clergy, the lack of the "most basic Christian religious instruction," the barriers faced by black preachers, and the "enduring African religious traditions" make "characterizations of slave religious conversion as 'Christian' . . . inadequate if not altogether inaccurate." The African-American Baptist experience in Kentucky indicates an ardent pursuit and embrace of Baptist identity; indeed, they seem to "out-Baptist" the white Baptists. William Courtland Johnson, "'A Delusive Clothing': Christian Conversion in the Antebellum Slave Community," *Journal of Negro History* 82 (Summer 1997): 295–311.

4. Ford, *Grace Truman*, 12; Ellen Eslinger, "The Beginnings of Afro-American Christianity Among Kentucky Baptists," in *The Buzzel About Kentuck: Settling the Promised Land*, ed. Craig Thompson Friend (Lexington: University Press of Kentucky, 1999), 203–11. Eslinger's research reveals pre-revival similarities between Methodist and Baptist rates of black membership. But after the revivals, the Methodist rate actually decreased while the Baptists' increased. Eslinger denies that slave owner influence was a factor in this outcome, but she does not explore a reason for the result.

5. Churches and their black/white membership ratios in 1845 include Clarksville 69/49, Elkton 46/36, Hopkinsville 92/84, and Russellville 105/96. Minutes of the Bethel Association, 1845, 1860, SBHLA.

6. Long Run Association churches and their black/white membership ratio include Jeffersontown 74/38, and Simpsonville 177/160. At the 1851 meeting of the Bracken Association, the church at Paris reported 117 black members compared to 93 white. The church at Yelvington, reporting to the Daviess County Association in 1860, noted their 181 black members compared to 93 white. In the same association, the Owensboro church reported 215 black members and 110 white. Minutes of the Long Run Association, 1860, SBHLA; Minutes of the Bracken Association, 1851, SBHLA; Minutes of the Daviess Country Association, 1860, SBHLA.

7. Hatch, *Democratization*, 102; Eslinger, "Afro-American Christianity," 209–10; Church Book, Providence Baptist Church, May–July 1802, UK. On committees, see S. H. Ford, "Committees," *Christian Repository* 5 (May 1856): 301–2. Ford writes, "This mischievous invention of special 'committees' . . . is an exotic amongst us; an imported plant, recent and unnatural."

8. Church Book, Providence Baptist Church, October 1810–April 1811, UK.

9. Church Book, Stamping Ground Baptist Church, September 1798, February 1818, August 1818, UK.

10. James Allen Lane recalled how one African-American preacher once filled a distant preaching appointment and returned home "after the hour forbidden for slaves to be abroad." The slave patrol detained him and the preacher was "cruelly whipped." Allen adds that "as the blows fell, his words were, 'Jesus Christ suffered for righteousness's sake, so kin I.'" James Allen Lane, *The Blue-Grass Region of Kentucky* (New York: n.p., 1911), 77–78, quoted in Ivan E. McDougle, *Slavery in Kentucky, 1792–1865* (Lancaster, PA: New Era Printing Company, 1918; reprint, Westport, CT: Negro Universities Press, 1970), 83. Church Book, Stamping Ground Baptist Church, November 1818, UK; Marion B. Lucas, *A History of Blacks in Kentucky*, vol. 1, *From Slavery to Segregation, 1760–1891* (Lexington: Kentucky Historical Society, 1992), 29–30.

11. Church Book, Mayslick Baptist Church, December 1798–July 1799, UK.

12. Madison Campbell, *Autobiography of Elder Madison Campbell: Pastor of the United Colored Baptist Church, Richmond, Ky.* (Richmond, KY: Pantograph Job Rooms, 1895), 35–37.

13. Since the early preachers in the state knew each other fairly well, Taylor knew many of the ministers who adopted and expressed emancipationist views. Still, his memoirs, written well after the emancipationists had separated from the majority, bear no sign of hostility on his part. In his recollection of the Hillsboro church, Taylor seems to characterize the emancipation movement in that body as simply a momentary hindrance to the church's eventual numerical prosperity. Taylor, *History of Ten Baptist Churches*, 19, 27–30, 242.

14. Taylor, *History of Ten Baptist Churches*, 19, 295–298; Masters, *A History of Baptists*, 84. The Bible verse Taylor cites is Acts 10:34.

15. Taylor, *History of Ten Baptist Churches*, 295–98.

16. Taylor, *History of Ten Baptist Churches*, 220, 351–52.

17. Church records used in this regard include those of Mount Pleasant, Mayslick, Providence, Paris, and Mount Zion Baptist Churches from 1780–1860. Randy J. Sparks found a similar phenomenon in his study of Mississippi churches. Randy J. Sparks, "Religion in Amite County, Mississippi, 1800–1861," in *Masters & Slaves in the House of the Lord: Race and Religion in the American South, 1740–1870*, ed. John B. Boles (Lexington: University Press of Kentucky, 1988), 75–76.

18. Church Book, Mount Pleasant Baptist Church, July 1812, UK.

19. Church Book, Stamping Ground Baptist Church, August 1803, April 1842, UK.

20. Wilson Thompson, *Elder Wilson Thompson*, 45–48. The Mouth of Licking Baptist Church changed its name to "Licking" in 1820 and then to "Cold Springs" in 1942. Masters, *A History of Baptists,* 84.

21. David T. Bailey, *Shadow on the Church: Southwestern Evangelical Religion and the Issue of Slavery, 1783–1860* (Ithaca, NY: Cornell University Press, 1985), 31–32; Asa Earl Martin, *The Anti-Slavery Movement in Kentucky Prior to 1850* (Louisville: Standard Publishing Company, 1918; reprint, New York: Negro Universities Press, 1970), 14–25. For the complicated Methodist struggle with slavery, see Wigger, *Taking Heaven by Storm,* 138–50.

22. Sweet, *Baptists,* 79–81; "The History of the Salem Baptist Association," in Minutes of the Salem Baptist Association, 1826, SBHLA. For other associational attitudes and difficulties with slavery, see Masters, *A History of Baptists,* 56, 69–70, and Sweet, *Baptists,* 82.

23. McDougle, 32; Sweet, *Baptists,* 82–83; Masters, *A History of Baptists,* 168–69.

24. Martin, 39–41; Minutes of the Baptized Licking-Locust Association, Friends of Humanity, 1807, in Sweet, *Baptists,* 564–65; Benedict, *A General History,* 2:248; Masters, *A History of Baptists,* 184. The calculation of organized emancipationist representation in 1812 is based upon the number reported by Benedict and an estimation of total membership based on Frank Master's figures for 1810. Masters reports a membership of about 20,000 in 1812. This yields 1.5 percent. A larger adherence rate would make that percentage actually much smaller.

25. Church Book, Stamping Ground Baptist Church, February–April 1798, UK; Minutes of the Elkhorn Baptist Association, 1786, in Sweet, *Baptists,* 420–21.

26. Church Book, Mayslick Baptist Church, 1789–1805, UK; Drake, *Pioneer Life in Kentucky,* 5, 179–80, 186, 190; Sweet, *Baptists,* 83; Spencer, *History,* 1:186.

27. Church Book, Mayslick Baptist Church, March 1800, May 1808, July 1809, April 1812, UK; Drake, *Pioneer Life in Kentucky,* 179, 207; Ira Berlin, *Slaves Without Masters: The Free Negro in the Antebellum South* (New York: Pantheon Books, 1974), 21–23; Minutes of the Licking Locust Association, 1807, in Sweet, *Baptists,* 564–565. On Jacob Grigg's emancipationist activities, see Spencer, *History,* 1:190–91.

28. David T. Bailey, *Shadow on the Church*, 22–30; Minutes of the Long Run Baptist Association, 1810, SBHLA; Minutes of the South District Baptist Association, 1810, SBHLA.

29. See notes 5 and 6 for specifics related to African-American participation in this association. Minutes of the Bethel Baptist Association, 1844, 1845, 1860, SBHLA; Lowell H. Harrison, *The Antislavery Movement in Kentucky* (Lexington: University Press of Kentucky, 1978), 4. In five of the ten churches in 1860 with a black majority, the percentage increase resulted partially from decrease in white membership. The Russell's Creek Association also recorded segregated preaching at their 1859 meeting; Minutes of the Russell's Creek Baptist Association, 1859, SBHLA.

30. In his formative study of slave religion in the antebellum South, Albert Raboteau noted the importance of worshipful spontaneity in black religious expressions. They "broke out in moaning, praying, singing, shouting." Raboteau connected such ecstatic expressions with vestiges of the African religious experience. Raboteau, *Slave Religion*, 59–75, 244.

31. Masters, *A History of Baptists,* 85; Hickman, *A Short Account*, 18; Church Book, Stamping Ground Baptist Church, May 1819, UK.

32. Charles Joyner, "'Believer I Know': The Emergence of African American Christianity," in *Religion and American Culture,* ed. David G. Hackett (New York: Routledge, 1995), 192–193; Church Book, Stamping Ground Baptist Church, May 1821, October 1840, February 1841, April 1841, June 1841, April 1842, UK. A similar, but less intense, account of concerns with disorder conjoined with eventual separation is found in Church Book, Paris Baptist Church, September 1849, September 1852, May 1857, UK.

33. Church Book, Stamping Ground Baptist Church, January–February 1855, UK. Studies which address the racially compromised nature of Baptist egalitarianism include Posey, *The Baptist Church*, 89–90; Sparks, "Religion in Amite County," 72–73; Butler, *Awash in a Sea of Faith*, 150–151; Berlin, *Slaves Without Masters*, 68–72; and Eugene D. Genovese, *Roll, Jordan, Roll: The World the Slaves Made* (New York: Pantheon Books, 1974), 234.

34. Berlin, *Slaves Without Masters*, 294; Sobel, *Trabelin' On*, 210, 333–43; Church Book, Stamping Ground Baptist Church, October 1825, February 1841, UK.

35. Minutes of the Baptist Association, 1850, SBHLA; *Baptist Banner and Western Pioneer,* 16 June 1842, 3; *Baptist Banner and Western Pioneer,* 2 June 1842, 6; *Baptist Banner and Western Pioneer,* 13 January 1842, 2.

36. Madison Campbell, *Elder Madison Campbell*, 37–40.

37. "Types of the Human Race," *Christian Repository* 8 (January 1859), 80–82.

38. William C. Buck, *The Slavery Question* (Louisville: Harney, Hughes & Hughes, 1849), 22–28; Harrison, *Antislavery Movement*, 56–60.

39. Buck, *The Slavery Question*, 22.

40. Minutes of the Long Run Baptist Association, 1842, SBHLA, 1843; Minutes of the Bracken Baptist Association, 1860, SBHLA; Minutes of the Tate's Creek Baptist Association, 1860, SBHLA. For another example of white representation of black churches, see Minutes of the Union Baptist Association, 1860, SBHLA, wherein the white messengers of the church at Paducah represented the "Colored church."

41. Green, *Rev. Elisha W. Green* 1–9; Minutes of the Bracken Baptist Association, 1860, SBHLA.

42. Masters, *A History of Baptists*, 346; Minutes of the Bracken Baptist Association, 1856, SBHLA; Spencer, *History*, 2:357; Sobel, *Trabelin' On*, 333, 339, 341.

43. Sobel, *Trabelin' On*, 336–37; Minutes of the Long Run Baptist Association, 1860, SBHLA.

44. Masters, *A History of Baptists*, 347–49; Spencer, *History*, 2:661; Sobel, *Trabelin' On*, 336–337.

7. Refining and Radiating the Impulse

1. Masters calculates the total Baptist population in 1860 as 94,759, with the Kentucky population at 1,155,684. Census records indicate that there were 793,215 Kentuckians age 10 and over in 1860. Minutes of the Tate's Creek Baptist Association, 1859, SBHLA; Smith, Diary, 27 January 1846, SBTS; Masters, *A History of Baptists*, 329; Newman and Halvorson, *Atlas of American Religion*, 39, 73, 100, 128; United States Bureau of the Census, *Population of the United States in 1860* (Washington DC: Government Printing Office, 1864), 168–179. On par with the sentiments of Waller and the Tate's Creek Association, S. H. Ford gave a similar statement in 1856. He wrote, "Infant membership and infant baptism, bubbles brought into being by the corrupting tide of Popery, are destined to perish with the breakers that gave them birth." S. H. F., "Decline of Infant Baptism in America," *Christian Repository* 5 (June 1856): 352.

2. McBeth, *Heritage*, 344–61, 381–91.

3. "The Great West," *Baptist Banner*, 17 October 1835, 3; *Baptist Banner and Western Pioneer*, 14 February 1839, 2; Editorial, *Baptist Banner*, 17 October 1835, 2.

4. "Our Country," *Baptist Banner and Western Pioneer*, 3 March 1842, 6; Minutes of the Bethel Baptist Association, 1844, SBHLA.

5. Minutes of the Long Run Baptist Association, 1845, SBHLA; McBeth, *Heritage*, 388–391.

6. Minutes of the West Union Baptist Association, 1846, SBHLA. As an example of this local orientation toward mission work, the Mayslick Baptist Church elected its own delegates to attend a meeting of the China Mission Society in Shelbyville. The church's 1847 associational letter also noted that the church members contributed money to educational institutions, to the state General Association, to the Indian Mission Society, and to the Bracken Association's Bible and Foreign Mission Society. Church Book, Mayslick Baptist Church, May 1845, August 1847, UK

7. Minutes of the Concord Baptist Association, 1846, SBHLA. Another example of the anxieties that derived from success can be found in Minutes of the Long Run Baptist Association, 1850, SBHLA.

8. Minutes of the Bethel Baptist Association, 1849, SBHLA. The Bracken Association made a similar case for Georgetown College, asserting that "as Americans we regard such institutions as of the highest importance to our national welfare." Minutes of the Bracken Baptist Association, 1845, SBHLA.

9. Minutes of the North Bend Baptist Association, 1854, SBHLA. The founding and success of Baptist colleges signals the incipient interest in ministerial education and gives an indication where and when this transition took hold. Pre-1845 Baptist colleges include: Rhode Island College (Brown), 1764; Hamilton (NY) Literary and Theological Institution (Colgate University), 1820; Waterville College (Colby College), 1820); Columbian College in the District of Columbia (George Washington University), 1821; Newton (MA) Theological Institution (Andover-Newton Theological School), 1825; Furman Academy and Theological Institution (Furman University), 1826; Rock Spring Seminary (Shurleff College), 1827; Georgetown College, 1829; Granville Literary and Theological Institution (Denison University), 1832; Richmond School (University of Richmond), 1832; Michigan and Huron Institute of Kalamazoo (Kalamazoo College), 1833; Mercer University, 1833; Wake Forest Institute (Wake Forest University), 1834; Indiana Baptist Manual Labor Institute (Franklin College), 1837; Judson

College, 1838; Howard College (Samford University), 1841; Hillsdale College, 1844. Like Georgetown College, many of these schools took ten to twenty years to become educational forces of notice. Robert G. Torbet, *A History of the Baptists* (Philadelphia: Judson Press, 1950), 322–335; Charles Allison Weed, "American Baptists and an Educated Ministry Prior to 1850" (M.Th. Thesis, Crozer Theological Seminary, 1935), 79–81. Beth Barton Schweiger's *The Gospel Working Up* models the impact these educational commitments had on late nineteenth century Baptist development and how it reflected a modern, forward-looking ethic.

10. Rorabaugh, *Alcoholic Republic*, 77–85; Spencer, *History*, 2:206; Ian R. Tyrrell, *Sobering Up: From Temperance to Prohibition in Antebellum America, 1800–1860* (Westport, CT: Greenwood Press, 1979), 56–57.

11. Based on a representative sample of eight churches: Bethel, Mayslick, McCormack's, Mount Pleasant, Mount Zion, Paris, Providence, and Williamstown. Whereas eighty-nine men were excluded by these churches, in the same time span five women suffered the same fate. Gregory A. Wills's study of Baptist discipline in Georgia notes that men were forty-five times more likely to be tried for drunkenness than women. Wills, *Democratic Religion*, 59.

12. Spencer, *History*, 1:400–1. For accounts of drunken pastors, see Spencer, *History*, 1:164, 191, 199, 283, 295, 416, 463; 2:133, 206, 233, 574. Though the associational records are largely silent on the issue of temperance in the 1830s, the Goshen Association advised in 1833 that churches not use the temperance issue as a bar to fellowship and communion. Masters, *A History of Baptists*, 239, 273.

13. Spencer, *History*, 1:708–710; Tyrrell, *Sobering Up*, 211–214, 260.

14. Church Book, Paris Baptist Church, August 1851, UK; Church Book, Stamping Ground Baptist Church, March 1852, UK; Church Book, Mayslick Baptist Church, March 1848, March 1853, UK; Minutes of the Campbell County Baptist Association, 1853, SBHLA. For other associational stances supporting temperance, see the associational minutes of Baptist (1852, 1854), Franklin, (1856), Liberty (1848, 1853, 1858), Little River (1854), Sulpher Fork (1853), and West Union (1860), SBHLA. Not all associations agreed, however. In 1850, the Greenup Association in eastern Kentucky split over the temperance issue, creating the pro-temperance Friendship Association. Masters, *A History of Baptists*, 314.

15. Lois W. Banner, "Religious Benevolence as Social Control: A Critique of an Interpretation," *Journal of American History* 60 (June 1973): 23–41.

16. Spencer, *History*, 1:718; Posey, *The Baptist Church*, 109; Isaac Russell, ed. *Selected Sabbath-School Hymns and Songs* (Louisville: J. LeBrun, 1860), 10; Mulder, *A Controversial Spirit*, 47, 120.

17. Minutes of the Bethel Baptist Association, 1849, SBHLA; McBeth, *Heritage*, 433; Minutes of the Russell's Creek Baptist Association, 1834, SBHLA; Minutes of the South District Baptist Association, 1845, SBHLA.

18. Minutes of the Long Run Baptist Association, 1842, SBHLA; Smith, *Diary*, 7 September 1845, 14 December 1845, 12 October 1845, 2 November 1845, SBTS.

19. Minutes of the Greenup Baptist Association, 1858, SBHLA; Minutes of the Daviess County Baptist Association, 1858, SBHLA; McBeth, *Heritage*, 435.

20. Pendleton, *Church Manual*, 153–156. For a more descriptive account of the impact of the Sabbath Schools in American religion, see Anne M. Boylan, *Sunday School: The Formation of an American Institution, 1790–1880* (New Haven, CT: Yale University Press, 1988).

21. James E. Tull, *A History of Southern Baptist Landmarkism in the Light of Historical Baptist Ecclesiology* (New York: Arno Press, 1980), 131.

22. John L. Waller, "The Validity of Baptism by Pedobaptist Ministers," *Western Baptist Review*, March 1848, 3:269, emphasis in the original. Waller came to this position after much investigation and hesitancy. Indeed, he had taken the opposite side in 1838. John L. Waller, "Query," *Baptist Banner*, 23 January 1838, 2. For Waller's evolution on the subject, see Bernard G. Holmes, "The Contribution of John Lightfoot Waller to Kentucky Baptists, 1830–1854," (Th.D. diss., Southwestern Baptist Theological Seminary, 1975), 239–244.

23. Waller, "Baptism by Pedobaptist Ministers," 3:271.

24. Ibid., 3:268.

25. "Fidus," letter to the editor, *Tennessee Baptist*, 25 May 1848. Many scholars have concluded with varying degrees of confidence that Fidus might have been Graves himself. Based on a gloss written by Graves's son-in-law in 1891 on the editor's own copy of the *Tennessee Baptist* (29 June 1848, page 2), historian W. W. Barnes accepted Fidus as Graves, leading others to the same conclusion. William Wright Barnes, *The Southern Baptist Convention, 1845–1953* (Nashville: Broadman Press, 1954), 103, n. 11. See also James Leo Garrett, *Baptist Theology: A Four-Century Study* (Macon, GA: Mercer University Press, 2009), 214 as one who builds on Barnes. Others, such as James E. Tull

and Stephen M. Stookey, accept Graves as Fidus, but not as unquestioningly as Barnes. See Tull, *A History of Southern Baptist Landmarkism*, 130, n. 3 and Stephen Martin Stookey, "The Impact of Landmarkism upon Southern Baptist Western Geographical Expansion," (Ph.D. diss., Southwestern Baptist Theological Seminary, 1994), 48, n. 100. Still others, notably a recent Graves biographer, remain unconvinced. James A. Patterson, *James Robinson Graves: Staking the Boundaries of Baptist Identity* (Nashville: B&H Publishing Group, 2012), 46. The debate is largely academic since Graves later offered a full-throated endorsement of Fidus's views. J. R. Graves, "The Western Review," *Tennessee Baptist,* 19 October 1848, 2.

26. J. R. Graves, "The Western Review," *Tennessee Baptist,* 25 May 1848, 2.

27. John L. Waller, "The Administrator of Baptism," *Western Baptist Review,* August 1848, 3:464–65, 467.

28. Ibid., 3:469, emphasis in the original.

29. John L. Waller, "Decline of Infant Baptism in America," *Western Baptist Review,* May 1849, 4:347–350.

30. John L. Waller, "The Evils and the Corrupting Influences of Infant Baptism," *Western Baptist Review,* August 1850, 5:89–103. Quotes are found on pages 89 and 103.

31. J. R. Graves, "A Chapter on Controversy," *Tennesssee Baptist,* 8 February 1849, 2.

32. J. R. Graves, "The War Begun," *Tennessee Baptist,* 23 November 1850, 2.

33. Tull, *History of Southern Baptist Landmarkism*, 131. For a fuller background on why Graves chose Cotton Grove for his meeting, see Joe Early, Jr., "The Cotton Grove Resolutions," *Tennessee Baptist History* 7 (Fall 2005): 47–50.

34. James A. Patterson, *James Robinson Graves*, 50–53; Early, Jr., "The Cotton Grove Resolutions," 50.

35. James A. Patterson, *James Robinson Graves*, 53–55.

36. James Madison Pendleton, *An Old Landmark* (Nashville: Graves & Marks, 1854). In later editions, Graves added the word "Re-Set" to the title.

37. John L. Waller, "Baptist High-Churchism," *Western Recorder,* 20 September 1854, 2. Waller died a month after writing this critique. S. H. Ford took over as editor of *The Western Recorder.* Waller's early and sudden death prompted J. R. Graves to observe, "Truly, a great man hath fallen in our Israel." Though they had disagreed in recent years, Graves warned, "Let no

one suppose for one moment that we were his enemy." J. R. Graves, "John L. Waller," *Tennessee Baptist,* 28 October 1855, 2.

38. J. R. Graves, "An Old Landmark," *Tennessee Baptist,* 4 November 1854, 2.

39. Ira V. (Jack) Birdwhistell, *Gathered at the River: A Narrative History of Long Run Baptist Association* (Louisville, KY: Long Run Baptist Association, 1978), 60–64.

40. W. W. Everts, "The Old Landmark Discovered," *Christian Repository* 4 (January 1855): 20–22.

41. Ibid., 22–25.

42. Ibid., 27–34.

43. J. M. Pendleton, "The 'Old Land-mark' Vindicated," *Christian Repository,* 4 (April 1855): 215–235, (May 1855): 265–272; W. W. Everts, "Review of 'Old Land-mark Vindicated,'" *Christian Repository,* 4 (April 1855): 235–46, (May 1855): 272–80.

44. W. Morgan Patterson, *Baptist Successionism: A Critical View* (Valley Forge, PA: Judson Press, 1969), 14–20; Henry Danvers, *A Treatise of Baptism* (1674), accessed November 23, 2012, http://baptisthistoryhomepage.com/danvers.h.treatise.baptsm.html; Thomas Crosby, *The History of the English Baptists, from the Reformation to the Beginning of the Reign of King George I,* 4 vols. (London: 1738–40); James Edward McGoldrick, *Baptist Successionism: A Crucial Question in Baptist History* (Metuchen, NJ: Scarecrow Press, 1994), 145–46

45. Robert Robinson, *Ecclesiastical Researches* (Cambridge: Francis Hodson, 1792), 475; W. Morgan Patterson, *Baptist Successionism,* 20–21.

46. See James A. Patterson, *James Robinson Graves,* 107–9, for a brief survey of early nineteenth century American Baptist articulations of successionism

47. J. R. Graves, introduction to *A Concise History of Foreign Baptists* by G. H. Orchard (Nashville: Graves, Marks & Rutland, 1855), xi

48. John L. Waller, "Reformation," *Christian Repository* 1 (January 1852): 5–14; 1 (September 1852): 543–48; 1 (October 1852): 631–36 (quote on 635)

49. S. H. Ford, "Past and Future of the Baptist Churches," *Christian Repository* 2 (February 1853): 89–108

50. S. H. Ford, *The Origin of the Baptists: Traced Back by Milestones on the Track of Time* (Memphis: Southwestern Publishing House, 1860).

51. Minutes of the Sulphur Fork Baptist Association, 1858, SBHLA; Minutes of the Sulphur Fork Baptist Association, 1859, SBHLA

52. W. C. Buck, "The National Question," *Baptist Banner and Western Pioneer*, 20 March 1850, 2. On the same page, Buck condemned Christian newspapermen who agitated rather than worked to conciliate, adding, "Surely such a spirit comes not of the Gospel of Christ." W. C. Buck, "A Reprehensible Spirit," *Baptist Banner and Western Pioneer*, 20 March 1850, 2.

53. John L. Waller, "The Political and the Religious Union of Our Country," *Baptist Banner and Western Pioneer*, 23 April 1851, 2.

54. Lowell H. Harrison and James C. Klotter, *A New History of Kentucky* (Lexington: University Press of Kentucky, 1997) 190–212; Minutes of the Long Run Baptist Association, 1861, SBHLA; Spencer, "Autobiography," 142–60; A. C. Graves, *Ministry of Faith: The Ardent Ministry, Times, Anecdotes, and Pulpit Selections of Rev. A. W. Larue, A. M.* (Louisville: Waller, Sherrill, and Co., 1865), 115–16

55. Minutes of the Ten Mile Baptist Association, 1859, SBHLA.

56. The language here is drawn directly from the circular letter issued by the Long Run Baptist Association in 1856. Minutes of the Long Run Association, 1856, SBHLA.

57. Finke and Stark, *The Churching of America*, 248.

Bibliography

Primary Sources

Church Record Books

Special Collections and Archives, Margaret I. King Library, University of
        Kentucky, Lexington.
Bethel Baptist Church, Wayne County
Mayslick Baptist Church, Mason County
McCormack's Baptist Church, Lincoln County
Mount Zion Baptist Church, Graves County
Mount Pleasant Baptist Church, Jessamine County
Paris Baptist Church, Bourbon County
Providence Baptist Church, Clark County
Sardis Baptist Church, Boone County
Stamping Ground Baptist Church, Scott County
Williamstown Particular Baptist Church, Grant County

Baptist Association Minutes

Southern Baptist Historical Library and Archives, Nashville, Tennessee
Baptist (Baptist) Association
Barren River Baptist Association
Bethel Baptist Association
Bracken Baptist Association
Campbell County Baptist Association
Concord Baptist Association
Cumberland River Baptist Association
Daviess County Baptist Association

Franklin Baptist Association
Freedom Baptist Association
Gaspar River Baptist Association
Goshen Baptist Association
Green River Baptist Association
Greenup Baptist Association
Liberty Baptist Association
Licking Baptist Association
Little River Baptist Association
Little Bethel Baptist Association
Long Run Baptist Association
Middle District Baptist Association
Nelson Baptist Association
Nolynn Baptist Association
North Bend Baptist Association
North District Baptist Association
Russell's Creek Baptist Association
Salem Baptist Association
South District Baptist Association
South Kentucky Baptist Association
Sulpher Fork Baptist Association
Tate's Creek Baptist Association
Ten Mile Baptist Association
Union Baptist Association
West Union Baptist Association

Periodicals

Baptist Banner (Lexington, Kentucky)
Baptist Banner and Western Pioneer (Lexington and Louisville, Kentucky)
Christian Repository (Louisville, Kentucky)
Tennessee Baptist (Nashville, Tennessee)
Western Baptist Review (Frankfort, Kentucky)
Western Recorder (Louisville, Kentucky)

Government Documents

United States Bureau of the Census. *Population of the United States in 1860.*
       Washington, DC: Government Printing Office, 1864.

Unpublished Sources

Bristow, Mary. Diary. Special Collections, James P. Boyce Centennial Library, Southern Baptist Theological Seminary, Louisville, KY.

Pratt, William Moody. Diary. Special Collections and Archives, Margaret I. King Library, University of Kentucky, Lexington, Kentucky.

Smith, Thomas, Jr., Diary. Special Collections, James P. Boyce Centennial Library, Southern Baptist Theological Seminary, Louisville, Kentucky.

Spencer, John H. "Autobiography of Dr. John Henderson Spencer." Special Collections, James P. Boyce Centennial Library, Southern Baptist Theological Seminary, Louisville, Kentucky.

Published Sources

Buck, William C. *The Slavery Question*. Louisville: Harney, Hughes & Hughes, 1849.

Campbell, Alexander. "Woman and Her Mission: An Address Delivered before the Henry Female Seminary, New Castle, Ky., May 30, 1856." In *The Writings of Alexander Campbell*, 442–458. Edited by W. A. Morris. Austin: Eugene Von Boeckmann, 1896.

Campbell, Madison. *Autobiography of Elder Madison Campbell: Pastor of the United Colored Baptist Church, Richmond, Ky*. Richmond, KY: Pantograph Job Rooms, 1895.

Conrad, William. *The Journal of Elder William Conrad, Pioneer Preacher*. Edited by Lloyd W. Franks. Lexington, KY: RF Publishing, 1976.

Edwards, Jonathan. "A Faithful Narrative of the Surprising Work of God (1737)." In *A Jonathan Edwards Reader*. Edited John E. Smith, Harry S. Stout, and Kenneth P. Minkema, 57–87. New Haven, CT: Yale University Press, 1995.

Edwards, Morgan. *The Customs of Primitive Churches*. Philadelphia: Printed by Andrew Stewart, 1768.

Ford, Sallie Rochester. *Grace Truman, or Love and Principle*. Philadelphia: American Baptist Publication Society, 1886. Reprint, 1903.

Gano, Stephen, ed. "Biographical Memoirs of the late Rev. John Gano. In *The Life and Ministry of John Gano, 1727–1804*, by Terry Wolever. Springfield, MO: Particular Baptist Press, 1998.

Green, Elisha W. *Life of the Rev. Elisha W. Green*. Maysville, KY: Republican Printing Office, 1888.

Hickman, William. *A Short Account of My Life and Travels*. N. p., 1828; reprint, Louisville: Kentucky Baptist Historical Society, 1969.

Manly, Basil, Jr., *The Kentucky Baptist Pioneers: A Discourse for the Kentucky Baptist Centennial, May 25, 1876, at Louisville, Ky*. Louisville, KY: Western Recorder, 1876.

Michaux, Francois Andre. *Travels to the West of the Allegheny Mountains*. In *Early Western Travels 1748–1846*. Edited by Reuben Gold Thwaites. 3rd Vol. Cleveland: Arthur H. Clark, 1904, 249.

Pendleton, J. M. *Church Manual, Designed for the Use of Baptist Churches*. Philadelphia: Judson Press, 1867.

Pendleton, James. *Reminiscences of a Long Life*. Louisville: Baptist Book Concern, 1891.

Pendleton, James M. *The Condition of the Baptist Cause in Kentucky in 1837: An Address Delivered at the Jubilee of the General Association of Kentucky Baptists, in Walnut Street Baptist Church, Louisville, October 20, 1887*. [Louisville?]: s. n., 1887.

Pendleton, James Madison. *An Old Landmark*. Nashville: Graves & Marks, 1854.

Russell, Isaac, ed. *Selected Sabbath-School Hymns and Songs*. Louisville: J. LeBrun, 1860.

Taylor, John. *Baptists on the American Frontier: A History of Ten Baptist Churches of Which the Author Has Been Alternately a Member*. Edited by Chester Raymond Young. 3rd ed. Macon, GA: Mercer University Press, 1995.

———. "The Rev. John Taylor's Experience," *Kentucky Missionary and Theological Magazine* 1 (May 1812): 33–36.

———. *Thoughts on Missions; Biographies of Baptist Preachers*, Frankfort, KY: s. n., 1820.

Thompson, Wilson. *The Autobiography of Elder Wilson Thompson: His Life, Travels, and Ministerial Labors*. Greenfield, IN: D. H. Goble, 1867; reprint, Conley, GA: Old School Hymnal Co., 1978.

Woodmason, Charles. *The Carolina Backcountry on the Eve of the Revolution: The Journal and Other Writings of Charles Woodmason, Anglican Itinerant*. Edited by Richard J. Hooker. Chapel Hill: University of North Carolina Press, 1953.

Secondary Sources

Books and Articles

Abzug, Robert H. *Cosmos Crumbling: American Reform and the Religious Imagination*. New York: Oxford University Press, 1994.

Alexander, Jon. *American Personal Religious Accounts, 1600–1980: Toward an Inner History of America's Faiths*. New York: Edwin Mueller Press, 1983.

Allen, Clifton J., ed. *Encyclopedia of Southern Baptists*. Nashville: Broadman Press, 1958.

Anders Sarah Frances and Marilyn Metcalf-Whittaker. "Women as Lay Leaders and Clergy: A Critical Issue." In *Southern Baptists Observed: Multiple Perspectives on a Changing Denomination*. Edited by Nancy Tatom Ammerman, 201–221. Knoxville: University of Tennessee Press, 1993.

Andrews, Dee. *The Methodists and Revolutionary America, 1760–1800: The Shaping of an Evangelical Culture*. Princeton, NJ: Princeton University Press, 2000.

Bailey, David T. *Shadow on the Church: Southwestern Evangelical Religion and the Issue of Slavery, 1783–1860*. Ithaca, NY: Cornell University Press, 1985.

Bailyn, Bernard. *The Ideological Origins of the American Revolution*. Cambridge: Harvard University Press, 1967.

Banner, Lois W. "Religious Benevolence as Social Control: A Critique of an Interpretation." *Journal of American History* 60 (June 1973): 23–41.

Barnes, William Wright. *The Southern Baptist Convention, 1845–1953*. Nashville: Broadman Press, 1954.

Beazley, George G., Jr. "Who Are the Disciples?" In *The Christian Church (Disciples of Christ): An Interpretive Examination in the Cultural Context*. Edited by George G. Beazley, Jr., 5–80. N.p.: Bethany Press, 1973.

Benedict, David. *A General History of the Baptist Denomination in America, and Other Parts of the World*. Vol. 2. Boston: Lincoln & Edmands, 1813; reprint, Freeport, NY: Books for Libraries Press, 1971.

Berlin, Ira. *Slaves Without Masters: The Free Negro in the Antebellum South*. New York: Pantheon Books, 1974.

Billington, Louis. "The Millerite Adventists in Great Britain, 1840–1850." In *The Disappointed: Millerism and Millenarianism in the Nineteenth Century*. Edited by Ronald L. Numbers and Jonathan M. Butler, 59–77. Bloomington: Indiana University Press, 1987.

Birdwhistell, Ira V. (Jack). *Gathered at the River: A Narrative History of Long Run Baptist Association*. Louisville, KY: Long Run Baptist Association, 1978.

Blevins, Carolyn DeArmond. "Women and the Baptist Experience." In *Religious Institutions and Women's Leadership: New Roles Inside the Mainstream*. Edited by Catherine Wessinger, 158–179. Columbia: University of South Carolina Press, 1996.

Blumin, Stuart M. *The Emergence of the Middle Class: Social Experience in the American City, 1760–1900*. New York: Cambridge University Press, 1989.

Boles, John B. *Masters & Slaves in the House of the Lord: Race and Religion in the American South, 1740–1870*. Lexington: University Press of Kentucky, 1988.

———. *The Great Revival, 1787–1805: The Origins of the Southern Evangelical Mind*. Lexington: University Press of Kentucky, 1972.

———. *Religion in Antebellum Kentucky*. Lexington: University Press of Kentucky, 1976.

Boylan, Anne M. *Sunday School: The Formation of an American Institution, 1790–1880*. New Haven, CT: Yale University Press, 1988.

Brackney, William H., ed. *Baptist Life and Thought: 1600–1980*. Valley Forge, PA: Judson Press, 1983.

Braude, Ann. "Women's History Is American Religious History." In *Retelling U. S. Religious History*. Edited by Thomas A. Tweed, 87–107. Berkeley: University of California Press, 1997.

Breen, T. H. "Persistent Localism." *William & Mary Quarterly* 32 (1975): 3–28.

Brekus, Catherine A. *Strangers and Pilgrims: Female Preaching in America, 1740–1845*. Chapel Hill: University of North Carolina Press, 1998.

Brooks, James P. *The Biography of Elder Jacob Locke, of Barren County, Ky*. Glasgow, KY: Times Print, 1881; reprint, South Central Kentucky Historical and Genealogical Society, 1976.

Brown, Kenneth O. *Holy Ground: A Study of the American Camp Meeting.* New York: Garland, 1992.

Bruce, Dickson D. *And They All Sang Hallelujah: PlainFolk CampMeeting Religion, 1800–1845.* Knoxville: University of Tennessee Press, 1974.

Bushman, Richard L. *Joseph Smith and the Beginnings of Mormonism.* Urbana: University of Illinois Press, 1984.

———. *The Refinement of America: Persons, Houses, Cities.* New York: Alfred A. Knopf, 1992.

Butler, Jon. *Awash in a Sea of Faith: Christianizing the American People.* Cambridge: Harvard University Press, 1990.

Caldwell, Patricia. *The Puritan Conversion Narrative: The Beginnings of American Expression.* Cambridge: Cambridge University Press, 1983.

Campbell, Alexander. *Memoirs of Elder Thomas Campbell.* Cincinnati: H. S. Bosworth, 1861.

Carpenter, Joel A. *Revive Us Again: The Reawakening of American Fundamentalism.* New York: Oxford University Press, 1997.

Chute, Anthony L. *A Piety Above the Common Standard.* Macon, GA: Mercer University Press, 2004.

Cody, Z. T. *History of the May's Lick Baptist Church.* Maysville: G. W. Oldham, 1890.

Conkin, Paul K. *Cane Ridge: America's Pentecost.* Madison: University of Wisconsin Press, 1990.

———. *The Uneasy Center: Reformed Christianity in Antebellum America.* Chapel Hill: University of North Carolina Press, 1995.

Cott, Nancy F. *The Bonds of Womanhood: "Woman's Sphere" in New England, 1780–1835.* New Haven, CT: Yale University Press, 1977.

Crismon, Leo Taylor and George Raleigh Jewell. *Kentucky Baptist Atlas.* Middletown: Kentucky Baptist Historical Society, 1964.

Crosby, Thomas. *The History of the English Baptists, from the Reformation to the Beginning of the Reign of King George I.* 4 vols. London, 1738–40.

Cross, Whitney R. *The BurnedOver District: The Social and Intellectual History of Enthusiastic Religion in Western New York, 1800–1850.* New York: Octagon Books, 1950.

Deweese, Charles W. *Baptist Church Covenants.* Nashville: Broadman Press, 1990.

Dolan, Jay P. *The American Catholic Experience: A History from Colonial Times to the Present.* Garden City, NY: Doubleday, 1985.

———. *Catholic Revivalism: The American Experience, 1830–1900.* Notre Dame: University of Notre Dame Press, 1978.

Donan, P. *Memoir of Jacob Creath, Jr.* Cincinnati: R. W. Carroll and Co., 1872.

Dorsey, Bruce. *Reforming Men and Women: Gender in the Antebellum City.* Ithaca, NY: Cornell University Press, 2002.

Drake, Daniel. *Pioneer Life in Kentucky: 1785–1800.* Edited by Emmet Field Horine. New York: Henry Schuman, 1948.

Eames, S. Morris. *The Philosophy of Alexander Campbell.* Bethany, WV: Bethany College, 1966.

Early, Joe, Jr. "The Cotton Grove Resolutions," *Tennessee Baptist History* 7 (Fall 2005): 41–52.

Epstein, Barbara Leslie. *The Politics of Domesticity: Women, Evangelism, and Temperance in Nineteenth-Century America.* Middletown, CT: Wesleyan University Press, 1981.

Eslinger, Ellen. "The Beginnings of Afro-American Christianity Among Kentucky Baptists." *In The Buzzel About Kentuck: Settling the Promised Land.* Edited by Craig Thompson Friend, 197–215. Lexington: University Press of Kentucky, 1999.

Eslinger, Ellen. *Citizens of Zion: The Social Origins of Camp Meeting Revivalism.* Knoxville: University of Tennessee Press, 1999.

Estep, William R. *Renaissance and Reformation.* Grand Rapids: William B. Eerdmans, 1986.

Finke, Roger and Rodney Stark. *The Churching of America, 1776–1990: Winners and Losers in Our Religious Economy.* New Brunswick, N.J.: Rutgers University Press, 1992.

———. "Turning Pews into People: Estimating Nineteenth-Century Church Membership." *Journal for the Scientific Study of Religion* 25 (1986): 180–192.

Foner, Eric. *The Story of American Freedom.* New York: W. W. Norton, 1998.

Ford, S. H. *The Origin of the Baptists: Traced Back by Milestones on the Track of Time.* Memphis: Southwestern Publishing House, 1860.

Foster, Lawrence. *Women, Family, and Utopia: Communal Experiments of the Shakers, the Oneida Community, and the Mormons.* Syracuse: Syracuse University Press, 1991.

Freehling, William W. *The Road to Disunion.* Vol 1. New York: Oxford University Press, 1990.

Fuller, A. James. *Chaplain to the Confederacy: Basil Manly and Baptist Life in the Old South, 1798–1868*. Baton Rouge: Louisiana State University Press, 2000.

Gardner, Robert G. *Baptists of Early America: A Statistical History, 1639–1790*. Atlanta: Georgia Baptist Historical Society, 1983.

Garrett, James Leo. *Baptist Theology: A Four-Century Study*. Macon, GA: Mercer University Press, 2009.

Garrison, Winfred E. *The Sources of Alexander Campbell's Theology*. St. Louis: Christian Publishing Company, 1900.

Genovese, Eugene D. *Roll, Jordan, Roll: The World the Slaves Made*. New York: Pantheon Books, 1974.

George, Timothy and Denise George, eds. *Baptist Confessions, Covenants, and Catechisms*. Nashville: Broadman & Holman, 1996.

Goen, Clarence C. *Revivalism and Separatism in New England, 1740–1800*. New Haven, CT: Yale University Press, 1962.

González, Justo L. *The Story of Christianity*. San Francisco: Harper & Row, 1985.

Graves, A. C. *Ministry of Faith: The Ardent Ministry, Times, Anecdotes, and Pulpit Selections of Rev. A. W. Larue, A. M.* Louisville: Waller, Sherrill, and Co., 1865.

Griffin, John R. *John Keble: Saint of Anglicanism*. Macon, GA: Mercer University Press, 1987.

Hardesty, Nancy A. *Women Called to Witness: Evangelical Feminism in the Nineteenth Century*. Knoxville: University of Tennessee Press, 1999.

Hardt, Philip F. *The Soul of Methodism: The Class Meeting in Early New York City Methodism*. Lanham, MD: University Press of America, 2000.

Harper, Keith and C. Martin Jacumin. *Esteemed Reproach: The Lives of Reverend James Ireland and Reverend Joseph Craig*. Macon, Georgia: Mercer University Press, 2005.

Harrell, David Edwin, Jr. *Quest for a Christian America: The Disciples of Christ and American Society to 1866*. Nashville: Disciples of Christ Historical Society, 1966.

Harrison, Lowell H. *The Antislavery Movement in Kentucky*. Lexington: University Press of Kentucky, 1978.

Harrison, Lowell H. and James C. Klotter. *A New History of Kentucky*. Lexington: University Press of Kentucky, 1997.

Hatch, Nathan O. "The Christian Movement and the Demand for a Theology of the People." *Journal of American History* 67 (December 1980): 545–567.

———. *The Democratization of American Christianity*. New Haven, CT: Yale University Press, 1989.

———. "The Puzzle of American Methodism." *Church History* 63 (June 1994): 175–189.

———. *The Sacred Cause of Liberty: Republican Thought and the Millennium in Revolutionary New England*. New Haven, CT: Yale University Press, 1977.

Hatch, Nathan O. and John H. Wigger, eds. *Methodism and the Shaping of American Culture*. Nashville: Kingswood Books, 2001.

Hempton, David. *The Religion of the People: Methodism and Popular Religion, c. 1750–1900*. London: Routledge, 1996.

Heyrman, Christine Leigh. *Southern Cross: The Beginnings of the Bible Belt*. New York: Knopf, 1997.

Hill, Marvin S. *Quest for Refuge: The Mormon Flight from American Pluralism*. Salt Lake City: Signature Books, 1989.

Holifield, E. Brooks. *The Gentlemen Theologians: American Theology in Southern Culture, 1795–1860*. Durham: Duke University Press, 1978.

———. "Theology as Entertainment: Oral Debate in American Religion." *Church History* 67 (September 1998): 499–520.

Innes, Stephen, ed. *Work and Labor in Early America*. Chapel Hill: University of North Carolina Press, 1988.

Isaac, Rhys. *The Transformation of Virginia, 1740–1790*. New York: W. W. Norton & Company, 1982.

Johnson, Charles A. *The Frontier Camp Meeting: Religion's Harvest Time*. Dallas: Southern Methodist University Press, 1955.

Johnson, Charles D. *Higher Education of Southern Baptists: An Institutional History, 1826–1954*. Waco, TX: Baylor University Press, 1955.

Johnson, Curtis D. *Islands of Holiness: Rural Religion in Upstate New York, 1790–1860*. Ithaca, NY: Cornell University Press, 1989.

Johnson, Paul E. *A Shopkeeper's Millennium: Society and Revivals in Rochester, New York, 1815–1837*. New York: Hill and Wang, 1978.

Johnson, Paul E. and Sean Wilentz. *The Kingdom of Matthias: A Story of Sex and Salvation in 19th-Century America*. New York: Oxford University Press, 1994.

Johnson, William Courtland. "'A Delusive Clothing': Christian Conversion in the Antebellum Slave Community." *Journal of Negro History* 82 (Summer 1997): 295–311.

Jonas, W. Glenn, Jr., ed. *The Baptist River: Essays on Many Tributaries of a Diverse Tradition*. Macon, GA: Mercer University Press, 2008.

Joyner, Charles. "'Believer I Know': The Emergence of African American Christianity." In *Religion and American Culture*. Edited by David G. Hackett, 187–207. New York: Routledge, 1995.

Juster, Susan. *Disorderly Women: Sexual Politics and Evangelicalism in Revolutionary New England*. Ithaca, NY: Cornell University Press, 1994.

Kerber, Linda. *Women of the Republic: Intellect and Ideology in Revolutionary America*. Chapel Hill: University of North Carolina Press, 1980.

King, Wilma. *Stolen Childhood: Slave Youth in Nineteenth-Century America*. Bloomington: Indiana University Press, 1995.

Leonard, Bill J. *Baptist Ways: A History*. Valley Forge, PA: Judson Press, 2003.

Lindley, Susan Hill. *"You Have Stept out of Your Place": A History of Women and Religion in America*. Louisville: Westminster John Knox Press, 1996.

Lindman, Janet Moore. *Bodies of Belief: Baptist Community in Early America*. Philadelphia: University of Pennsylvania Press, 2008.

Lindner, Eileen W., ed. *Yearbook of American and Canadian Churches*. Nashville: Abingdon Press, 2001.

Long, Loretta M. *The Life of Selina Campbell: A Fellow Soldier in the Cause of Restoration*. Tuscaloosa: University of Alabama Press, 2001.

Lucas, Marion B. *A History of Blacks in Kentucky*. Vol. 1, *From Slavery to Segregation, 1760–1891*. Lexington: Kentucky Historical Society, 1992.

Lumpkin, William L. *Baptist Confessions of Faith*. Valley Forge, PA: Judson Press, 1959.

———. *Baptist Foundations in the South: Tracing through the Separates the Influence of the Great Awakening, 1754–1787*. Nashville: Broadman Press, 1961.

Lyerly, Cynthia Lynn. *Methodism and the Southern Mind, 1770–1810*. New York: Oxford University Press, 1998.

Malone, Dumas, ed. *Dictionary of American Biography*. New York: Charles Scribner's Sons, 1964.

Marsden, George M. *Religion and American Culture*. San Diego: Harcourt
   Brace Jovanovich, 1990.
Martin, Asa Earl. *The Anti-Slavery Movement in Kentucky Prior to 1850*.
   Louisville: Standard Publishing Company, 1918; reprint, New York:
   Negro Universities Press, 1970.
Masters, Frank M. *A History of Baptists in Kentucky*. Louisville: Kentucky
   Baptist Historical Society, 1953.
Mathews, Donald G. *Religion in the Old South*. Chicago: University of
   Chicago Press, 1977.
Mathis, James Rhett. *The Making of the Primitive Baptists: A Cultural and
   Intellectual History of the Antimission Movement, 1800–1840*. New
   York: Routledge, 2004.
McBeth, H. Leon. *The Baptist Heritage: Four Centuries of Baptist Witness*.
   Nashville: Broadman Press, 1987.
———. *Women in Baptist Life*. Nashville: Broadman Press, 1979.
McDougle, Ivan E. *Slavery in Kentucky, 1792–1865*. Lancaster, PA: New Era
   Printing Company, 1918; reprint, Westport, CT: Negro Universities
   Press, 1970.
McGoldrick, James Edward. *Baptist Successionism: A Crucial Question in
   Baptist History*. Metuchen, NJ: Scarecrow Press, 1994.
McGuire, Meredith B. *Pentecostal Catholics: Power, Charisma, and Order in a
   Religious Movement*. Philadelphia: Temple University Press, 1982.
McLoughlin, William G. *Isaac Backus and the American Pietistic Tradition*.
   Boston: Little, Brown, 1967.
———. *New England Dissent, 1630–1833: The Baptists and the Separation of
   Church and State*. 2 Vols. Cambridge: Harvard University Press, 1971.
Mead, Frank S. and Samuel S. Hill. *Handbook of Denominations in the United
   States*. 8th ed. Nashville: Abingdon Press, 1985.
Miller, Perry. *Errand into the Wilderness*. New York: Harper & Row, 1956.
Miyakawa, T. Scott. *Protestants and Pioneers: Individualism, and Conformity
   on the American Frontier*. Chicago: University of Chicago Press,
   1964.
Morgan, Edmund S. *The Puritan Family: Religion & Domestic Relations in
   SeventeenthCentury New England*. New York: Harper & Row, 1966.
———. *Visible Saints: The History of a Puritan Idea*. New York: New York
   University Press, 1963.

Mulder, Philip N. *A Controversial Spirit: Evangelical Awakenings in the South*. New York: Oxford University Press, 2002.

Mullins, E. Y. *Baptist Beliefs*. 6th ed. Philadelphia: Judson Press, 1951.

Murch, James DeForest. *Christians Only: A History of the Restoration Movement*. Cincinnati: Standard Publishing, 1962.

Newman, William M., and Peter L. Halvorson. *Atlas of American Religion: The Denominational Era, 1776–1990*. Walnut Creek, CA: AltaMira Press, 2000.

Noll, Mark A. *America's God: From Jonathan Edwards to Abraham Lincoln*. New York: Oxford University Press, 2002.

———. *A History of Christianity in the United States and Canada*. Grand Rapids, MI: William B. Eerdmans, 1992.

Orchard, G. H. *A Concise History of Foreign Baptists*. Nashville: Graves, Marks & Rutland, 1855.

Owen, Christopher H. *The Sacred Flame of Love: Methodism and Society in NineteenthCentury Georgia*. Athens: University of Georgia Press, 1998.

Patterson, James A. James *Robinson Graves: Staking the Boundaries of Baptist Identity*. Nashville: B&H Publishing Group, 2012.

Patterson, W. Morgan. *Baptist Successionism: A Critical View*. Valley Forge, PA: Judson Press, 1969.

Pettit, Norman. *The Heart Prepared: Grace and Conversion in Puritan Spiritual Life*. New Haven, CT: Yale University Press, 1966.

Pogue, Blair A. "'I Cannot Believe the Gospel That Is So Much Preached': Gender, Belief, and Discipline in Baptist Religious Culture." In *The Buzzel About Kentuck: Settling the Promised Land*. Edited by Craig Thompson Friend, 217–241. Lexington: University Press of Kentucky, 1999.

Posey, Walter Brownlow. *The Baptist Church in the Lower Mississippi Valley, 1776–1845*. Lexington: University of Kentucky Press, 1957.

Potter, David M. *The Impending Crisis, 1848–1861*. New York: Harper & Row, 1976.

Potts, David B. *Baptist Colleges in the Development of American Society, 1812–1861*. New York & London: Garland Publishing, 1988.

Raboteau, Albert J. *Slave Religion: The "Invisible Institution" in the Antebellum South*. New York: Oxford University Press, 1978.

Redford, A. H. *The History of Methodism in Kentucky*. Nashville: Southern Methodist Publishing House, 1868–1870.

Richardson, Robert. *Memoirs of Alexander Campbell*. Philadelphia: J. B. Lippincott & Co., 1870.

Richey, Russell E. *Early American Methodism*. Bloomington: Indiana University Press, 1991.

Roberts, Phil. "Andrew Fuller." In *Baptist Theologians*. Edited by Timothy George and David S. Dockery, 121–139. Nashville: Broadman Press, 1990.

Robinson, H. Wheeler. *The Life and Faith of the Baptists*. 2nd ed. London: Kingsgate Press, 1946.

Robinson, Robert. *Ecclesiastical Researches*. Cambridge: Francis Hodson, 1792.

Rogers, James A. *Richard Furman: Life and Legacy*. Macon, GA: Mercer University Press, 1985; reprint, 2001.

Rohrer, James R. *Keepers of the Covenant: Frontier Missions and the Decline of Congregationalism, 1774–1818*. New York: Oxford University Press, 1995.

Rorabaugh, W. J. *The Alcoholic Republic: An American Tradition*. New York: Oxford University Press, 1979.

Ross, James. *Life and Times of Elder Reuben Ross*. Philadelphia: Grant, Faires & Rodgers, 1882.

Ryan, Mary P. *Cradle of the Middle Class: The Family in Oneida County, New York, 1790–1865*. New York: Cambridge University Press, 1981.

———. "A Woman's Awakening: Evangelical Religion and the Families of Utica, New York, 1800–1840." *American Quarterly* 30 (1978): 602–623.

Sassi, Jonathan D. *A Republic of Righteousness: The Public Christianity of Post-Revolutionary New England Clergy*. New York: Oxford University Press, 2001.

Schaff, Philip. *The Creeds of Christendom*. Grand Rapids, MI: Baker Books, 1996.

Schlesinger, Arthur M. "What Then is the American, This New Man." *American Historical Review* 48 (1943): 225–244.

Schmidt, Leigh Eric. *Holy Fairs: Scottish Communions and American Revivals in the Early Modern Period*. Princeton, NJ: Princeton University Press, 1989.

Schneider, A. Gregory. *The Way of the Cross Leads Home: The Domestication of American Methodism*. Bloomington: Indiana University Press, 1993.

Schweiger, Beth Barton. *The Gospel Working Up: Progress and the Pulpit in NineteenthCentury Virginia*. New York: Oxford University Press, 2000.

Sellers, Charles Grier. *The Market Revolution: Jacksonian America, 1815–1846*. New York: Oxford University Press, 1991.

Sheriff, Carol. *The Artificial River: The Erie Canal and the Paradox of Progress, 1817–1862*. New York: Hill and Wang, 1996.

Shipps, Jan. *Mormonism: The Story of a New Religious Tradition*. Urbana: University of Illinois Press, 1985.

Short, Roy Hunter. *Methodism in Kentucky*. Rutland, VT: Academy Books, 1979.

Shurden, Walter B. *Associationalism among Baptists in America, 1704–1814*. New York: Arno Press, 1980.

———. "The Southern Baptist Synthesis: Is It Cracking?" *Baptist History and Heritage*, April 1981: 2–11.

Smith, Timothy L. "The Evangelical Kaleidoscope and the Call to Christian Unity," *Christian Scholar's Review* 15 (1986): 125–140.

Sobel, Mechal. *Teach Me Dreams: The Search for Self in the Revolutionary Era*. Princeton, NJ: Princeton University Press, 2000.

———. *Trabelin' On: The Slave Journey to an Afro-Baptist Faith*. Westport, CT: Greenwood Press, 1979.

Spangler, Jewel L. "Becoming Baptists: Conversion in Colonial and Early National Virginia." *Journal of Southern History* 67 (May 2001): 243–286.

Sparks, Randy J. *On Jordan's Stormy Banks: Evangelicalism in Mississippi, 1773–1876*. Athens: University of Georgia Press, 1994.

———. "Religion in Amite County, Mississippi, 1800–1861." In *Masters & Slaves in the House of the Lord: Race and Religion in the American South, 1740–1870*. Edited by John B. Boles, 58–80. Lexington: University Press of Kentucky, 1988.

Spencer, J. H. *A History of Kentucky Baptists*. 2 Vols. N.p.: Printed for the Author, 1886; reprint, Lafayette, TN: Church History Research and Archives, 1976.

Sprague, William B. *Annals of the American Pulpit*. Vol. 6, *Baptist*. New York: Robert Carter and Brothers, 1865; reprint, New York: Arno Press, 1969.

Stevenson, Edward. *Biographical Sketch of the Rev. Valentine Cook*. Nashville: Southern Methodist Publishing House, 1858.

Stout, Harry S. *The Divine Dramatist: George Whitefield and the Rise of Modern Evangelicalism*. Grand Rapids: William B. Eerdmans, 1991.

———. *The New England Soul: Preaching and Religious Culture in Colonial New England*. New York: Oxford University Press, 1986.

Sutton, William R. *Journeymen for Jesus: Evangelical Artisans Confront Capitalism in Jacksonian Baltimore*. University Park, Pa.: Pennsylvania State University Press, 1998.

Sweeney, Douglas A. *Nathaniel Taylor, New Haven Theology, and the Legacy of Jonathan Edwards*. New York: Oxford University Press, 2003.

Sweet, Leonard I. *The Minister's Wife: Her Role in Nineteenth-Century American Evangelicalism*. Philadelphia: Temple University Press, 1983.

Sweet, William Warren. *Religion on the American Frontier*. Vol. 1, *The Baptists*. New York: Henry Holt and Co., 1931.

———. *Religion on the American Frontier*. Vol. 2, *The Presbyterians*. New York: Harper & Brothers Publishers, 1936.

———. *Religion on the American Frontier*. Vol. 4, *The Methodists*. Chicago: University of Chicago Press, 1946.

———. *Revivalism in America: Its Origin, Growth, and Decline*. New York: Abingdon Press, 1944.

Taylor, Alan. *William Cooper's Town: Power and Persuasion on the Frontier of the Early American Republic*. New York: A.A. Knopf, 1995.

Taylor, George Rogers. *The Transportation Revolution, 1815–1860*. New York: Harper Torchbooks, 1951.

Taylor, William Carey, Sr. *Biography of Elder Alfred Taylor*. Louisville, KY: Caperton and Cates, 1878; revision and reprint, published by Wendell Holmes Rone, Sr., 1983.

Thomas, George M. *Revivalism and Cultural Change: Christianity, Nation Building, and the Market in the NineteenthCentury United States*. Chicago: University of Chicago Press, 1989.

Torbet, Robert G. *A History of the Baptists*. Philadelphia: Judson Press, 1950.

Touchstone, Blake. "Planters and Slave Religion in the Deep South." In *Masters & Slaves in the House of the Lord: Race and Religion in the American South, 1740–1870*. Edited by John B. Boles, 99–126. Lexington: University Press of Kentucky, 1988.

Tull, James E. *A History of Southern Baptist Landmarkism in the Light of Historical Baptist Ecclesiology*. New York: Arno Press, 1980.

———. *Shapers of Baptist Thought*. Valley Forge, PA: Judson Press, 1972.

Tyrrell, Ian R. *Sobering Up: From Temperance to Prohibition in Antebellum America, 1800–1860*. Westport, CT: Greenwood Press, 1979.

Ulrich, Laurel Thatcher. *Good Wives: Image and Reality in the Lives of Women in Northern New England, 1650–1750*. New York: Vintage Books, 1980.

———. *A Midwife's Tale: The Life of Martha Ballard, Based on Her Diary, 1785–1812*. New York: Vintage Books, 1990.

Vaughan, Thomas M. *Memoirs of Rev. Wm. Vaughan, D. D.* Louisville: Caperton & Cates, 1878.

Vine, W. E. *Expository Dictionary of Bible Words*. London: Marshall, Morgan & Scott, 1981.

Walters, Ronald G. *American Reformers, 1815–1860*. New York: Hill and Wang, 1978.

Watkins, Owen C. *The Puritan Experience: Studies in Spiritual Autobiography*. New York: Schocken Books, 1972.

Watts, Steven A. *The Republic Reborn: War and the Making of Liberal America, 1790–1820*. Baltimore: Johns Hopkins University Press, 1987.

Weisberger, Bernard A. *They Gathered at the River: The Story of the Great Revivalists and Their Impact upon Religion in America*. Boston: Little, Brown and Company, 1958.

Welter, Barbara. "The Cult of True Womanhood, 1820–1860." *American Quarterly* 18 (Summer 1966): 151–174.

West, Robert Frederick. *Alexander Campbell and Natural Religion*. New Haven, CT: Yale University Press, 1948.

Wigger, John H. *Taking Heaven by Storm: Methodism and the Rise of Popular Christianity in America*. New York: Oxford University Press, 1998.

Wilentz, Sean. *Chants Democratic: New York City & the Rise of the American Working Class, 1788–1850*. New York: Oxford University Press, 1984.

Williams, David R. *Wilderness Lost: The Religious Origins of the American Mind*. Selinsgrove, PA: Susquehanna University Press, 1987.

Wills, Gregory A. *Democratic Religion: Freedom, Authority, and Church Discipline in the Baptist South, 1785–1900*. New York: Oxford University Press, 1997.

Wood, Gordon S. *The Creation of the American Republic, 1776–1787*. Chapel Hill: University of North Carolina Press, 1969.

———. *The Radicalism of the American Revolution*. New York: Vintage Books, 1991.

Theses and Dissertations

Bailey, Fred Arthur. "The Status of Women in the Disciples of Christ Movement, 1865–1900." Ph.D. diss., University of Tennessee, 1979.

Compton, Bob. "Baptist Church Manuals in America: A Study in Baptist Polity and Practice." Th.D. diss., Southern Baptist Theological Seminary, 1967.

Corkern, Randall Allen. "A Study of the Education, Morals, Salary, and Controversial Movements of the Frontier Baptist Preacher in Kentucky from its Settlement until 1830." Ph.D. diss., Southern Baptist Theological Seminary, 1952.

Dain, Michael Andrew. "The Development of the Primitivist Impulse in American Baptist Life, 1707–1842." Ph.D. diss., Southwestern Baptist Theological Seminary, 2001.

Deweese, Charles William. "The Origins, Development, and Use of Church Covenants in Baptist History." Th.D. diss., Southern Baptist Theological Seminary, 1973.

Halbrooks, Guy Thomas. "Francis Wayland: Contributor to Baptist Concepts of Church Order." Ph.D. diss., Emory University, 1971.

Haynes, Melissa G. "Piety, Purity, and Baptist Femininity: Gender and Religious Discipline in Wilkes County, North Carolina, 1777 to 1890." M.A. Thesis, Appalachian State University, 2001.

Holmes, Bernard G. "The Contribution of John Lightfoot Waller to Kentucky Baptists, 1830–1854." Th.D. diss., Southwestern Baptist Theological Seminary, 1975.

Humphrey, James Edward. "Baptist Discipline in Kentucky, 1781–1860." Th. D. diss., Southern Baptist Theological Seminary, 1959.

Lindman, Janet Moore. "A World of Baptists: Gender, Race, and Religious Community in Pennsylvania and Virginia, 1689–1825." Ph.D. diss., University of Minnesota, 1994.

Lup, John R., Jr. "A History of the Nineteenth Century Women's Issue in the Restoration Movement." M.A. Thesis, Cincinnati Bible Seminary, 1993.

Smith, Larry Douglas. "The Historiography of the Origins of Antimissionism Examined in the Light of Kentucky Baptist History." Ph.D. diss., Southern Baptist Theological Seminary, 1982.

Stookey, Stephen Martin. "The Impact of Landmarkism upon Southern Baptist Western Geographical Expansion." Ph.D. diss., Southwestern Baptist Theological Seminary, 1994.

Taylor, Jeffrey Wayne. "Self-Definition in the Formation of the Primitive Baptist Movement as Expressed in their Three Major Periodicals, 1832–1948." Ph.D. diss., Baylor University, 2000.

Weed, Charles Allison. "American Baptists and an Educated Ministry Prior to 1850." M.Th. Thesis, Crozer Theological Seminary, 1935.

Young, Doyle L. "The Place of Andrew Fuller in the Developing Modern Mission Movement." Ph.D. diss., Southwestern Baptist Theological Seminary, 1981.

Internet Sources

"An Evening Hymn." Hymnary.org. Accessed April 11, 2014. http://www.hymnary.org/text/all_praise_to_thee_my_god_this_night.

Danvers, Henry. *A Treatise of Baptism*. 1674. Accessed November 23, 2012. http://baptisthistoryhomepage.com/danvers.h.treatise.baptsm.html.

Index

Page numbers in **boldface** refer to illustrations.

ministers (*cont.*)

of, 44–51; ordination, 51–55; populist influence 37–38, 40–41; preaching style, 59–60, 62–64; professionalization, 82–85

Mississippi, 1, 241n17

Missouri, 23, 64, 82

Mormonism, 4, 5, 79, 222n19

Morris, Zachariah, 54

Morrow, Orson Holland, 40, 187

Mount Pleasant Baptist Church (Adair Co.), 148

Mount Pleasant Baptist Church (Jessamine Co.), 32–33, 79–80, 82, 88, 143, 147, 165, 237n37, 246n11

Mount Tabor Baptist Church, 45

Mount Zion Baptist Church, 122

Mouth of Licking Baptist Church, 165

Mullins, E. Y., 111

Muscle Shoals Baptist Association, 190

Nall, James, 39

Nelson Baptist Association, 156

New Castle (Kentucky), 49, 189

New Light, 2, 6, 12, 63, 111, 134

New York, 6, 105, 153, 169, 195

Nixon, Richard W., 40

Noe, Parmelia, 142

Noel, Silas Mercer, 40, 49, 62, 112–13, 118, 123–24

Noll, Mark, 4, 6

Nolynn Baptist Association, 118

North Bend Baptist Association, 186

North Carolina, 2, 24, 117, 166, 237n37

North District Baptist Association, 112, 168

North Fork Baptist Church, 53

Ohio County, 32

Ohio River, 3, 29, 53, 61, 163, 164, 198

O'Neal, Nelly, 54

Orchard, G. H., 196

Paducah (Kentucky), 198

Paris Baptist Church, 78, 85, 94, 147–48, 157–58, 174, 239n1, 240n6

Particular Baptists, 20, 234n11, 236n27

Peck, John Mason, 105–6

pedobaptism, 24, 29, 32, 101, 103, 181, 186, 190–92, 194, 196–97

Pendleton, James M., 17, 39, 47–49, **50**, 52, 54–55, 83–85, 193–95, 197, 222n24, 223n27, 225n33

Penney, William White, 40, 63

Pierson, Moses, 55

pluralism, 1, 6, 23–24, 35, 66, 185, 193

Pogue, Blair A., 133, 145–46

prayer meetings, 26, 42, 134–36

predestination, 20, 22, 42, 52, 68, 77, 115–18, 141

Presbyterianism, 5, 28, 38, 73, 81, 100–101, 108, 121, 140, 146, 153–55, 158, 166, 185, 192, 210n9, 220n9

primitivism, 72, 79, 87, 101, 104, 106, 124, 127–29, 143–47, 179, 187–88

protracted meetings, 110, 120–21, 127–28, 193, 231n32, 231n33

Providence Baptist Church (Clark Co.), 34, 71, 106, 134, 160

Providence Baptist Church (Jessamine Co.), 106

Puritanism, 4, 6, 41, 65, 72, 75, 205n10, 209n9, 212n17

Quakers, 5

Ramey, Elizabeth, 29–30
Ramey, William, 30
rebaptism, 2, 57
Red River Baptist Association, 117
Redding, Isaac, 12–13
Redding, Joseph, 12
Rees, Farmer, 40
refinement, 8–9, 121–22, 126, 149, 171,
   174–75, 177, 185, 218n33, 234n3
Regular Baptists, 6, 77, 111–12, 115–16, 134
   208n20
republicanism, 34, 66, 71, 81, 83, 85, 92, 105,
   122, 140, 188, 212n17, 223n27, 235n23
revivalism, 4, 6, 64, 99, 120, 159, 172,
   205n10, 235n11
revivals, 2–3, 6, 17–22, 27, 30, 53, 63, 108,
   110, 116, 120–21, 128, 136, 139, 145,
   159–60, 205n10, 231n32, 240n4
Rhode Island, 3, 61, 65, 245n9
Rice, David, 28, 166
Rice, Luther, 104–5, 118
Richardson, Henry H., 185
Ricketts, Robert W., 40
Robinson, Landon, 49
Robinson, H. Wheeler, 111
Robinson, Robert, 196
Rolling Fork Baptist Church, 167
Ross, Reuben, 17, 84, 117
Russell's Creek Baptist Association, 148, 189

Sabbath schools, 103, 127, 175, 178, 188–90,
   247n20
Salem Baptist Association, 97, 113–14, 166–67
salvation, 7, 13–14, 17, 20–21, 27, 42, 53, 60,
   68, 76–77, 107, 115–16, 158, 193, 210n9,
   213n21, 221n16; accessibility of, 116;

experience, 35, 213n26; loss of, 52, 77, 115;
   validity of, 43
Sardis Baptist Church, 33, 68–69, 76
Scearce, Martha "Patsy," 21
Second Colored Baptist Church
   (Louisville), 179
Second Great Awakening, 4–5, 8, 70–71,
   145, 199, 234n3
Separate Baptists, 6, 77, 97, 111–12, 115–16,
   134, 208n20
Severn's Valley Church, 3, 167
Shackleford, John, 82
Shakers, 4
Sinking Creek Baptist Church, 81
Smith, Mrs. A. O., 151
Smith, George S., 82
Smith, John, 81–82
Smith, Joseph, 18, 99
Smith, Thomas Jr., 17, 21–22, 26, 30, 35, 41,
   165, 189
South Carolina, 2, 24, 67, 184
South District Baptist Association, 148,
   170, 189
South Elkhorn Baptist Church, 3, 33, 82
South Kentucky Association, 116
Southern Baptist Convention, 183–84
Spencer, John Henderson, 49, 54, 67–69,
   136, 187, 198
Stamping Ground Baptist Church, 78, 84,
   94, 133, 142–43, 160–61, 165, 168, 172–73
Steele, Isaac, 54
Stockton, Robert, 40
Stone, Barton, 62, 114
Stout, Harry S., 41
Suggett, James, 53, 64, 172
Sulpher Fork Baptist Association, 128, 144

Tanner, John, 21–22

Tarrent, Carter, 167

Tate's Creek Baptist Association, 111, 118, 181, 245n1

Tate's Creek African Baptist Church, 178

Taylor, Alfred, 29, 47, 231n33

Taylor, Jane, 17, 21

Taylor, John, 11–14, 17, 20, 27, 28–30, 34, 48, 54, 60, 62–64, 74–75, 83–84, 94, 105–6, 112, 133, 135–37, 162–64, 209n1, 216n11, 220n11, 223n26, 241n13

Taylor, Joseph, 54

temperance, 94, 96, 127, 148, 175, 186–88, 246n12, 247n14

Ten Mile Baptist Association, 128, 198

Tennessee, 6, 54, 60, 117, 171, 185, 191, 192–94, 238n50

Thompson, Wilson, 18–19, 27–29, 42–44, 46, 62–63, 136, 138, 141, 165

Tinsley, Thomas, 3

Town Fork Baptist Church, 93

Trott, Samuel, 39

Tuggle, Henry, 82

union meetings, 97

United Baptist Church, Colored, Richmond, 175

Vancleave, Samuel, 18

Vardeman, Jeremiah, 17, 103, 119, 231n31

Vaughan, William, 17–18, 40, 108, 117

Vickers, Moses, 75

Virginia, 2–3, 11, 14, 24, 38, 53, 62, 65, 67, 74, 84, 135, 166, 169, 184, 208n20, 216n5

voting (in the church), 21, 32–33, 78, 80, 81, 85–86, 89, 93, 95–96, 106, 109, 122, 134,

143–45, 150, 160, 164, 166, 175, 178–79, 187

voting (political), 2, 177

Waller, Edmund, 82

Waller, John Lightfoot, 118, 128, 149–51, 181–83, **182**, 190–92, 194, 196–97, 244n1, 247n22, 249n37

Walnut Street Baptist Church, 194

Warder, Walter, 23, 39, 48, 82, 107–8, 123, 179

Warfield, William C., 62

Wayland, Francis, 6

West Union Baptist Association, 185, 196

westward expansion, 2, 16, 38, 58, 115, 198

Williamstown Baptist Church, 54, 111, 142, 147

women, 2, 8, 19, 89–90, 131–56, 158–60, 165, 187, 198, 231n21, 225n35, 225n37, 234n3, 234n6, 234n11, 235n18, 236n23, 237n45, 238n47; African-American (*see also* African Americans); associations, 144–45; discipline, 14, 21, 44–46, 237n37; education, 139–40, 151; exclusion of, 145–48, 165, 246n11; family, 139–41, 151–52; fundraising, 148–49; home, 154; influence of, 134–37, 139, 148; leadership, 133–34; membership rates, 133; poverty, 143; restrictions, 132–33, 134, 150; voting rights, 134

Wood, William, 60–61

Woodmason, Charles, 21, 24

Woolfolk, Polly, 20

Worley, Zachariah, 186

worship, 6, 12–13, 21, 58, 63–65, 69, 74–75, 78, 81, 88, 92, 94, 97, 120, 136, 157–58, 162–63, 171–72, 174, 177, 190, 243n30

Young, John W., 40